BILL JOHNSON

WITH JENNIFER MISKOV, PhD

DEFINING MOMENTS

WHITAKER
HOUSE

DEFINING MOMENTS:
God-Encounters with Ordinary People Who Changed the World

Bill Johnson
bjm.org

ISBN: 978-1-62911-547-4
eBook ISBN: 978-1-62911-549-8
Printed in the United States of America
© 2016 by Bill Johnson

Whitaker House
1030 Hunt Valley Circle
New Kensington, PA 15068
www.whitakerhouse.com

Library of Congress Cataloging-in-Publication Data
Names: Johnson, Bill, 1951- author.
Title: Defining moments : God-encounters with ordinary people who changed the world / Bill Johnson with Jennifer A. Miskov, Ph.D.
Description: New Kensington, PA : Whitaker House, 2016. | Includes bibliographical references.
Identifiers: LCCN 2015041748 | ISBN 9781629115474 (hardcover : alk. paper)
Subjects: LCSH: Christian biography.
Classification: LCC BR1700.3 .J64 2016 | DDC 270.8092/2—dc23 LC record available at http://lccn.loc.gov/2015041748.

1 2 3 4 5 6 7 8 9 10 11 ⨃ 23 22 21 20 19 18 17 16

I dedicate this book to the following:

The Assemblies of God:

My entire upbringing was in the Assemblies of God. Some of the finest people I've ever met are a part of that movement. I am so thankful to have been raised in such an environment, where both the Holy Spirit and the Word of God were honored at such a high level. From that family of believers, I received a passion for the work of the Holy Spirit and the missionary endeavors around the world. The cry of the nations will always be in my ears because the people of the Assemblies of God said yes to the Great Commission. I am forever grateful for such a wonderful heritage.

Jack Hayford and the Foursquare Church:

Initially, it was my dad who was profoundly impacted by Dr. Jack Hayford, which, in turn, affected my life. In time, I was also exposed to this *general in God's army*. His impact is beyond my ability to describe. The annual pastors' conference at Church on the Way was life-changing in every possible way. I saw pastoral ministry modeled in a way that was rare and inspiring, and learned firsthand how to lead people in the ultimate ministry of worship. There we had the privilege of hearing from a great number of Foursquare leaders of that era. Dr. Hayford's friendship has been a great strength and encouragement to me. I am forever grateful for the wisdom and grace that has left an eternal mark on how I think, live, and serve.

John Wimber and the Vineyard Movement:

The Vineyard helped me to see that the realm of the Holy Spirit that I thought was reserved for the *super saints* was actually for everyone. Through their example, I lost all excuses and felt required (of the Lord) to take risks to see what God would do through me. While I never had the privilege of meeting John, the simple opportunity to attend two conferences at which he spoke completely changed my life. The year was 1987. The humility and total absence of hype gave me hope that I, too, could be used by God to display the power of the gospel. I am forever indebted to the Wimber family and the Vineyard Movement.

Rodney Howard-Browne:

This man left his homeland of South Africa to be a missionary to the United States. And I'm so thankful. He carries such a powerful Spirit of breakthrough that countless people have been forever changed by his ministry—and I am one of them. He carries revival in his bones. His ability to stay committed to what he feels God is doing, regardless of public opinion, has inspired courage in many of us. His emphasis on the Holy Spirit *and* the Word of God has brought an ongoing level of revival that in times past was thought to be out of reach. It's not so. He has taught us how the move of the Holy Spirit can be the norm. And I am forever grateful.

Revival Alliance:

This group is comprised of six couples, each with corresponding networks of churches, ministries, and leaders. They are John and Carol Arnott, Randy and DeAnne Clark, Rolland and Heidi Baker, Ché and Sue Ahn, Georgian and Winnie Banov, and Beni and me. Each couple leads a movement of thousands of churches and leaders around the world and could easily be on my above list of their own accord. I am forever indebted to each of them. Their selfless lifestyles, passion for the lost, cry for the increasing move of the Holy Spirit, and willingness to pay any price for the "more of God" have left a permanent mark upon my life. I will never ever be the same. These are some of my most treasured friends.

Bethel Church Pastoral Team:
These are the people who have paid the biggest price to follow the things God has put in my heart. There are no words—at least there are no adequate words—to describe my love and value for each member of this amazing team. We've shared victories that I'd only read of on the pages of Scripture or in the books on church history. But we've also endured tragedy and loss in ways that either cause shipwreck and fear to rule the day or forge an immutable bond between people who truly become family. This group has repeatedly chosen the latter, embracing the privilege of "family" over and above personal ministry goals. To these my friends, I owe my life.

—*Bill Johnson*

Contents

Foreword

I wish I had written this book!

As I moved from the introduction and first chapter through the body of *Defining Moments*, I was prophetically moved and inspired. A large portion of my ministry has always been concerned with church history, and this book—so wonderfully written by Bill Johnson with Jennifer Miskov—will be a treasured part of my personal library.

From John Wesley to Heidi Baker, we have the joy and privilege of experiencing these leaders' extraordinary encounters with God, as well as their lowest moments. We witness their complete dependence on Him who empowers them to rise again and again, stronger and wiser and more powerful than before. And He will do the same for us!

Anyone who has loved and served the Lord for any length of time has had times of trial and testing. Trial and testing is "Bible speak" for a really terrible time! The devil tells us that God's promises are just whims and that our dreams will become nightmares. When we go through such times, we need to read this book. But if we are doing well and everything in our lives is bright and beautiful, we also need to read this book!

Today, we must have a revelation that the church is not broken up into segments of time and movements through history. We must see ourselves as our Father sees us: a body that is coming to maturity in loving submission to our glorious Head and carrying His resurrection Light within! We have been the bride of Christ from the moment Jesus breathed His Spirit into and upon His followers, and we will be His bride until the last soul enters His kingdom—and throughout eternity. The church includes all generations of believers.

We hear people say, "Let's not reinvent the wheel." Our wheel was "invented" the moment Jesus rose from the dead—and He is the Wheel! It has taken us centuries to learn how to live and move and have our being in Him, but I believe the church is in a position right now to become fully operational, doing the greater works of Jesus in the earth to the glory of God.

The insight and revelation that Bill and Jennifer give us in this book help us to grow into the full stature of Christ for the challenges of these final days. The lives and ministries of the giants of faith they describe impart immeasurable wisdom with regard to revival: obeying the Word and trusting the Spirit as we experience all the wonder and excitement—as well as the shock, demonic activity, and messiness—that come with a great awakening. We need always to be reminded of who we are, *whose* we are, and how we are to relate to one another as members of Jesus' body.

Let us glean from this great work and faithfully forge ahead in the Holy Spirit momentum of our brothers and sisters, these great men and women of God who have gone before us. We must stand with them by moving in Him. Jesus is calling us to walk through powerful doors to disciple nations, doors that those who have had extraordinary encounters with God have opened for us.

Read and be inspired to be brave and bold!

—*Roberts Liardon*
Author, God's Generals series

Introduction

Defining Moments is about the unusual encounters that various individuals have had with God that changed absolutely everything about their life. Their thought life changed, as did their ministry gifts and their sense of what might be possible in their lifetime. Each person's worldview also experienced radical transformation, as he or she was positioned to see the "big picture" through God's eyes. But for most of them, perhaps their biggest paradigm shift came in relation to their idea of the nature of God and their ability to feel His heart for other people. Seeing these things more clearly always carries a summons with it. They said *yes* to the call of God and, as a result, became people who shaped the course of world history.

Here is the remarkable truth about each of these individuals: not one of them was unusually gifted for such a task. Their gift was God Himself. All of our heroes of the faith were pretty normal people. But that changed when the touch of God upon their lives transformed everything.

In some ways, *Defining Moments* is the most unusual book I have written. I coauthored this work with Dr. Jennifer A. Miskov. I asked her to help with this project because of her passion for revival, her love for history, and her gift for research. This made her an obvious choice. I knew what I was looking for in the lives of some of our heroes in church history, but I needed help in finding it. She not only found the important information, but she also wrote it in a way that didn't need my help in rewriting. As a result, Jen wrote the lion's share of this work. I am thankful for the help, and I hope that you will find this book to be a great encouragement.

These things are written to stir up a passion in each of our lives for *the tomorrows that hold great promise*! This is a book of hope. It speaks of the *more* that God alone can offer.

Dreaming with God,
Bill Johnson

Brace Yourself!

I have had the privilege of meeting many high-profile men and women of God throughout my years as a pastor and a leader. Thankfully, it is extremely rare to find someone whose integrity outside the pulpit is less than it is inside. They have paid a high price for being in their place of responsibility and influence, and they deserve undying respect and love from the people of God. I know of few who look for attention or credit for what God does in and through them. They are truly Christlike in their approach to life and ministry, and I am better off just for knowing them.

Interestingly, those positions of influence were never anything they desired or sought after. Instead, God gave positions to people whom He could trust to lead—and to lead well. They first hungered for Him. Their longing for more of God is what brought them into life-changing encounters in which God entrusted them with Himself. "[He was] *not ashamed to be called their God*" (Hebrews 11:16). This must be the ultimate crowning touch on a life—having God want to manifest Himself upon you and with you. That was His message to Moses, who questioned his own qualifications for service. God's answer to him was, *"Certainly I will be with you"* (Exodus 3:12 NASB). There is no greater qualification than that.

If there is one thing I have noticed about all these leaders, it is that they are very normal people. Media reports and rumors (and sometimes the legitimate report of God's blessing on their lives) have created larger-than-life images of these down-to-earth people. Each has idiosyncrasies, for sure, as we all do. But each also has very strong giftings, or graces, from God. Gifts are common; every one of us has them. What's more important is that each one of these leaders has possessed a love for God that dominates everything they are and everything they do. It is their simple devotion to Christ that stands out above every other feature in their lives.

A Secret Life in God

Whenever I've had the opportunity to look a bit more behind the scenes of these leaders' lives, I've discovered that they usually have had a moment or an encounter with God that changed everything. For some, there were several such moments. When the normal encounters the extraordinary, everything changes. It must.

All these leaders have always been willing to share their story if it would help to encourage and inspire others. But I have not seen any of them use their testimony for self-promotion or to appear "spiritual." People who have had extreme encounters with God never feel super-spiritual. The apostle Paul is a great example of this. He had one of the most profound encounters with Jesus ever recorded. (See Acts 9:1–22.) The result was that he considered himself to be the least of all the apostles—not even qualified to be called an apostle—because of his persecution of the church. (See 1 Corinthians 15:9.) In fact, he thought himself as the least of all saints. (See Ephesians 3:8.) I don't believe that Paul was attempting to project an image of humility. He was baring his soul in a way that must have been painful. Never do we grow beyond our realization of our need of God's grace. And the apostle illustrated this truth very well.

Real God-encounters don't manifest in pride. And such encounters are measured by the impact on the person who had them, and then on those who were under that person's influence. Week after week, I stand amazed at the impact that so many people today have on the world around them when I know that, just a short time ago, none of them would have been picked as the most likely to succeed. Of such is the kingdom of God.

A Theology of Encounter

It fascinates me to see how change is brought into people's lives. Exposure to the divine truly transforms everything about us: how we think, how we live, and how we plan for the future. While I don't understand the way in which this happens, it is biblical, and I've seen this reality in countless individuals' lives.

The apostle John stated that Jesus is the light that enlightens everyone who comes into the world. (See John 1:9.) John then expounded on the subject by describing the *authority to become* that is given to those who receive this light. (See John 1:12.) The most interesting outcome is what happens to those who receive this light. They become light! (See Matthew 5:14.) Lest there be any misunderstanding, Jesus is the light Source within every believer. But the Scripture does not command us to "'arise and *reflect*,' for your light has come." It says to "arise and shine"! (See Isaiah 60:1.) The follower of Jesus is able to shine.

In another metaphor, Jesus encourages us to come to Him and drink. (See John 7:37.) In the very next verse, He states that out of our innermost being will flow rivers of living water. Think of it—those who drink become givers of water themselves. In other words, when water was received, water could flow. Another way to put it is that once life is received, life flows. We become givers of the very thing that has transformed us.

This truth is quite profound. The way God touches us changes who we are and what we are capable of doing in His name. These *defining moments* transform us into fully equipped servants of the Lord.

Prepare for What Is Coming!

At first glance, *Defining Moments* appears to be a book about history. In part, that is true. But I honestly wouldn't spend my time writing a book solely about the past. That has already been done brilliantly over and over again by people much more qualified for such a task. This work is prophetic in nature, because it is about tomorrow. Page after page describes what has been promised to happen again.

I live for what is coming. My whole life is about what I believe God wants to do in my lifetime and beyond. So, let me whet your appetite for something almost everyone is concerned with—the future. This book is a prophecy over our lives. Read it with a sense of readiness and watch what happens.

These stories carry a prophetic anointing for all who have ears to hear. In a sense, each chapter is a summons to appear in the courts of heaven, where the course of history is determined. From this position, we will together hear His heart for this "planet of orphans" by looking at His works of the past.

God gives people encounters with Him, and these encounters make a supreme difference in their lives from that point on. Here are accounts of real people who changed the course of world history. But their stories are much more than a glance into the past. In fact, the high points of church history reveal to us more about God and His purposes in the earth. The low points simply reveal what happens when people interfere with those purposes. The following chapters are just a handful of the countless thousands of reported encounters with God that could be studied. Yet what you are about to read will prophesy about our future from God's perspective.

The Power of Testimonies

Testimonies prophesy. They reveal the nature of God, which never changes. The two profound truths upon which this book is built are (1) *God does not show partiality* (see Acts 10:34), and (2) *God is the same yesterday, today, and forever* (see Hebrews 13:8). These realities qualify every reader for the seemingly impossible task of seeing *"the kingdoms of this world… become the kingdoms of our [God]"* (Revelation 11:15).

Can we expect an outpouring of the Holy Spirit in our day that changes the atmosphere and the values of the whole body of Christ? Can we expect a move of God that brings a transformational effect on entire cities and nations? It has happened before. History is now looking for a generation who will rise up and live in such a way that it will happen again—but this time through the accumulated effect of *all* past revivals and awakenings. We are not looking for a simple repeat of a past event or even an unusual season of divine favor. On the contrary, we are looking for a full expression of God's interventions throughout history to culminate in these days that are upon us. We are dependent on this happening to complete what He has assigned us to accomplish—to disciple nations, *until the kingdoms of this world become the kingdoms of our God.*

I'd like to conclude this chapter with an excerpt about restoration from my book *Release the Power of Jesus:*

HISTORY PROPHESIES

On July 17, 1859, Charles Spurgeon brought forth a message entitled, "The Story of God's Mighty Acts." One hundred and fifty years ago, he declared this truth that had the power to shape the culture of the Church until there was a full restoration of God's historic interventions among mankind. Listen to his prophetic cry:

When people hear about what God used to do, one of the things they say is: "Oh, that was a very long while ago."... I thought it was God that did it. Has God changed? Is he not an immutable God, the same yesterday, today and forever? Does not that furnish an argument to prove that what God has done at one time he can do at another? Nay, I think I may push it a little further, and say *what he has done once, is a prophecy of what he intends to do again....* *Whatever God has done...is to be looked upon as a precedent....* [Let us] with earnestness seek that God would restore to us the faith of the men of old, that we may richly enjoy his grace as in the days of old. [Emphasis mine][1]

In 1859, through this great prophetic preacher, the chance was given to initiate a full recovery of all that had been lost. History tells us the Church did little with this truth, except perhaps to applaud another great sermon. We are now presented with a similar opportunity.

In a relay race there are four runners. The first three do not leave the racetrack and go into the showers before the last one finishes the race, because they all receive a prize according to how the last runner finishes. At this moment the *cloud of witnesses* are waiting to see what we will do with what we've been given (see Heb. 12:1). Let's not miss our opportunity to see a full restoration of God's works with mankind until Jesus is accurately *re-presented* and His glory fills the earth. This must happen through the obedience of a generation who captures the momentum of history through *keeping the testimony, thereby fully releasing the power of Jesus.*[2]

Read on—and brace yourself to receive God's restoration in our time!

2

Love:
John Wesley

"I put myself wholly into thy hands: put me to what thou wilt,
rank me with whom thou wilt; put me to doing, put me to
suffering, let me be employed for thee, or laid aside for thee,
exalted for thee, or trodden under foot for thee; let me be full, let
me be empty, let me have all things, let me have nothing, I freely,
and heartily resign all to thy pleasure and disposal."[3]
—*John Wesley*

God-encounters are the greatest experiences a person can have. God is overwhelmingly powerful, yet He moves with such grace and intentionality in His dealings with us. He knows our weaknesses and frailties and takes all these things and more into consideration whenever His presence falls upon someone. He often works beyond our comfort zones yet is determined not to extinguish a dimly burning wick. (See Isaiah 42:3.) The result is that we are forever changed. John Wesley is a major historical figure who still impacts our lives today. He was transformed through a profound encounter with God's love.

A Significant Player

John Wesley (1703–1791) was a significant player in sparking and releasing the First Great Awakening. Moravian missionaries were instrumental in setting the stage for Wesley's defining moment. His first interaction with them took place on a boat ride to America in 1735–1736 where he observed their peace in God and assurance of salvation in the midst of storms. In February 1738, while in London, Wesley met another Moravian missionary named Peter Böhler. His interactions with the Moravians caused him to rethink his earlier theological training. Then, on May 24, 1738, Wesley reluctantly attended a Moravian meeting at Aldersgate Street in London. While he was listening to a portion of Martin Luther's preface to the book of Romans, his heart was "strangely warmed." From that point on, he had full confidence in his salvation by faith, rather than by works. Almost immediately after this encounter, he went to Herrnhut, Germany, to spend time with the Moravians in order to learn more. By New Year's Eve that same year, he was back in England at an all-night prayer meeting with his brother Charles, evangelist George Whitefield, and about sixty others. God "crashed in" on them in the early hours of New Year's Day. This became fuel for the Great Awakening, and shortly after, Wesley began open-air preaching. John and Charles Wesley later became founders of the Methodist movement, which gave birth to the Holiness Movement and greatly influenced Pentecostalism.

Early Life

John Wesley was the fifteenth of nineteen children (only ten of whom lived to adulthood). He was born on June 17, 1703, into an Anglican family in Epworth, England.[4] In 1709, at the age of six, Wesley was miraculously saved from the flames of a burning house. When he was a teenager, he was marked by God when he came across a poor individual employed as a luggage carrier who was nonetheless overflowing with joy. This caused Wesley to rethink his own Christianity. He began to fast, pray, and discipline himself to find more of God. In 1720, he moved to Oxford. By 1725, he was ordained as a deacon in the Anglican Church (at Christ Church Cathedral). A year later, he became a fellow at Lincoln College in Oxford.[5]

During this time, Wesley was heavily influenced by *The Imitation of Christ* by Thomas à Kempis, *Holy Living and Dying* by Jeremy Taylor, and *A Serious Call to a Devout and Holy Life* and *Christian Perfection* by William Law.[6] In 1728, he was ordained a priest. Then, in 1729, he joined the "Holy Club," which was a group that regularly met together to observe daily disciplines and to love those less fortunate. George Whitefield and John's brother Charles were instrumental in helping to form the group. The students at Oxford named them "Methodists" because of their strict spiritual disciplines.[7]

The Moravian Influence

Faith in the Midst of Storms

Shortly after their father's death, John and Charles headed by ship to Georgia with two others from the Holy Club with the intent to evangelize the Native Americans. During their journey to America, from October 1735 to February 1736, they faced heavy storms. John and his British friends were afraid they might die, and they were unsure of their salvation if that were to happen. Their attitude contrasted with the positive outlook of the German Moravians, also on board, who were singing praises and holding services in the midst of the storms. Recalling that dangerous Sunday, February 25, Wesley wrote in his journal the following:

> At noon our third storm began. At four it was more violent than before. At seven I went to the Germans. I had long before observed the great seriousness of their behaviour. Of their humility they had given a continual proof.... In the midst of the psalm wherewith their service began, the sea broke over, split the mainsail in pieces, covered the ship, and poured in between the decks, as if the great deep had already swallowed us up. A terrible screaming

began among the English. The Germans calmly sung on. I asked one of them afterwards, "Was you not afraid?" He answered, "I thank God, no." I asked, "But were not your women and children afraid?" He replied, mildly, "No; our women and children are not afraid to die."[8]

Wesley was shocked by their response and their steadfast faith amid the storm, and he carried the memory with him long after their ship safely docked in Georgia. While Wesley originally wanted to do evangelistic work among the Native Americans, he was instead appointed as a minister in Savannah.[9] While there, he pursued Sophia Hopkey, a woman who had come on the same ship with him from England. However, taking the advice of a Moravian leader he trusted, he decided to stop courting her. When she decided to marry someone else, he then refused to administer Communion to her. This tangled him up in a lawsuit that discredited his ministry. On December 22, 1737, he headed back to England, marred by his troublesome time in Georgia and struggling greatly with self-doubt.

A Significant Friendship Is Born

On February 7, 1738, the same week that he returned to London, he met a twenty-five-year-old Moravian missionary named Peter Böhler, who had just been ordained by Moravian leader Nikolaus von Zinzendorf. Wesley began to converse regularly with him over theological matters.[10] On March 5, 1738, Böhler encouraged Wesley to preach faith regardless of his struggles with it.

> Immediately it struck into my mind, "Leave off preaching. How can you preach to others, who have not faith yourself?" I asked Böhler whether he thought I should leave it off or not. He answered, "By no means." I asked, "But what can I preach?" He said, "Preach faith till you have it; and then, because you have it, you will preach faith." Accordingly, Monday, 6, I began preaching this new doctrine, though my soul started back from the work. The first person to whom I offered salvation by faith alone, was a prisoner under sentence of death.[11]

Several things happened during this time that caused Wesley to do some deep reflection. His brother Samuel died the week after he met Böhler. Then, on May 14 and May 20, Wesley wrote two very direct letters to a mentor, William Law, who had influenced his thinking for twelve years up to that point. He challenged Law's views and asked why he had never taught him about saving faith before.[12] The old teaching brought torment under the law, while the newer revelation Böhler taught made it easy to have full assurance by faith in Christ alone. Rather than having to work for salvation and live in suspense waiting to know if one had received it, immediate assurance of one's conversion was possible. Around this same time, John's brother Charles was sick, so Böhler visited him.[13] Charles became convinced of this new teaching and was the first from the Holy Club to experience assurance of salvation. He was also healed that same day, Sunday, May 21, 1738.[14]

A Heart "Strangely Warmed" (May 24, 1738)

After his theological understanding had been shaken and his brother had received assurance of salvation, Wesley's heart was opened wide. Earlier in the week, Wesley said he "had had continual sorrow and heaviness in [his] heart."[15] Then, at about five in the morning on Wednesday, May 24, 1738, he opened his Bible to 2 Peter 1:4, and it was highlighted to him that he could become a partaker of the divine nature. He was also struck by Mark 12:34 and realized that he was not far from the kingdom of God. Later that same day, Wesley was invited to go to St. Paul's in London where "the anthem was, 'Out of the deep have I called unto Thee, O Lord: Lord, hear my voice.'"[16] After wrestling with a potential paradigm shift in his theology for weeks beforehand, Wesley hesitantly went to another meeting that night. It is interesting to note the opposition in his heart leading up to going to this meeting.

> In the evening I went very unwillingly to a society in Aldersgate Street, where one was reading Luther's preface to the Epistle to the Romans.[17]

> About a quarter before nine, while he was describing the change which God works in the heart through faith in Christ, I felt my

heart strangely warmed. I felt I did trust in Christ, Christ alone, for salvation; and an assurance was given me that He had taken away my sins, even mine, and saved me from the law of sin and death. I began to pray with all my might for those who had in a more especial manner despitefully used me and persecuted me. I then testified openly to all there what I now first felt in my heart.[18]

Immediately after this love encounter, however, Wesley was bombarded with doubt and a spiritual attack. The enemy quickly attempted to discount and to steal what God had just done in him. Wesley recalled,

After my return home, I was much buffeted with temptations, but I cried out, and they fled away. They returned again and again. I as often lifted up my eyes, and He "sent me help from his holy place." And herein I found the difference between this and my former state chiefly consisted. I was striving, yea, fighting with all my might under the law, as well as under grace. But then I was sometimes, if not often, conquered; now, I was always conqueror.[19]

If Wesley had partnered with the enemy's lies and discarded his spiritual experience as mere emotionalism, he might have missed out on the more that God had for him.

Immediate Effects of the Aldersgate Experience

After his heart was "strangely warmed," Wesley no longer felt conquered, as he had many times before; now, he was "always the conqueror." He realized that salvation came by faith in Christ alone and that God's grace was freely available for all. He also prayed for his enemies and testified openly of what God had done in him. He overcame fear, doubt, and temptation. The very next day, Thursday, May 25, 1738, Wesley was in a state of bliss with his Savior.

The moment I awakened, "Jesus, Master," was in my heart and in my mouth; and I found all my strength lay in keeping my eye fixed upon Him and my soul waiting on Him continually…. Yet the enemy injected a fear, "If thou dost believe, why is there not a more sensible change?" I answered (yet not I), "That I know not. But, this I know, I have 'now peace with God.' And I sin not today, and Jesus my Master has forbidden me to take thought for the morrow."[20]

The Great Awakening Is Launched

Shortly after his encounter, Wesley spent three months learning from the Moravians in Herrnhut, Germany, before returning to England just prior to the end of the year. After a night of prayer and worship with his community on New Year's Eve, something similar to Pentecost hit them in the early morning hours. Wesley recorded,

> Mon. Jan. 1, 1739. Mr. Hall, Kinchin, Ingham, Whitefield, Hutchins, and my brother Charles, were present at our love-feast in Fetter-lane, with about sixty of our brethren. About three in the morning, as we were continuing instant in prayer, the power of God came mightily upon us, insomuch that many cried out for exceeding joy, and many fell to the ground. As soon as we were recovered a little from that awe and amazement at the presence of his Majesty, we broke out with one voice, "We praise thee, O God, we acknowledge thee to be the Lord."[21]

As the result of this community of saints choosing to seek God together into the New Year, the Great Awakening was launched. A few months later, in March 1739, with the encouragement of Whitefield, Wesley began open-air preaching.[22] Rather than speak about salvation through good works and righteous living, he began to preach about salvation through faith in Christ alone. God began to move over the people with deep conviction. It was when Wesley stepped outside of his comfort zone that he activated his deposited anointing with even greater success. Wesley continued to preach at churches when he was invited, but he also preached in fields, in cottages, and in halls when the churches would not receive him. He eventually broke away from the Moravians to form his own Methodist classes. By

May 12, 1739, a stone was laid in Bristol for the first Methodist meeting-house.[23] Wesley also began to approve and release local people to preach who were not ordained by the Anglican Church. This was untraditional at the time but became a key factor in the rapid spread of Methodism.

Newer Manifestations of the Holy Spirit

Wesley began to see manifestations of the Holy Spirit that he was not accustomed to seeing. In the summer of 1739, Wesley and Whitefield conversed on this subject.

> I had an opportunity to talk with him [Whitefield] of those outward signs which had so often accompanied the inward work of God. I found his objections were chiefly grounded on gross misrepresentations of matter of fact. But the next day he had an opportunity of informing himself better: for no sooner had he begun (in the application of his sermon) to invite all sinners to believe in Christ, than four persons sunk down close to him, almost in the same moment. One of them lay without either sense or motion. A second trembled exceedingly. The third had strong convulsions all over his body, but made no noise, unless by groans. The fourth, equally convulsed, called upon God, with strong cries and tears. From this time, I trust, we shall all suffer God to carry on his own work in the way that pleaseth him.[24]

It is hard to comprehend how something so impossible to understand could bring people to Christ. What many people think will offend others actually attracts them. It is the mystery of this wonderful gospel for God to display Himself as He pleases and then expect humanity to adjust. Such is this privileged invitation to be a disciple of Jesus.

Mysterious Encounters with Eternal Fruit

Besides seeing people exhibit unusual physical manifestations, Wesley also saw people who had been "slain in the Spirit" or been led into extraordinary trances. On June 12, 1742, when Wesley was preaching on "the righteousness of the law and the righteousness of faith," he recalled that as he was preaching, "several dropped down as dead; and among the rest, such a cry was heard, of sinners groaning for the righteousness of faith, as almost drowned [his] voice. But many of these soon lifted up their heads with joy, and broke out into thanksgiving; being assured they now had the desire of their soul—forgiveness of their sins."[25]

The signs continued to occur. Years later, Wesley interviewed people who had fallen into trances to learn more about what was happening.

> I talked largely with Ann Thorn, and two others, who had been several times in trances. What they all agreed in was, 1. That when they went away, as they termed it, it was always at the time they were fullest of the love of God: 2. That it came upon them in a moment, without any previous notice, and took away all their senses and strength: 3. That there were some exceptions: but in general, from that moment, they were in another world, knowing nothing of what was done or said, by all that were round about them.
>
> About five in the afternoon I heard them singing hymns. Soon after, Mr. B. came up, and told me, Alice Miller (fifteen years old) was fallen into a trance. I went down immediately, and found her sitting on a stool, and leaning against the wall, with her eyes open and fixed upward. I made a motion as if going to strike, but they continued immovable. Her face showed an unspeakable mixture of reverence and love, while silent tears stole down her cheeks. Her lips were a little open, and sometimes moved; but not enough to cause any sound. I do not know whether I ever saw an human face look so beautiful; sometimes it was covered with a smile, as from joy, mixing with love and reverence; but the tears fell still though not so fast.[26]

Another time, on March 29, 1782, Wesley assisted a friend in a service and experienced an unusual sign of "a low, soft, solemn sound."

> I preached for him morning and afternoon; and we administered the sacrament to about thirteen hundred persons. While we were

administering, I heard a low, soft, solemn sound, just like that of an Aeolian harp. It continued five or six minutes, and so affected many, that they could not refrain from tears. It then gradually died away. Strange that no other organist (that I know) should think of this. In the evening I preached at our room. Here was that harmony which art cannot imitate.[27]

Miraculous Protection from Persecution

Wesley was willing to preach the gospel and was compelled to do the work that God had called him to do, no matter what the cost. He boldly proclaimed,

I look upon all the world as my parish; thus far I mean, that, in whatever part of it I am, I judge it meet, right, and my bounden duty, to declare unto all that are willing to hear, the glad tidings of salvation. This is the work which I know God has called me to; and sure I am that his blessing attends to it.[28]

This great pioneer of the faith experienced extreme opposition and suffered persecution. For example, in July 1745, Wesley had an experience similar to one that Jesus had when He walked right through an angry mob unscathed.[29] (See Luke 4:28–30.) In February 1748, crowds enclosed Wesley and others in a house and started to throw stones, trying to kill them. Wesley recorded the following testimony of God's deliverance.

After we were gone into the house, they began throwing great stones, in order to break the door. But perceiving this would require some time, they dropped that design for the present. They first broke all the tiles on the pent-house over the door, and then poured in a shower of stones at the windows. One of their captains, in his great zeal, had followed us into the house, and was now shut in with us. He did not like this, and would fain have got out; but it was not possible; so he kept as close to me as he could, thinking himself safe when he was near me: but, staying a little behind when I went up two pair of stairs, and stood close on one side, where we were a little sheltered a large stone struck him on the forehead, and the blood spouted out like a stream. He cried out, "O Sir, are we to die to-night? What must I do? What must I do?" I said, "Pray to God. He is able to deliver you from all danger." He took my advice, and began praying in such a manner as he had scarce done ever since he was born. Mr. Swindells and I then went to prayer; after which I told him, "We must not stay here; we must go down immediately." He said, "Sir, we cannot stir; you see how the stones fly about." I walked straight through the room, and down the stairs; and not a stone came in, till we were at the bottom. The mob had just broke open the door when we came into the lower room; and exactly while they burst in at one door, we walked out at the other. Nor did one man take any notice of us, though we were within five yards of each other.[30]

Another time, in August 1748, Wesley faced great danger and possible stoning while he was in the midst of preaching. Just as God guided the stones that David flung at Goliath, so He guided the stones meant to harm Wesley.

At one I went to the Cross in Bolton. There was a vast number of people, but many of them utterly wild. As soon as I began speaking, they began thrusting to and fro; endeavoring to throw me down from the steps on which I stood. They did so once or twice; but I went up again, and continued my discourse. They then began to throw stones; at the same time some got upon the Cross behind me to push me down; on which I could not but observe, how God overrules even the minutest circumstances. One man was bawling just at my ear, when a stone struck him on the cheek, and he was still. A second was forcing his way down to me, till another stone hit him on the forehead: it bounded back, the blood ran down, and he came no farther. The third, being got close to me, stretched out his hand, and in the instant a sharp stone came upon the joints of his fingers. He shook his hand, and was very quiet till I concluded my discourse and went away.[31]

In yet another attempt to escape danger, Wesley was miraculously left unscathed after his horse tumbled over him.[32]

Final Years

As John Wesley's theology developed, tension and division arose between him and Whitefield over the Calvinist view of predestination, which Wesley did not agree with. Eventually, the two men reconciled their differences by putting friendship above their disagreements.[33] Then, in 1749, Wesley wanted to marry Grace Murray, a woman who had nursed him back to health, but his brother Charles would not release his blessing. John was going forward with it anyway until Charles intercepted and encouraged her to marry her other suitor. This brought a rift between the brothers until, ironically, Whitefield helped them to reconcile.

On October 18, 1751, Wesley injured his ankle while walking across the London Bridge. He continued on to preach that day and even preached on his knees the next few days. He went into the care of Mary "Molly" Vazeille to recuperate. To everyone's surprise, he married her after a week.[34] She soon became bitter and resentful of his ministry, and she left him years later. Wesley continued to preach right up until nearly the end of his life. Even in his seventies, he preached to over thirty thousand people.[35] He died on March 2, 1791, at the age of eighty-seven.

Legacy

The Methodist movement that Wesley helped to start consisted of classes or societies and circuit riders.[36] It is believed that Wesley rode over two hundred fifty thousand miles on horseback to preach. He even figured out a way to read while on horseback. Through the years, he preached over forty thousand sermons and published over five thousand books, sermons, and other literature. He received a sum of over twenty thousand pounds for his books but gave most of this money away. He put together societies, opened new chapels, released and launched itinerant preachers, helped the sick, was an avid abolitionist, and helped with schools and orphanages.

When Wesley died, there were over 79,000 Methodists in England and nearly 50,000 in North America. By 1830, Methodism was the largest denomination in the United States.[37] In 1901, there was recorded over 104,000 local preachers, over 89,000 churches, over 861,000 students, and over 7,659,000 members of Methodism as a whole.[38] According to the World Methodist Council, in 2015, there were 39,414,488 members and 51,289,800 who could take Communion worldwide.[39]

Reflections

Journey played a role in the life of John Wesley. It was while he was on his way to the mission field that he crossed paths with the Moravians for the first time. The same week he returned home from the mission field, he again came across a Moravian missionary, who led him to have his encounter shortly afterward. Journey helps to open people up to encounter God in new ways. Many times, it is in the movement of leaving what is familiar and of exploring something new that creates space for people to go after things they might otherwise have been unaware of or blind to.

Receiving from those in the body of Christ both inside and outside his religious tradition also impacted him greatly. It was the Moravians who played a significant part in influencing him to have his defining moment at Aldersgate on May 24, 1738. Then, after he spent a night of prayer and worship with a small community of saints at Fetter Lane in the early hours of New Year's Day, January 1, 1739, the Great Awakening was birthed. Before Wesley's God-encounter, in which his heart was "strangely warmed," he had been rigorous about practicing spiritual disciplines in order to try to gain assurance of his salvation. After his encounter at Aldersgate, he received full assurance and the confidence that he was saved. Not long after he prayed with friends into New Year's Day, he started open-air preaching. This activated his anointing in a powerful way, resulting in great exploits for the kingdom. He received strategies from heaven for launching lay people into ministry, which accelerated the spread of Methodism.

Prophetic Inheritance

Structured Spontaneity

The Methodists became a major contributor to the Pentecostal movement, which would burst on the scene in full force one hundred fifty years later. This movement has brought more people into the kingdom than all the others combined. The themes of power in preaching, discipline in lifestyle, and holiness are all the fruit of a profound encounter with God's love.

One of Wesley's slogans was "Organizing to beat the devil." Such an approach to life gave the church the power of the Spirit in spontaneous, radical obedience to God, as seen in Wesley's meetings in open fields. But working in tandem was the believers' ability to live with great personal discipline and corporate organization without structuring the Holy Spirit out of their gatherings or their movement. They illustrate the perfect blend of structure and strategy, combined with the power and spontaneous elements of the move of the Holy Spirit. Both of these aspects are necessary for us today. History shows us it can be done.

Sustained Revival

Tragically, many great moves of God come and go with little or no impact on the culture or society. Thankfully, that was not the case here. The Wesleys and their partners had the wisdom to sustain the fires of revival that they had been given. While the circuit preachers served to ignite and reignite revival fires, as needed, the local church leaders stayed at the home base and worked on the task of discipleship. Their combined efforts made it possible for this move of God to last.

John Wesley's personal journey to experience the assurance of his salvation became a focus of the Methodist movement. Its members were then able to live with confidence and boldness in their missional responsibilities.

Living accountably in a small group of believers was an extremely important part of the discipling process. If someone sinned, he would confess to the rest of the members of the group and receive much-needed support to live a holy life. This biblical lifestyle became the system by which personal victories became corporate blessings. By having both the fire of revival and the structure of discipline in community, they beat the odds of having a move of God that lasted only a short time. Instead, they became a people who had great and lasting impact on the world around them.

Unity Through Diversity

A huge part of understanding Wesley's story is to recognize the profound influence that the Moravians had upon his life and eventually his movement. What must be noted is that he felt no need to try to become just like the Moravians or to duplicate their model for life and ministry. The principles that the Moravians lived by were valued, taught, celebrated, and honored by Wesley throughout his life, but he felt no need to copy the group.

Another part of this thread is the obvious value that John Wesley placed on other streams in the body of Christ. It is obvious that the Moravians made their mark on his life. But so did George Whitefield, who, in some ways, was his theological opposite. The two men learned how to value their friendship and their commitment to the harvest fields above their need to agree on everything. The legacy of their relationship is profound. They modeled how two are really better than one if united. (See Ecclesiastes 4:9–12.) It must also be noted that two are less than one if divided.

Each of us was meant to be an original, but most of us die merely a copy. Anyone who discovers who God made him or her to be would never want to be anyone else. Tragically, religious systems seldom value this kind of diversity. They work hard to fit all of us into the same mold. Yet, while issues of character and integrity are the same for all of us, our unique expressions of our gifts and personalities are to be protected and treasured.

We must realize that we are all a part of what God is doing in our world, but none of us carries it all. This is an easy statement to make, in the sense of acknowledging that it is true. But it really isn't an effective statement until we place value, in word and deed, on those who differ from us the most. In such a culture of honor, we can celebrate who a person is without stumbling over who he or she is not.

Holy Spirit Manifestations

John Wesley provides us with a great example of how not to quickly judge what we do not understand. Fruit takes time to manifest, and he seemed willing to wait and examine. Most everything we've seen in today's outpouring of the Spirit had already been witnessed in the Great Awakening, under the influence of leaders like Wesley and Whitefield, over two hundred fifty years ago. And while George Whitefield initially expressed concern about what he heard was happening in Wesley's meetings, he changed his tune when he saw the fruit in people's lives. Another convincing factor was how the Holy Spirit began to do the same thing in his meetings. He knew that he did nothing out of emotionalism or the power of suggestion, so he acknowledged that these manifestations were the result of a sovereign invasion of the Spirit of God. He wholeheartedly embraced what God was doing. None of these heroes of the faith dared to lay a hand on what God was doing in order to protect their reputations in front of the often-critical masses. As a result, God was able to trust them with more.

Empowering People

John Wesley knew that the role of preaching the gospel was never to be reserved for only a special class of people with certain kinds of religious training. While training is important, Wesley also knew that to bring about cultural change, there had to be a revolution in the way people thought about following Christ. They had to move from being pew-sitters to participants in the ministry of the gospel. This is one of the most important aspects of Wesley's life—he empowered countless others to preach the gospel. And because he caused the focus of opposition to shift from one person to the many, there was no clear target for the opponents (or rather, the enemy) to discourage or destroy. While he still faced serious persecution, he put something into motion that could not be stopped if he was removed from the picture. Empowering the people of God to do what all disciples were commanded to do is an essential part of effective leadership.

The temptation for many is to create a system in which the leaders become necessary in order for things to work well. But in fact, the leaders are to equip the saints for the work of service. (See Ephesians 4:11–12.) Or, as John Wimber put it, referring to a life of miracles, "We all get to play."

Paying the Price

Few could criticize John Wesley's devotion to Christ. His passion to preach the gospel is almost beyond comprehension. From his devotion to training others through the writing of more than five thousand articles and books, to traveling on horseback over two hundred fifty thousand miles, the man just *had* to declare the good news. His encounter with the love of God made it impossible for him to be passive about life. He discovered that Jesus hadn't accomplished everything in order that we would do nothing.

During Wesley's time, the existing church leadership considered him and his gift to be of little value. He was way too unconventional for their taste. But the real issue that challenged their thinking and the security of their positions of influence was that he preached with power. God showed up when he preached. The demonstration of power forces people to make decisions. Sometimes that power is for us. Sometimes it is against us. But seldom can we remain solely observers of it. Wesley's powerful preaching resulted in leaders either joining the ranks of what God was doing in the earth or opposing and criticizing it. Many clergymen locked Wesley out of their churches. Others tried to destroy his ministry or, worse yet, kill him. But his passion to preach was unparalleled. Consequently, he was a threat to those in established positions of power.

Passion born out of an encounter with God cannot be quenched. Its continuance is not dependent on external circumstances. It is explosive, almost volcanic, in nature. It is the activity of God within the believer that must be expressed to others so that they might taste His love for themselves.

Postscript

We must pray for the church in this hour to have the kinds of encounters with God that enable us to endure the criticisms of opponents of the gospel, both within the religious systems and outside of them. Then, and only then, will we have the same breakthroughs, resulting in another Great Awakening.

Holiness:
Charles G. Finney

"As I closed the door and turned around,
my heart seemed to be liquid within me. All my feelings seemed
to rise and flow out; and the utterance of my heart was,
'I want to pour my whole soul out to God.'"[40]
—*Charles G. Finney*

Holiness is the beauty of God—not a punishing part of His nature to keep us from pleasure or success. Quite the opposite, it is the essence of all that is beautiful and right in the world, which is an expression of the Artist Himself. For this reason, the powers of darkness work hard to distort our understanding of this most wonderful of God's attributes. Seeing His holiness changes us as we become what we behold. If we discover the wonder and beauty of holiness, nothing will be impossible for us.

This aspect of God's person and nature is to be fully seen in believers' lives and expressed through them to the surrounding world. That, in part, is what draws people to Him. When Jesus lived on earth, people sought opportunities to be with Him. He lived the essence of holiness, and still people wanted to be with Him. True holiness is both attractive and convicting. That's why the *Holy* Spirit has been given to us. As He is holy, so are we to be holy. (See, for example, Leviticus 11:44.) Living in a way that displays God's nature in the earth is key for sustaining any move of God. One of the great proponents of this lifestyle was the revivalist Charles Finney, whose encounter with God launched him into becoming a true world-changer.

New Methods for Bringing and Sustaining Revival

Charles Grandison Finney (1792–1875), often referred to as "the Father of Modern Revivalism," was a significant revivalist who taught about—and implemented—new methods for bringing and sustaining revival. Finney had two major encounters that deeply impacted his life. The first was in 1821 when he had his conversion experience, followed by a baptism of "liquid love" the same day. This experience totally transformed him. Immediately following, he quit his job and went into full-time ministry. He saw many revivals break out as a result of his efforts. Over twenty years later, during the winter of 1843–1844, Finney became disillusioned when he observed that his earlier converts had lost their zeal. This led him to study holiness. During this time, he was stirred to make an act of consecration to the Lord. Following this, he received a fresh baptism of the Holy Spirit, which resulted in a peace he had not experienced until that point. He also shifted the focus of his teaching to the fullness of Christ. Finney wanted sustainable revival, and he saw that holiness could be a means to help sustain revival and carry it into future generations. His methods and his literature reshaped American evangelicalism's approach to revival.

The Week When Everything Changed

Charles Finney was born on August 29, 1792, in Warren, Connecticut. He grew up in New Jersey before eventually moving to New York. His parents were not believers, so he did not receive religious training as a child. From 1818–1821, he studied law and became an apprentice to a judge in New York.[41] It was during his studies that he noticed many references to Scripture, which led him to buy his first Bible.

In 1821, at twenty-nine years old, Finney entered into a week that would change his life forever. On Sunday, October 7, he was stirred to make peace with God and to give himself "wholly to the work of securing the salvation of [his] soul."[42] He had resolved to put aside all business and any other distractions so that he could focus on this one thing. Over the next few days, the conviction and surge in his heart continued to build. He longed for a safe place to pray boldly and to encounter God. He wrote that "Tuesday night I had become very nervous; and in the night a strange feeling came over me as if I was about to die. I knew that if I did I should sink down to hell; but I quieted myself as best I could until morning."[43]

Conversion in the Woods

The next morning, Wednesday, October 10, Finney's hunger for God led him to find a secret place to pray. He remembered,

> At an early hour I started for the office. But just before I arrived at the office, something seemed to confront me with questions like these: indeed, it seemed as if the inquiry was within myself, as if an inward voice said to me, "What are you waiting for? Did you not promise to give your heart to God? And what are you trying to do? Are you endeavoring to work out a righteousness of your own?"…
>
> Without being distinctly aware of it, I had stopped in the street right where the inward voice seemed to arrest one. How long I remained in that position I cannot say. But after this distinct revelation had stood for some little time before my mind, the question seemed to be put, "Will you accept it now, to-day?" I replied, "Yes; I will accept it to-day, or I will die in the attempt."
>
> …Nevertheless, instead of going to the office, I turned and bent my course toward the woods, feeling that I must be alone, and away from all human eyes and ears, so that I could pour out my prayer to God….

...As I turned to go up into the woods, I recollect to have said, "I will give my heart to God, or I never will come down from there."...

...But when I attempted to pray I found that my heart would not pray.... The thought was pressing me of the rashness of my promise, that I would give my heart to God that day or die in the attempt. It seemed to me as if that was binding upon my soul; and yet I was going to break my vow. A great sinking and discouragement came over me, and I felt almost too weak to stand upon my knees.[44]

Finney was not going to back down from his resolve to find God. Even in his intensity, he continued to struggle with an overwhelming sense of his sin until it broke him down before the Lord.[45]

Just at that point this passage of Scripture seemed to drop into my mind with a flood of light: "Then shall ye go and pray unto me, and I will hearken unto you. Then shall ye seek me and find me, when ye shall search for me with all your heart." I instantly seized hold of this with my heart. I had intellectually believed the Bible before; but never had the truth been in my mind that faith was a voluntary trust instead of an intellectual state....The question of my being converted, had not so much as arisen to my thought; but as I went up, brushing through the leaves and bushes, I recollect saying with great emphasis, "If I am ever converted, I will preach the Gospel."[46]

Baptism of "Liquid Love"

Following his prayers in the woods, Finney experienced a peace he had never before known.[47] Later that same night, as Finney began to worship, his heart melted in the overwhelming presence and love of God.

I went to my dinner, and found I had no appetite to eat.... I took down my bass-viol, and, as I was accustomed to do, began to play and sing some pieces of sacred music. But as soon as I began to sing those sacred words, I began to weep. It seemed as if my heart was all liquid; and my feelings were in such a state that I could not hear my own voice in singing without causing my sensibility to overflow.... After trying in vain to suppress my tears, I put up my instrument and stopped singing....

...Just at dark Squire W—, seeing that everything was adjusted, bade me good-night and went to his home. I had accompanied him to the door; and as I closed the door and turned around, my heart seemed to be liquid within me. All my feelings seemed to rise and flow out; and the utterance of my heart was, "I want to pour my whole soul out to God." The rising of my soul was so great that I rushed into the room back of the front office to pray.[48]

Face-to-Face Encounter with Jesus

In the midst of encountering God's love, Finney saw Jesus in a way he never had before.

There was no fire, and no light, in the room; nevertheless it appeared to me as if it were perfectly light. As I went in and shut the door after me, it seemed as if I met the Lord Jesus Christ face to face. It did not occur to me then, nor did it for some time afterward, that it was wholly a mental state. On the contrary it seemed to me that I saw him as I would see any other man. He said nothing, but looked at me in such a manner as to break me right down at his feet. I have always since regarded this as a most remarkable state of mind; for it seemed to me a reality, that he stood before me, and I fell down at his feet and poured out my soul to him. I wept aloud like a child, and made such confessions as I could with my choked utterance. It seemed to me that I bathed his feet with my tears; and yet I had no distinct impression that I touched him, that I recollect.[49]

Waves of Electricity

Finney's defining day continued into the evening hours. The waves of God's presence flowed so powerfully over him that he felt like he might die if they did not stop.

I must have continued in this state for a good while.... I returned to the front office, and found that the fire that I had made of large wood was nearly burned out. But as I turned and was about to take a seat by the fire, I received a mighty baptism of the Holy Ghost. Without any expectation of it, without ever having the thought in my mind that there was any such thing for me, without any recollection that I had ever heard the thing mentioned by any person in the world, the Holy Spirit descended upon me in a manner that seemed to go through me, body and soul. I could feel the impression, like a wave of electricity, going through and through me. Indeed it seemed to come in waves and waves of liquid love; for I could not express it in any other way. It seemed like the very breath of God. I can recollect distinctly that it seemed to fan me, like immense wings.

No words can express the wonderful love that was shed abroad in my heart. I wept aloud with joy and love; and I do not know but I should say, I literally bellowed out unutterable gushings of my heart. These waves came over me, and over me, and over me, one after the other, until I recollect I cried out, "I shall die if these waves continue to pass over me." I said, "Lord, I cannot bear any more"; yet I had no fear of death.[50]

Holy Laughter

Finney's encounter caused him to weep loudly, which attracted some concern. When people came to check on him, they broke out in holy laughter. After seeing the power of God on Finney's life, one person was immediately struck to the ground and cried out for more of God. Even in the midst of his life-changing encounter, Finney imparted and released what he had received to those who came to him.

How long I continued in this state with this baptism continuing to roll over me and go through me, I do not know. But I know it was late in the evening when a member of my choir—for I was the leader of the choir—came into the office to see me. He was a member of the church. He found me in this state of loud weeping, and said to me, "Mr. Finney, what ails you?" I could make him no answer for some time. He then said, "Are you in pain?" I gathered myself up as best I could, and replied, "No, but so happy that I cannot live."

He turned and left the office, and in a few minutes returned with one of the elders of the church, whose shop was nearly across the way from our office. This elder was a very serious man; and in my presence had been very watchful, and I had scarcely ever seen him laugh. When he came in, I was very much in the state in which I was when the young man went out to call him. He asked me how I felt, and I began to tell him. Instead of saying anything, he fell into a most spasmodic laughter. It seemed as if it was impossible for him to keep from laughing from the very bottom of his heart....

Soon after this they all retired and left me alone.... I soon fell asleep, but almost as soon awoke again on account of the great flow of the love of God that was in my heart. I was so filled with love that I could not sleep. Soon I fell asleep again, and awoke in the same manner. When I awoke, this temptation would return upon me, and the love that seemed to be in my heart would abate; but as soon as I was asleep, it was so warm within me that I would immediately awake. Thus I continued till, late at night, I obtained some sound repose.[51]

Activation

The morning after this encounter, Thursday, October 11, Finney was still experiencing a continued baptism of love.

When I awoke in the morning the sun had risen, and was pouring a clear light into my room.... Instantly the baptism that I had received the night before, returned upon me in the same manner. I arose upon my knees in the bed and wept aloud with joy, and remained for some time too much overwhelmed with the baptism of the Spirit to do anything but pour out my soul to God.[52]

Instant Evangelist

Finney went to his office with the intention to work that day. However, in response to the inquiry of a client about an upcoming trial, he said, "I have a retainer from the Lord Jesus Christ to plead his cause, and I cannot plead yours."[53] He then walked out of the office and stopped at the shoemaker's shop to talk about God with anybody he might meet.[54] He joined in on a conversation to refute Universalism. The young man who was countered in that discussion left and went toward the woods. He returned later to tell Finney that he had given his heart to God. Finney recalled, "I spoke with many persons that day, and I believe the Spirit of God made lasting impressions upon every one of them. I cannot remember one whom I spoke with, who was not soon after converted."[55]

Later that night, a local family found out that Finney had been converted and invited him to dinner. They asked him to give a blessing before the meal, something he had never done before. After he began the blessing, he was overcome with compassion and then "burst into weeping." He could not continue on, and everyone sat speechless. Then one of the young men rushed out and locked himself in his room, only to reappear the next morning confessing his new hope in Christ.[56]

When word spread that Finney was converted, the whole village was in a stir. He went to a crowded place of worship, and since no one was ready to start the meeting, Finney shared his testimony. He recalled, "We had a wonderful meeting that evening; and, from that day, we had a meeting every evening for a long time. The work spread on every side."[57] Many were brought to Christ in that town because of Finney's passion to share the gospel. He also went to his parents' house and prayed with them to know Christ.

Ministry of Revival

Finney began theological training under George Gale and, by 1822, started to minister full-time; he was later licensed as an evangelist with the Presbyterian church. In 1824, he married Lydia Root, with whom he had six children. In 1825, he was invited to preach in Utica, New York, where revival broke out as he ministered there and in the surrounding areas of Rome and Syracuse.[58] At Utica, five hundred conversions were reported within only a few weeks.[59] In the spring of 1826, Finney went to a factory in that city and saw a move of God break out among the workers there.

I approached slowly, looking on each side at the machinery, as I passed; but observed that this girl grew more and more agitated, and could not proceed with her work. When I came within eight or ten feet of her, I looked solemnly at her. She observed it, and was quite overcome, and sunk down, and burst into tears. The impression caught almost like powder, and in a few moments nearly all in the room were in tears. This feeling spread through the factory. Mr. W—, the owner of the establishment, was present, and seeing the state of things, he said to the superintendent, "Stop the mill, and let the people attend to religion; for it is more important that our souls should be saved than that this factory run." The gate was immediately shut down, and the factory stopped; but where should we assemble? The superintendent suggested that the mule room was large; and, the mules being run up, we could assemble there. We did so, and a more powerful meeting I scarcely ever attended. It went on with great power. The building was large, and had many people in it, from the garret to the cellar. The revival went through the mill with astonishing power, and in the course of a few days nearly all in the mill were hopefully converted.[60]

By 1826–1827, revival spread to western New York in what later would be termed "the burned-over district." As the years went on, revival continued to follow Finney. In 1830–1831, during his meetings in Rochester, New York, businesses closed down and the owners put notices on their doors "urging people to attend Finney's meetings." Crime in the city also dropped by two-thirds during this time.[61] Many leading businessmen, lawyers, and doctors were saved during the revivals.

In 1832, Finney moved to New York City and preached at Chatham Street Chapel. Over five hundred people were converted under his ministry there.[62] He later founded and pastored New York City's Broadway Tabernacle. In 1835, he moved to Ohio to be a professor at Oberlin College, eventually becoming the institution's president (1851–1866). He also published his *Lectures on Revivals of Religion* in 1835, which countered the prevalent Calvinism of the day.[63] Later, he and Asa Mahan (1799–1889) developed what became known as "Oberlin Theology."[64] Finney also became an avid abolitionist and helped Oberlin College become one of the earliest schools in America to integrate African-Americans and also women.[65]

"New Measures"

As Finney began to see God move, he looked at patterns and developed a methodology for revivals. He pioneered a way of revivalism called "New Measures." Influenced by John Wesley, he integrated the Methodists' "anxious bench" into his meetings. This is somewhat similar to today's altar call.[66] He also allowed mixed congregations of men and women and regularly made space for women to pray publicly in the meetings. He used a style of preaching that sought to evoke an immediate response and called people to action in the moment.[67] While many preachers of the day read their sermons and referenced only historical examples, Finney spoke inspired by the Holy Spirit and rarely used many notes. He preached in a way that the people could easily relate to, drawing on examples from everyday life to illustrate his points. Some complained that Finney "talked like a lawyer at the bar," "talked to the people in a colloquial manner," and addressed people as "'you,' instead of preaching about sin and sinners, and saying 'they.'"[68] It didn't matter to Finney, though, because he burned for "the unalterable necessity of a radical change of heart by the Holy Ghost."[69] He had his heart set on releasing the gospel, so much so that he would sometimes even ride horseback through storms to the point of coughing blood in order to travel to meetings.[70]

Finney also recognized the significance that prayer played in releasing the kingdom. He regularly sent his intercessor, Daniel Nash, into cities three or four weeks before him to covenant with a handful of believers in the area to pray. Nash's job was to break up the fallow ground so that when Finney arrived, the community would be ready to receive the seeds. Other times, Finney called people to set apart times of prayer as the only means to release revival.[71]

Finney saw God move in powerful ways as he continued to minister. There were times when people fell out under the power of God, and other times when Finney gave words of knowledge without even knowing it.[72] At one meeting, an illiterate woman was instantly able to read the Bible after her conversion.[73] Another time, Finney prayed intensely for his friend's wife to be healed. After the Lord had given him "power to prevail," the woman was healed the next morning.[74]

In one town Finney visited, there was a notorious man who ridiculed Christians and sought to oppose the Christian work. This man owned a tavern where "all the opposers of the revival" would gather. Finney's intercessor, Nash, added the man to his prayer list. One night during Finney's meeting, this tavern owner showed up, and many people feared what he might do. When Finney recognized him, he noticed that the tavern owner had not come to oppose but was rather sitting in anguish. The man then arose to offer a testimony that "thoroughly broke up the fallow ground in many hearts." Finney recalled that "it was the most powerful means that could have been used, just then, to give an impetus to the work."[75] Following this, the tavern owner banned profanity and opened up his tavern for a prayer meeting nearly every night.

When Finney went to Auburn, New York, there was opposition because bad reports had been given to the people about him before he got there. He called out to God for help to rise above the storms. In communion with God, he saw a vision and found strength to stand.

> The sense of God's presence, and all that passed between God and my soul at that time, I can never describe. It led me to be perfectly trustful, perfectly calm, and to have nothing but the most perfectly kind feelings toward all the brethren that were misled, and were arraying themselves against me.[76]

Finney continued to encounter God in various ways after his initial conversion and profound life-changing experience. One time, he got caught up in the glory of God and saw a light that "seemed to be like the brightness of the sun in every direction." This vision of God's glory sent him "into a flood of tears."[77]

Another Fresh Baptism of the Holy Spirit

As the years went on, Finney observed some of the long-term effects of his revivals. He was troubled because while some converts were still burning bright, others had backslidden or lost their zeal for the Lord.[78] He was stirred to search for ways to increase holiness so that the transformation in his converts would be permanent. He began to develop talks about holiness and to teach them to his students at Oberlin. In the winter of 1843–44, he spent time preaching in Boston at Marlborough Chapel. There, he was burdened because he saw that the believers were not able to release what had been imparted to them to bring transformation to the city, but were rather weakened by their surroundings.

> But this winter, in particular, my mind was exceedingly exercised on the question of personal holiness; and in respect to the state of the church, their want of power with God; the weakness of the orthodox churches in Boston, the weakness of their faith, and their want of power in the midst of such a community. The fact that they were making little or no progress in overcoming the errors of the city, greatly affected my mind.

> I gave myself to a great deal of prayer. After my evening services, I would retire as early as I well could; but rose at four o'clock in the morning, because I could sleep no longer, and immediately went to the study, and engaged in prayer.[79]

During this season of meditating on God's holiness, Finney was stirred to an extreme level of consecration. He was even prompted to surrender, and to trust God in, the posture of his heart toward his wife. After an intense struggle, he finally yielded and was able to surrender all. Following this, Finney "had a deeper view of what was implied in consecration to God, than ever before." He was so surrendered that he experienced a "deep and perfect…resting in the will of God" that he had not previously experienced.[80] God also gave his "soul a very thorough overhauling, and a fresh baptism of his Spirit."[81]

Results of Renewed Baptism of the Holy Spirit

After this second blessing of a fresh baptism of the Holy Spirit, Finney experienced a "perfect rest, body and soul." Additionally, he experienced calmness, greater religious freedom, and "freshness" of his first love.[82] He claimed that this "new and enlarged experience" was the most significant he had had up to that point.[83] He also shifted the focus of his preaching more to fullness in Christ. He saw that this new emphasis affected the people in Boston in a life-changing way.

Final Years

In 1847, Finney's wife died, and the next year he married Elizabeth Atkinson.[84] In 1849–1851, he took his first international trip, traveling to England to release revival. In 1859–1860, he took a second trip to England and also visited Scotland. After his second wife died in 1863, he married Rebecca Allen Rayl in 1865. From 1866–1875 he taught in Oberlin, Ohio. He continued to preach until the day the Lord took him home, August 16, 1875, just before his eighty-third birthday.

Legacy

Throughout his ministry, Finney had a great impact on the Second Great Awakening, leading over five hundred thousand people to Christ and developing a new methodology for releasing revival. Finney changed the way sinners approached God. He called them to act now to be saved instead of "waiting" on Him for salvation. He also pioneered a scientific method called "New Measures" in order to bring revivals. Throughout the years, he was an advocate for women, abolition, and other social causes. Finney paved the way for evangelists like Dwight L. Moody, Billy Sunday, Billy Graham, Oral Roberts, and others.

Reflections

It was Finney's conversion and baptism of "liquid love" on October 10, 1821, that caused the most extreme shift in his life. Immediately following this, he quit his job, prepared for full-time ministry, and then began to release revival fires wherever he went. Twenty years later, as he spent time studying the topic of holiness, he had a "fresh baptism of the Holy Spirit," which resulted in greater anointing and a shift in focus for preaching. Both encounters were profound in Finney's life. The first one was a crisis encounter that catapulted him into his destiny of releasing revival fire. The second experience came gradually as he pursued holiness, and it had a deep, personal impact on his spirit, mind, emotions, and heart. It also led him to preach holiness as a means for sustaining revival.

Prophetic Inheritance

There is nothing in me that could ever be satisfied with having merely "good church meetings," as wonderful as they are. While it is a great honor to see the demonstration of God's power to transform lives, such an encounter is incomplete until it impacts the world around us. Awakenings, which bring about global shifts in the awareness of God and His purposes, are always in the heart of God. Charles Finney was used powerfully in what was called the Second Great Awakening. The breakthroughs in which he lived are now our inheritance and must be rediscovered and modeled for yet another Great Awakening—greater in every way than all previous moves because we live in the momentum created by such a glorious inheritance.

Joyful Holiness

Today, our most common understanding of holiness is that it is very somber. In fact, many people today reject joy as a frivolous experience in their pursuit of holiness. It is not the idea of joy that is rejected, for that would be unbiblical. It is the experience of joy that so many find offensive. To such people, joy sometimes appears to be the opposite of holiness. Yet the Bible teaches us that holiness and joy are related.

Nehemiah 8:10 says, "*Then he said to them, 'Go your way, eat the fat, drink the sweet, and send portions to those for whom nothing is prepared; for this day is holy to our Lord. Do not sorrow, for the joy of the* LORD *is your strength.'*" The context of this verse is quite interesting. The Word of God had just been read, and the people of Israel knew that they didn't measure up to God's standards. But instead of allowing the people to give a mournful response to God, the priests led them into celebration. The reason? They understood the words that were read. Think of it: the joy that starts with understanding God's heart is what takes us into maturity and strength. This passage puts *joy* and *holiness* together: "*This day is holy.... The joy of the* LORD *is your strength.*"

This truth is vital to understand. Charles Finney, a man who preached the holiness message with great effect, was in fact first transformed by joy. There is something profound about the effect of the joy of the Lord in a person's life, taking him or her deeper into the beauty of holiness (living fully for God). It is tangible.

In the experience of my church, joy has been central. In fact, whenever this quality seems to be waning, I tell our people to find where they left their joy. Following Jesus must remain a life of joy. Joy, fully realized, has a profound effect on how people live. As a result, it impacts the sustainability of all revivals. Without joy, revivals end up falling short of becoming awakenings; therefore, they never develop into God's ultimate goal—reformation. When church leadership chokes the joy out of the move of God, their wrong control also kills liberty and freedom, which are the true evidences that God is present and is doing as He pleases.

Joy is such a priceless commodity in heaven that it was used to inspire and motivate Jesus to endure the cross. He suffered crucifixion "*for the joy that was set before Him*" (Hebrews 12:2). If it brought such strength to Jesus in the ultimate earthly challenge, it certainly can enable us to experience a move of God that does not diminish.

Valuing the Presence of God

Charles Finney is one of the best examples of the principles I discussed in my book *Hosting the Presence*. In essence, because of the impact of the Holy Spirit on his life, and because he gave place for the Spirit to rest upon him, he was a catalyst for transformation in any environment he walked into. The day he had his face-to-face encounter with Jesus, everyone he talked to was soon converted. There was something, or rather *Someone*, upon him that made surrendering to the Lord the only logical response for those whom he encountered. Learning how to maintain this sense of Presence is really what drove Finney to seek a greater baptism of the Spirit.

One of my favorite stories in all of church history is when Finney walked into a factory, and, though he said nothing, the Spirit of God upon him brought such an overwhelming conviction of sin and an awareness of need for God that the owner, who was an unbeliever, shut down the factory to give room for revival. Many church leaders will not make room for a move of God, yet this unbeliever stopped everything that would profit him so that his workers could find peace with God. That man models a value that too few pastors and leaders hold. Great moves of God happen when people long for God to invade their environment and do as He pleases. He often starts with what is most sacred to us—our Sunday services.

Embarking on the Journey

It has been said, "Wise men still travel." And it is true. There must be a willingness to move out of our comfort zones, where we are in charge of everything, and let our hunger for God take over. For Charles Finney, it wasn't a trip to a foreign land. It was a walk in the woods. Seldom do people find what they're crying out for when they hold to their agenda and routine. There is something to be said about being outside of what we are accustomed to and plunged into something that is new and risky. It seems that God likes those moments and those conditions. People once brought a blind man to Jesus to be healed. They thought if Jesus would just touch him, he'd be made whole. Mark 8:23 says, *"So He took the blind man by the hand and led him out of the town. And when He had spit on his eyes and put His hands on him, He asked him if he saw anything."* The result, of course, was that this man was healed. But it is the process that is worth noting. Jesus took the man by the hand and led him out of town. To remove a blind man from familiar settings might almost seem cruel. But for this man, it was key to his miracle. Jesus often requires us to move beyond convenience to discover the kingdom.

One of the most offensive things I've heard leaders say is, "God knows we want revival. He can touch us here as well as He can touch us in Toronto, Brownsville, or any other such place." It sounds so spiritual, but it's foolish. Most of the individuals examined in this book were on a journey somewhere. It's important to leave our convenience and comfort zones to find that pearl of great price. (See Matthew 13:45–46.) Wise men still travel!

Prayer for Breakthroughs

Sometime after Finney's conversion, he discovered that believers in his community had partnered together in prayer for his salvation. There is little doubt that this discovery left a profound mark on his thinking in regards to massive revivals, the kind where great multitudes of people would be saved. This resulted in prayer being a central theme of his ministry—specific, calculated prayer for breakthroughs over certain cities and churches that led to the conversion of great numbers of people. Sometimes, extra focus was taken for a specific situation. Occasionally, his prayers were simple groanings beyond words. He learned that prayers that don't move us won't move God.

Some years ago, a friend of mine was training people in the ministry of intercession, with a specific bent—they were to pray for pastors. I'll never forget the day I received a letter from the person assigned to me. They made a covenant before God to pray for me at least fifteen minutes a day for the next year. I felt like the richest man in the world. I can't think of a greater gift than to have someone pray for us consistently. Charles Finney received a similar gift. His name was Daniel Nash. This great prayer warrior would become the individual whose intercessions set the stage for countless thousands to come into the kingdom during Finney's meetings. There's little doubt that without those prayers going before him, Finney wouldn't have had nearly the success or impact on the nation that he did. Breakthrough happened because of the prayers of Nash combined with the bold obedience of Charles Finney. The role of prayer was so vital that after Nash's death, Charles Finney traveled very little in revival ministry. It was that crucial.

Perhaps the most delightful part of Finney's encounters with God was the deep affection and tenderness that the Lord showed him. Stories of these encounters provide an intimate picture of a lawyer becoming a lover and friend of God. This is the basis for everything else. To construct our lives and ministries with any other building materials is to build with straw.

Involvement in Social Causes

It should also be noted that many, if not all, of the heroes of the faith mentioned in this book gave themselves to the poor and fought hard against the social ills of the day. For example, Charles Finney was a strong opponent of racial inequality, helping Oberlin College to become one of the earliest schools in America to integrate African-Americans and also women.

Relevance in impacting the ills of the day is essential as an expression of the kingdom on earth. These are manifestations of God's dominion, as He is a God of justice. Defending the defenseless and speaking for those who have no voice are a huge part of the effects of revival.

Many Baptisms

One of the most important aspects of Finney's personal life and ministry is that he always hungered for more of God. His encounters with God are legendary. The fruit of those encounters is also legendary, establishing some of the high points of the Second Great Awakening. And yet he knew there was more. This hunger marked him in a profound way. Although he had experienced some of the greatest harvests of souls anyone has ever seen, he knew there was more.

Regardless of our various definitions of the baptism of the Holy Spirit, we can all probably agree it was essential in the life of the early church. And as we look through history at the greatest world changers, they all sought for and experienced this gift from God, viewing it as absolutely essential. For Charles Finney, there were at least two major baptisms.

Postscript

It's rather strange to the natural mind, but there is a spiritual hunger that comes only from fullness and satisfaction. In the same way that we are exalted by humbling ourselves, or that we receive by giving, so we experience our greatest hunger from our greatest satisfaction or fullness.

Such was the case for Finney. His overwhelming sense of the presence of God upon his life was just enough for him to cry for more. These God-encounters became his new norm, as they should be for any believer. It was this second touch that made such an increased impact on him and the world around him. These baptisms of the Spirit are the defining moments that shape the course of history. It is time for those who claim to have had this experience to actually hunger for more until the world around us stands up and takes notice that the living God is among us.

4

Laying Foundations for Legacy:
Dwight L. Moody

"I do not know of anything that America needs more today than men and women on fire with the fire of heaven; and I have yet to find a man or a woman on fire with the Spirit of God that is a failure. I believe it is utterly impossible. They are never discouraged or disheartened. They rise higher and higher and it grows better and better all the while. My dear friends, if you haven't this illumination, make up your mind you are going to have it. Pray, 'O God, illuminate me with Thy Holy Spirit!'"[85]
—D. L. Moody

Every new move of God brings back to the church a spiritual truth or reality that had been missing from it. Many people call this a restoration movement, because God is restoring to us what once existed in the early church. Jesus taught that giving new things to His people is like putting new wine in a container made of animal skin. New wine expands.

If the animal skin is already stretched, it will tear and be unusable. But if the wineskin is new also, it will stretch with the expanding new wine. (See, for example, Matthew 9:17.) God is concerned for the new wine (His present outpouring) and the old wineskin (what God gave in the previous move). New structures and systems have to be created that can expand with the new thing God is doing.

Formulas and Patterns for Revival

Using formulas and patterns for revival doesn't in any way control God. Instead, because God honors His Word, we are invited to learn His ways so that we might more fully co-labor with Him. His ways are hidden for us to discover, not hidden from us that they might remain a secret. Discovering His ways enables His coworkers to labor with much more confidence. Again, it is not that we don't need to hear from God or follow His leading. Quite the opposite. God honors those who have the heart to discover His ways. And one of the great revivalists leading the charge to discover those ways was D. L. Moody. We must relearn what he found for us.

Moody also paved the way for preaching that focused primarily on the goodness of God. This was a refreshing change to those who had grown up hearing only of the threats of God's punishment for sin. God is not okay with sin, period. Yet it's wonderful to find those in history who encountered God's extreme goodness so profoundly that they rediscovered the truth that it's God's kindness that leads to repentance. (See Romans 2:4.)

A Series of Events

Dwight L. Moody (1837–1899) was a great American evangelist who pioneered new forms of evangelism and invited churches from various denominations to work together to bring in the harvest. In 1861, Moody's interaction with a dying Sunday school teacher sparked a fire within him to reach lost souls and inspired him to quit his job to enter full-time ministry. Then, in 1867, a seventeen-year-old British preacher influenced Moody to receive God's love in a way that transformed his ministry. As a result, rather than preach about punishment against sinners, Moody emphasized God's love and mercy.

A series of events in 1871 positioned Moody to step into one of the most significant shifts of his life. First, he encountered two women who regularly prayed for him and encouraged him to pray for power from on high. During his season of prayer for this power, the great Chicago fire burned down his church and his home and killed many in his congregation. Following this tragedy, he took his family on a trip to New York. One day, while walking down the street, he was overwhelmed with God's presence and a hunger to be filled with more of the Holy Spirit. Needing to satisfy this urge, he knocked on the door of a friend's home nearby and asked to use one of his rooms to pray. There, he received power from on high like never before. After this, even though Moody preached the same messages as before, people responded in new waves. Rather than one or two conversions here or there, thousands were converted at once. It was while ministering in England that Moody saw the initial impact of his encounter. He also partnered there with musician Ira D. Sankey. The two had great success in England, where they ministered to millions of people.

Conversion

Dwight Lyman Moody, originally from Northfield, Massachusetts, was born into a poor family on February 5, 1837. When he was four years old, his father died suddenly, and the creditors came and took nearly everything.[86] The sixth of nine children, Moody worked on a farm at a young age to help the family. At the age of seventeen, he left home to seek work in Boston. He was unsuccessful until his uncle, Samuel Holton, hesitantly gave him a job at his shoe store. The only requirement for Moody was compulsory church attendance at the nearby Congregational church.[87] In just three months, Moody became the leading salesman at the store.[88] Then, on April 21, 1855, Moody's Sunday school leader, Edward Kimball, visited him at his workplace to share about the love of Jesus. Moody surrendered and made a commitment to Jesus that day. Years later, Moody repaid the favor when he had the opportunity to lead Kimball's seventeen-year-old son to the Lord.[89]

"Then God Opened My Eyes"

Eventually, Moody moved to Chicago and became successful in selling shoes there as well. In 1858, while continuing his day job, he opened North Market Hall Sabbath School, where he reached out to the children on the streets. Moody also started a Sunday school class in Chicago that met at the Young Men's Christian Association (YMCA). He became more involved in the organization over the next few years (1857–1862), and in 1863 was officially appointed a missionary with the YMCA. By 1860, attendance of his Sunday school class reached fifteen hundred, and even President Lincoln came to visit.[90] His mission Sunday school focused on reaching out to the unsaved and poor youth in the city. This ministry grew so much that Moody, still only in his mid-twenties, started a church on February 28, 1864, called Illinois Street Church. At a time when people often had to rent seats in the pews to attend church, Moody invited all, especially the poor, to come to church for free. In 1865, he became the vice president of the Chicago Sunday School, and a year later the president of the Chicago chapter of the YMCA.[91] Moody recalled,

> When I went to Chicago, I hired four pews in a church, and used to go out on the street and pick up young men and fill these pews. I never spoke to those young men about their souls; that was the work of the elders, I thought. After working for some time like that, I started a mission Sabbath-school. I thought numbers were everything, and so I worked for numbers. When the attendance ran below one thousand, it troubled me; and when it ran to twelve or fifteen hundred, I was elated. Still none were converted; there was no harvest. Then God opened my eyes.[92]

In 1861, a dying Sunday school teacher told Moody how discouraged he was that none of the ladies in his class had been converted. Recognizing the impact that personal visits had had on his own life, Moody encouraged him to meet with them at their homes to lead them to Christ. Moody accompanied the teacher on this venture, and all of the ladies in the class got converted. Following this harvest of souls, they arranged an evening prayer meeting for the Sunday school class. Moody recalled that on that day, "God kindled a fire in my soul that has never gone out."[93] The next day, he and the class went to say good-bye to the teacher whom they would never see again. Moody remembered the impact that this whole experience had on the course of his life:

> I didn't know what this was going to cost me. I was disqualified for business; it had become distasteful to me. I had got a taste of another world, and cared no more for making money. For some days after, the greatest struggle of my life took place. Should I give up business and give myself to Christian work, or should I not? I have never regretted my choice.[94]

As a result of his interaction with the Sunday school teacher, Moody decided to quit his business job so he could minister full-time. He had already put enough money aside to cover a year's salary. With some of this money, he purchased a pony to widen his reach.[95] When his money ran out sooner than he expected, he tried to follow the way of George Müller by living completely by faith. George Müller (1805–1898), who was originally from Prussia but later relocated to England, had opened an orphanage in Bristol in 1835. Choosing to rely upon God alone for his provision, he financed his center through prayer based on the principle found in Philippians 4:19. Many who came after him followed his faith model.[96]

Moody went so far as to sleep on the bench in the prayer room and to eat only cheese and crackers so he could afford to continue ministering. He did not tell anyone of his needs, but when some of his friends found out, they quickly came to his aid. During this time, Moody pursued Emma C. Revell and married her on August 28, 1862.[97] Not long after, their friends surprised them with a fully furnished home, rent free, given to them early on New Year's morning.[98]

When the Civil War broke out, Moody organized a group to minister to troops that were stationed near Chicago. From 1861–1865, he ministered to thousands of soldiers, both Union and Confederate, on and off the battlefield.[99] Around this time, Moody and his wife met Emma Dryer, who partnered with them to build a school specifically for training women for evangelism.

First Trip to England

In 1867, Moody went on a trip to England with a desire to meet Charles H. Spurgeon and George Müller and learn more about their methods for ministry.[100] In a letter Moody wrote to his mother, he mentioned how "the great orphan schools of George Müller are at Bristol. He has 1,150 children in the house, but never asks a man for a cent to support them. He calls on God, and God sends money to him. It is wonderful to see what God can do with a man of prayer."[101]

At that time, Moody was known to only a few in England; nonetheless, he established a noon prayer meeting for the YMCA in Aldersgate Street, and about one hundred men were present for the first meeting. It is interesting to note that Aldersgate is the same street where John Wesley had his "strangely warmed heart" encounter. As the days went on, several hundred began to gather. This prayer meeting spurred others in England to start similar meetings. While there, Moody heard the saying, "The world has yet to see what God will do with and for and through and in and by the man who is fully and wholly consecrated to Him."[102] These words marked him, and he sought to be that man.

New Epoch of God's Love:
The Boy Preacher and John 3:16

Moody had heard about Henry Moorehouse, "the Boy Preacher" from England, but had never met him until his first trip to the United Kingdom. Moorehouse was only about seventeen years old when he approached Moody and told him that he would like to come to Chicago to preach at his church. He asked Moody which ship he was returning to America on so he could accompany him. Moody didn't think this zealous teenager could really preach, so he never followed up with him.

Several weeks after Moody returned to Chicago, he received a letter from Moorehouse stating that he was in America and could come to Chicago and preach for him if he wanted. Moody responded by telling him to look him up if he came to town. Moody received a second letter to the same effect. Then Moody received a third letter saying that on Thursday of that week, Moorehouse would come to Chicago and preach for Moody if he wanted. Moody had already made up his mind that Moorehouse couldn't preach, so he was not sure what to do about this boy, especially since he was scheduled to be out of town on Thursday. Moody told his leaders to let Moorehouse have a try at preaching in a smaller meeting and then, if he did well, to proceed accordingly.

When Moody returned on Saturday, he discovered from his wife and the leaders that the boy had been a great success. On Sunday, Moorehouse preached from John 3:16 about God's great love for sinners. He backed up everything with Scripture and went through an overview of the whole Bible to prove how *"God so loved the world."* Moody recalled, "I never knew up to that time that God loved us so much. This heart of mine began to thaw out; I could not keep back the tears. It was like news from a far country: I just drank it in."[103]

Even though the next night was a Monday, crowds came with their Bibles. Moorehouse expounded on John 3:16 once more. This impacted Moody again, and he recalled that Moorehouse

> struck a higher note than ever, and it was sweet to my soul to hear it. He just beat that truth down into my heart, and I have never doubted it since. I used to preach that God was behind the sinner with a double-edged sword ready to hew him down. I have got done with that. I preach now that God is behind him with love, and he is running away from the God of love.[104]

At the Tuesday meeting, Moorehouse talked about John 3:16 yet again, and Moody recalled that the love of God "seemed to strike a higher chord still. *'God so loved the world, that He gave His only begotten Son, that whosoever believeth in Him should not perish, but have'*—not going to have when you die, but have it right here, now—*'eternal life.'* By that time we began to believe it, and we have never doubted it since."[105] Moorehouse continued to preach this text for seven straight nights.

It is also recorded that Moorehouse later said to Moody, "You are sailing on the wrong track. If you will change your course and learn to preach God's words instead of your own, He will make you a great power."[106] This caused Moody to focus on preaching the Bible exclusively.[107] Moody's son later recognized that "a new epoch in Mr. Moody's religious experience and preaching was marked by his friendship with Henry Moorehouse."[108] Moorehouse returned to Chicago several times after his first visit and ministered alongside Moody. He was also one of the first to welcome Moody in his future visits to England.

The Music of Revival: Synergy with Sankey

In June 1870, Moody met a musician named Ira D. Sankey while in Indianapolis. Moody immediately recognized him in the Spirit and told him he had been praying for eight years for someone like Sankey to accompany him.[109] Sankey came out to visit Moody for a week to see if it would be a good fit. He arrived at Moody's home in the midst of family prayers. Moody immediately asked Sankey to sit at the organ and play a hymn. That same day, they visited the sick from Moody's congregation; Sankey sang over them, and Moody released the Word and "offered prayer for the healing of both body and soul."[110] During this visit, Moody also stood on a box on the sidewalk, gathered a crowd, had Sankey sing, and then began to preach.[111] It took several months, but eventually Sankey quit his job and came to minister alongside Moody.[112]

Moody and Sankey were a great "tag team" and partnered together for nearly thirty years. One of Moody's biographers wrote:

> Mr. Moody's words would bring a sinner to the point of conviction, and then the tender pathos of Mr. Sankey's singing would let a great flood of blessing into that sinner's soul, and the softening influences would work until he would cry out in his joy, "I am saved!" And, on the other hand, when a meeting had just begun, and away back in the farthest corners men were sitting who had come in a scoffing

mood, or out of curiosity, to hear the evangelists, the preliminary song of Mr. Sankey would rouse the attention of those persons, and they would try to get nearer the platform, and by the time Mr. Moody was ready to speak, they would have forgotten why they had come, in their eagerness to hear the preacher's message.[113]

Two Women Pray for Moody

In June 1871, "two holy women" from Moody's congregation, Sarah Cook and Mrs. Snow, approached him and told him they were praying for him to have the baptism of the Holy Spirit and power.[114] He remembered,

It was delightful to see them there, for when I began to preach, I could tell by the expression on their faces they were praying for me. At the close of the Sabbath evening services they would say to me, "We have been praying for you." I said, "Why don't you pray for the people?" They answered, "You need power." "I need power," I said to myself; "why, I thought I had power." I had a large Sabbath school and the largest congregation in Chicago. There were some conversions at the time, and I was in a sense satisfied. But right along these two godly women kept praying for me, and their earnest talk about "the anointing for special service" set me thinking. I asked them to come and talk with me, and we got down on our knees. They poured out their hearts, that I might receive the anointing of the Holy Ghost. And there came a great hunger into my soul. I knew not what it was. I began to cry as I never did before. The hunger increased. I really felt that I did not want to live any longer if I could not have this power for service. I kept on crying all the time that God would fill me with His Spirit.[115]

The Chicago Fire

Moody's hunger for more of God continued to grow over the next several months. He agreed to meet with the two women on Fridays to specifically pray for power from on high. Then, on Sunday night, October 8, 1871, after Moody had finished preaching to a crowd of about twenty-five hundred, an alarm bell rang in the city. This warning cry alerted them to what would later be known as the Great Chicago Fire.[116] Moody's church, house, and nearly everything he owned were destroyed in the fire, along with eighteen thousand other buildings and fifty churches. It killed about three hundred people and displaced over one hundred thousand. The death toll included members of Moody's own congregation.[117]

After making sure his family was safe in the home of friends, Moody devoted himself to relief work in the city.[118] Additionally, he raised enough funds to build North Side Tabernacle on December 24, 1871, less than three months after the fire.[119] This period was a time of refining for him as he reevaluated what he was building with his life and ministry. The sermon he had given the night of the fire had offered people a week to think about coming to Christ before having to make a commitment. However, after that dreadful day in which hundreds perished, there was a new urgency in his voice. He began to call people to come to Christ in the moment, without hesitating.[120] Moreover, following this devastation, Moody decided to focus more on his call to preach the gospel, and he immediately started evangelistic campaigns. He went from being a pastor, a conference speaker, a fundraiser, a relief worker, a Sunday school director, and the president of several associations to primarily being an evangelist.[121]

Endued with Power from on High: New York

After the fire, Moody took his family to New York for a break, and he continued to seek God for power from on high. He remembered that during this intense season, "four months of wrestling went on within me, and I was a miserable man. But after four months, the anointing came. It came upon me as I was walking the streets of New York."[122] Evangelist R. A. Torrey, who worked with Moody, recounted the story:

> Not long after, one day on his way to England, he was walking up Wall Street in New York (Mr. Moody very seldom told this and I almost hesitate to tell it) and in the midst of the bustle and hurry of

that city his prayer was answered; the power of God fell upon him as he walked up the street and he had to hurry off to the house of a friend and ask that he might have a room by himself, and in that room he stayed alone for hours; and the Holy Ghost came upon him, filling his soul with such joy that at last he had to ask God to withhold His hand, lest he die on the spot from very joy. He went out from that place with the power of the Holy Ghost upon him, and when he got to London (partly through the prayers of a bed-ridden saint in Mr. Lessey's church), the power of God wrought through him mightily in North London, and hundreds were added to the churches; and that was what led to his being invited over to the wonderful campaign that followed in later years.[123]

Moody recognized the profound impact of his encounter that day.

Well, one day, in the city of New York—O, what a day! I cannot describe it; I seldom refer to it; it is almost too sacred an experience to me. Paul had an experience of which he never spoke for fourteen years. I can only say, God revealed Himself to me, and I had such an experience of His love that I had to ask Him to stay His hand. I went on preaching again. The sermons were not different; I did not present any new truths, and yet hundreds were converted. I would not be placed back where I was before that blessed experience if you would give me all of Glasgow.[124]

This power encounter from on high proved to be a critical defining moment that launched Moody's ministry into exponential growth.

Revivals Break Out in England

When Moody stepped out in faith to journey to a new land, the anointing that he had recently received was activated in a greater measure. In the summer of 1872, Moody went to England for a short visit, intending only to learn more of the Bible. While there, a pastor at a church in London asked him to preach, and he consented. Moody's son recalled that the morning service seemed very dead and cold. The people did not show much interest, and he felt that it had been a morning lost. But at the next service, which was at half-past six in the evening, it seemed, while he was preaching, as if the very atmosphere was charged with the Spirit of God. There came a hush upon all the people, and a quick response to his words, though he had not been much in prayer that day, and could not understand it. When he had finished preaching he asked all who would like to become Christians to rise, that he might pray for them. People rose all over the house until it seemed as if the whole audience was getting up. Mr. Moody said to himself: "These people don't understand me. They don't know what I mean when I ask them to rise." He had never seen such results before, and did not know what to make of it…. The minister was surprised, and so was Mr. Moody. Neither had expected such a blessing. They had not realized that God can save by hundreds and thousands as well as by ones and twos.[125]

The next day, Moody headed to Ireland but immediately received correspondence calling him back to London. More inquirers had come to the church that week seeking to know more about God. Moody returned and spent ten additional days in London, where four hundred people were brought into the church.[126]

Moody went back home but returned to England again in June 1873. He had been invited by several people who promised to cover his expenses. When he had made all the preparations to go, he had yet to receive their funds. He went anyway, counting on them to reimburse him when he arrived. Once there, he discovered that the three people who had invited him had all passed away. Moody was not comfortable ministering without an invitation, and he contemplated returning to America. Just then, he found a letter in his pocket from a minister in York who had invited him to come preach. He went there immediately. After some time, God began to move, and many were led to the Lord. From there, many more doors were opened for Moody and Sankey to minister throughout the United Kingdom.[127] This trip proved to be catalytic in Moody's ministry. Before this time in England, Moody was relatively unknown. After it, he was one of England's most sought-after evangelists.

Moody went back and forth with Sankey from the United States to England and ministered regularly on both continents.[128] It was during one of Moody and Sankey's England tours that the famous "Cambridge Seven" committed to becoming missionaries with China Inland Mission under Hudson Taylor. Moody and Sankey spread revival fires across the land, preaching to a crowd of over twenty thousand people in London alone. They inspired many people to begin children's ministries and training schools for women. They also ministered in Ireland during a dangerous conflict there between Catholics and Protestants. In Scotland, Moody preached to crowds of over thirty thousand.[129] It is believed that during Moody's travels with Sankey in the UK, the two men ministered to over 2.5 million people in just three years. By the end of this time of ministering in England, Moody became known as one of the greatest evangelists of his era.

The Work Continues

After this, Moody and his family moved back to his hometown of Northfield, Massachusetts, to prepare for evangelism. From October 1875 to May 1876, Moody traveled around the country on evangelistic crusades. On January 19, 1876, President Ulysses S. Grant attended one of these meetings. In 1879, Moody opened Northfield Seminary for Young Women so that women would have an opportunity to receive an education. He founded Mount Hermon School for Boys to give poorer children access to education as well. In 1886, with a friend's help, he founded the Chicago Evangelization Society (now Moody Bible Institute), a school that emphasized practical training, urban evangelism, and prayer. Later in 1886, Moody gathered 251 college students from over eighty-nine colleges for about a month at his Northfield conference. The organic connections that were formed within this student body would later give birth to the Student Volunteer Movement for Foreign Missions. By 1911, over five thousand volunteers had already come out of this movement.[130] The movement eventually spread around the world, inspiring the cause of foreign missions. In 1893, at the same time as the World's Fair in Chicago, Moody and his students led a revival that touched millions of lives. Over one hundred thirty thousand people were evangelized. In 1894, Moody set up a publishing company to help spread the gospel.

Moody regularly released impartation of what he had received in his Spirit baptism encounter. R. A. Torrey gave an account of how 456 people were baptized in the Spirit in one day.

> I shall never forget the eighth of July, 1894, to my dying day. It was the closing day of the Northfield Students' Conference—the gathering of the students from the eastern colleges. Mr. Moody had asked me to preach on Saturday night and Sunday morning on The Baptism with the Holy Ghost. On Saturday night I had spoken about, "The Baptism With the Holy Ghost: What It Is; What It Does; the Need of It and the Possibility of It." On Sunday morning I spoke on "The Baptism With the Holy Spirit: How to Get It." It was just exactly twelve o'clock when I finished my morning sermon, and I took out my watch and said: "Mr. Moody has invited us all to go up to the mountain at three o'clock this afternoon to pray for the power of the Holy Spirit. It is three hours to three o'clock. Some of you cannot wait three hours. You do not need to wait. Go to your rooms; go out into the woods; go to your tent; go anywhere where you can get alone with God and have this matter out with Him." At three o'clock we all gathered in front of Mr. Moody's mother's house (she was then still living), and then began to pass down the lane, through the gate, up on the mountainside. There were four hundred and fifty-six of us in all; I know the number because Paul Moody counted us as we passed through the gate.
>
> After a while Mr. Moody said: "I don't think we need to go any further; let us sit down here." We sat down on stumps and logs and on the ground. Mr. Moody said: "Have any of you students anything to say?" I think about seventy-five of them arose, one after the other, and said: "Mr. Moody, I could not wait till three o'clock; I have been alone with God since the morning service, and I believe I have a right to say that I have been baptized with the Holy Spirit." When these testimonies were over, Mr. Moody said: "Young men, I can't see any reason why we shouldn't kneel down here right now and ask God that the Holy Ghost may fall upon

us just as definitely as He fell upon the apostles on the Day of Pentecost. Let us pray." And we did pray, there on the mountainside. As we had gone up the mountainside heavy clouds had been gathering, and just as we began to pray those clouds broke and the rain-drops began to fall through the overhanging pines. But there was another cloud that had been gathering over Northfield for ten days, a cloud big with the mercy and grace and power of God; and as we began to pray our prayers seemed to pierce that cloud and the Holy Ghost fell upon us. Men and women, that is what we all need—the Baptism with the Holy Ghost.[131]

Besides leading people into life-changing encounters with God, Moody was a gracious man who was not afraid to go against the tide. One time, a baby was crying in one of his meetings, and Moody saw the embarrassed mother look for an escape from the glares she was receiving from members of the audience. Moody told her to remain in the meeting. Then, at the close of the service, he called for a meeting the next day where "he would preach to mothers with babies in their arms, and no one unaccompanied by a baby would be admitted." It was a tremendous time, and Moody said afterward "that a good many of the women present must have borrowed babies for the occasion."[132]

Final Years

Throughout the years, Moody consistently woke up early to spend several hours with God and to read the Bible before beginning his day.[133] He also valued and honored revival history. He even had Charles H. Spurgeon's Bible in his possession and would regularly refer to it before preaching a sermon to see if Spurgeon had written any notes on the same passage.[134] Before he died on December 22, 1899, at the age of sixty-two, Moody continued to evangelize all around North America.

Legacy

Prior to Moody's defining Spirit baptism encounter in 1871, he had already experienced great favor and success. He had started Sunday schools and training schools, planted one of the largest churches in Chicago, and spent much time evangelizing the marginalized, the poor, and the outcast. He had also already quit his business to work for the Lord alone. Rather than preach hellfire and brimstone in order to pressure people into conversion, Moody (likely influenced by Moorehouse) preached about the goodness and love of God to draw people to repentance.[135] But after the Chicago fire, followed by his "enduement from on high" encounter in New York in 1871, there was a sense of urgency and power in his preaching like never before. After this, increasing numbers of people began to respond to the same messages he had given previously. Moody is believed to have reached over one hundred million people with the gospel.[136] Furthermore, Moody inspired future preachers like Billy Sunday and R. A. Torrey. It was said that Moody was a "marked man in a crowd, and every one turned to look at him because the very atmosphere that surrounded him was commanding."[137] The secular newspapers even applauded him after his death. The *Chicago Times-Herald* wrote:

> Chicago at one time claimed this mighty preacher. But when he died the whole world claimed him, so wide was the range of his evangelizing activities. He stirred the hearts of two great English-speaking nations with his militant enthusiasm. He was the field marshal of the hosts that cling to the belief that the Gospel itself suffices for all the spiritual needs of humanity. The moral effect of his life-work upon humanity was greater than that of any other man of the nineteenth century.[138]

Moody truly was one of the greatest evangelists this world has seen. He saw the value of integrating the Word of God and worship into his meetings. He also laid the foundation for the Moody Bible Institute and the Student Volunteer Movement, which continue even to this day.

Prophetic Inheritance

Hunger

Hunger in any form significantly influences how one's life is lived. Solomon almost excuses stealing when it comes from a place of hunger, saying, "*Men do not despise a thief if he steals to satisfy himself when he is hungry*" (Proverbs 6:30 NASB). (He goes on to say in verse 31 that the thief still has to return many times over what he stole.)

Hunger indeed affects our conduct dramatically, and there really isn't a hunger that can be compared to an all-consuming passion for God. It is anything but casual. Such hunger changes our value system and alters what we think about, making us willing to risk everything to satisfy it. This passion impacts our sleep, our friendships, our leisure activities, and our money—absolutely everything. The life of D. L. Moody profoundly illustrates this reality. It was this kind of hunger that paved the way for this good but average minister to become one of the greatest evangelists who ever lived. But it wasn't the hunger itself that changed him. It was hunger that attracted the divine encounter, the defining moment that altered everything about his life.

In church history, we find radical stories of transformation that came about in two basic ways. The first way is the sovereign invasion of God. The apostle Paul is the perfect example here. We don't see him crying out for the Lord. We don't see him fasting and praying for more of God. We just see God sovereignly choose him in the midst of his opposition to the gospel. God is God. He can and will do as He pleases. But it's a great mistake to reduce God to that one example. He has also made a covenant with His people, saying that if we hunger and thirst for Him, we will be satisfied. (See, for example, Jeremiah 29:13; Matthew 5:6.) In a sense, one example portrays God invading earth. The other seems to imply that there are people whose hunger enables them to invade heaven. This is not a violation of God's sovereignty, for even crying out for God would be impossible without God's invitation.

My personal story is not like Paul's. In fact, I once discounted my role in the gospel because I never had an encounter like these heroes of the faith who had been so overtly chosen by God. Then I saw the other side of the same coin—God responds to hunger. Sometimes, it's the hunger and the corresponding reckless pursuit that actually prepares and shapes us for the answer we have prayed for. This process changes us and makes us ready for the *more of God*. And so, perhaps my personal favorite high point of Moody's life was his hunger for more of God.

Being Filled with the Holy Spirit

Moody also seemed to recognize the need to *remain* filled with the Holy Spirit. He understood that we are cracked vessels in need of continual filling. Here are two quotes from Moody that illustrate this idea:

> Some one asked a minister, if he had ever received a second blessing since he was converted. "What do you mean?" was his reply, "I have received ten thousand since the first." A great many think because they have been filled once, they are going to be full for all time after; but O, my friends, we are leaky vessels, and have to be kept right under the fountain all the time in order to keep full.[139]

> I believe this is a mistake a great many of us are making; we are trying to do God's work with the grace God gave us ten years ago. We say, if it is necessary, we will go on with the same grace. Now, what we want is a fresh supply, a fresh anointing and fresh power, and if we seek it, and seek it with all our hearts, we will obtain it.[140]

For years, I have watched people point back to an experience they had with God many years ago, thinking they still have what they had immediately after that encounter. But the effect of the encounter has not been kept current, and they are living off the memory of what used to be. Thankfully for all of us, Dwight L. Moody was not one of those individuals. He knew that he always needed more, and that he always needed to remain current in his surrender to the Holy Spirit. Even a life-changing encounter with God needs to be stewarded. It must be maintained.

Recognizing Anointing and the Need for Partnerships

We don't always know whom God intends to have us partner with for life and ministry. To put in another way, such partnerships are not always reasonable from our perspective. The boy preacher, Henry Moorehouse, became a monumental tool in God's hands to shape the heart of this evangelist. It was not a partnership that Moody would ever have chosen for himself. Yet God knew exactly what he needed. Moody had a special quality that would become the hallmark of his life—he could recognize the anointing of God upon another person. And once he saw the presence of God upon this seventeen-year-old preacher from the UK, everything changed. As a result, Moody was launched on a journey that would affect the lives of millions of people.

D. L. Moody also recognized the anointing of God upon the two women who prayed for him to be baptized in the Holy Spirit. While he was initially a bit offended by his interaction with them, he recognized God upon them. This added focus to his pursuit of God, and his passion truly became all encompassing.

These two partnerships, one with the boy preacher and the other with the two praying women, launched Moody into a pursuit of God that became empowered by God Himself. It was supernatural hunger. It was as though God gave him His own passion in his quest for God's face to shine upon his life. This hunger was one that God refused to ignore. The story of His coming upon Moody that day on the streets of New York is legendary for so many reasons. The first is that it is God who chooses the time and the means. It is our responsibility to respond to His summons. The second is that a token prayer will never take us to where we want to go. The prayer that moves us is the one that will move Him. Moody's corresponding hours of prayer brought about the greatest encounter of His life, and thereby enabled him to preach with such power that thousands would be saved at a time. But perhaps more important, he preached from an understanding of God's heart for humanity and was personally overflowing with great joy from his encounter with the God of joy. This was the actual platform from which he preached. Finally, not many can say that their defining moment came while walking the streets of New York City!

Those two partnerships helped to take Moody to his *promised land*, so to speak, but it was his subsequent partnership with Ira D. Sankey that enabled him to thrive while there. Sankey became the partner in ministry that made these two men golden in both word and song. Not only did Moody preach the gospel as *good news*, but Sankey's anointed voice melted the hardest hearts, igniting them with a hunger for God. The music brilliantly prepared people for Moody's preaching. Once again, Moody's ability to recognize the anointing of God upon another person would multiply the effectiveness of his own gift.

John Wesley had his brother Charles, who became the great hymn writer of his day. Charles was able to take John's theology and put it to music. It became an important tool to educate and train the people of their day to think biblically. And while that approach still has value today, it perhaps could be said that Sankey's gift was more of a worship expression. Through his music, people became convinced that God was good and was drawing them to Himself. And so we see the God-born partnership of preaching and worship.

In these three cases, it is easy to see the benefit that relationships provided for Moody and his ministry. But it must be clearly recognized that these relationships were not for his personal benefit. The partnerships came about because Moody was already of true value to the Holy Spirit. The benefits to his ministry were the fruit of that core value.

Postscript

Each of the above realms of breakthrough is absolutely necessary for the church in this hour. They are all expressions of the kingdom of God, which is still *"at hand"* (Mark 1:15) and within reach. But once again, these breakthroughs are all products of the overwhelming effect of a life-changing encounter with God. It was the baptism in the Holy Spirit that made these fruits even possible. None of them were obtained because of hard work, personal discipline, or unique gifting. The hard work, personal discipline, and unique gifting all became effective because of the God-encounter.

This encounter brought revival to one man, D. L. Moody; but because he was then truly burning with the fires of heaven, revival spread to many, and revival brought the fruits. Many people think it's the fruits that bring the Spirit of revival on the scene. That really is backwards. So now it's time to cry out for the fullness of the Holy Spirit to burst upon our lives in unprecedented ways, knowing that the purposes of God will be more fully realized on the earth in our lifetime if we do.

5

Courage:
Maria Woodworth-Etter

"My prayers have always been, and now are for more Light, and more Wisdom at any cost. This must be our cry and faith. Then go forward in His name, no matter about the results, or persecutions, then the Blood will continuously cleanse, and we will be kept in love with one another; and have sweet fellowship with our Lord and Saviour, Jesus Christ."[141]
—*Maria Woodworth-Etter*

Few people I've ever read about have affected my life in the realm of courage as much as this amazing woman of God. She is a wonderful example of how God alone can cause a person's greatest weakness to become their greatest strength. She was fearful and timid, looking for reasons *not* to respond to the call of God on her life. She felt unqualified in both biblical understanding and in the anointing. But through a series of experiences with God, she was transformed. Once again, a God-encounter became a defining moment that changed everything. As someone once said, "God doesn't call the qualified. He qualifies the called." Maria Woodworth-Etter's life perfectly illustrates this truth.

Powerful Signs and Wonders

Maria Woodworth-Etter (1844–1924), said by many to be the "grandmother" of the Pentecostal movement, moved in unique and powerful signs and wonders throughout her ministry. Even though she experienced tremendous personal loss with the deaths of five of her six children, God continued to remind her of His early call on her life to be an evangelist. She had struggled to step into this call because she had never seen another woman preach. However, after a subsequent healing, a series of visions, a prayer to have the same power as the disciples, and an encounter of "liquid fire," she finally stepped out to evangelize at the age of thirty-five. She immediately saw powerful results, as many people were converted. After moving out from the local level to minister nationally, she saw people "slain in the Spirit" and falling into trances in her meetings. Many lay prostrate for hours, sometimes even days, before they jumped up and praised the Lord, completely converted, healed, or transformed. Maria later integrated prayer for the sick into her meetings and saw many healings. She boldly went into the darkest places to bring the gospel and planted church after church. Over the years, she led thousands to Christ and became a trailblazer for other women in ministry.

Conversion and Calling

Maria Beulah Woodworth-Etter (maiden name Underwood) was born in New Lisbon, Columbiana County, Ohio, on July 22, 1844. She was introduced to Christianity in 1854 when her parents started going to a local Disciples of Christ church. When her father suddenly died of sunstroke in July 1855, her mother was left to care for their eight children on her own.[142] When Maria was eight years old, her "heart went out in strong desires to know of God."[143] When two of her sisters were converted in a Methodist meeting, she wanted to join them but felt shunned because of her age. At thirteen, she was finally able to make a full commitment to Christ after hearing the story of the cross. She was baptized the next day, which she later counted as her true conversion.[144] She then received her life calling. Her account follows:

> Soon after I was converted I heard the voice of Jesus calling me to go out in highways and hedges and gather the lost sheep. Like Mary, I pondered these things in my heart, for I had no one to hold counsel with. The Disciples did not believe that women had any right to work for Jesus…. I had never heard of women working in public except as missionaries, so I could see no opening—except, as I thought, if I ever married, my choice would be an earnest Christian and then we would enter upon the mission work.[145]

Struggle to Embrace the Call: Tragedy, Healing, and Promise

Maria later married Philo Harris Woodworth, and they had six children, five of whom died young. Her husband was not interested in religion, nor was he very supportive of her dream of ministry. She remembered that "in all these trials God was preparing me and opening the way for the great battle against the enemy of souls…."[146] Maria also became very sick, to the point that she was willing to die and leave her family behind. However, she said,

> The work God was calling me to do, loomed up before me. All these years God had been preparing me—for I was not willing. I felt like a worm in his sight. It seemed impossible for me to undertake the work for the salvation of souls; but the time had come to promise or die. I promised God that if he would restore my health, and prepare me, and show me the work, I would try to do it: I began to get better immediately.[147]

Even though God answered Maria's prayers for healing, she continued to struggle with stepping into her calling as an evangelist. She had never seen any women preachers before, and she questioned her role. However, a burden for the lost continued to consume her.

> There was all this time a secret monitor within telling me that I should be calling sinners to repentance. I could not get clear of that reflection by day or by night. Waking or dreaming, I seemed to have a large congregation before me, all in tears, as I told them the story of the cross. This for months and years did I debate; and yet did I falter and hesitate.[148]

Visions from Heaven

Into her thirties, God continued to call Maria to step into her destiny. While she was testifying at her local church one day, God gave her a vision confirming her call.

> I was very timid, and bound as with chains in a man-fearing spirit. When I arose to testify I trembled like a leaf, and began to make excuses—"O God, send some one else!" Then the Lord in a vision caused me to see the bottomless pit open in all its horror and woe. There was weeping and wailing and gnashing of teeth. It was surrounded by a great multitude of people who seemed unconscious of their danger, and without a moment's warning they would tumble into this awful place. I was above the people on a narrow plank-walk, which wound up toward heaven; and I was exhorting and pleading with the people to come upon the plank and escape that awful place. Several started. There was a beautiful bright light above me, and I was encouraging them to follow that light and they would go straight to heaven.
>
> This vision left quite an impression on my mind…. But I had so much opposition to contend with. My people were opposed; my husband and daughter fought against it; and my whole nature shrunk from going to stand as a gazing-stock for the people. But the Lord was showing in many ways that I must go and perform the work he had for me to do.[149]

After the first vision, Maria was still reluctant to step into ministry because of her lack of training. Yet God was merciful and gave her another vision to answer her concerns.

> The dear Savior stood by me one night in a vision and talked face to face with me, and asked what I was doing on earth. I felt condemned, and said, "Lord, I am going to work in thy vineyard." The Lord said, "When?" and I answered, "When I get prepared for the work." Then the Lord said to me, "Don't you know that while you are getting ready souls are perishing? Go now, and I will be with you." I told him that I could not talk to the people; I did not know what to say, and they would not listen to me. Jesus said, "You can tell the people what the Lord has done for your soul; tell of the glory of God and the love of Jesus; tell sinners to repent and prepare for death and the judgment, and I will be with you." Still I made one excuse after another, and Jesus would answer, "Go, and I will be with you."
>
> I told him I wanted to study the Bible; that I did not understand it well enough. Then there appeared on the wall a large open Bible, and the verses stood out in raised letters. The glory of God shone around and upon the book. I looked, and I could understand it all. Then Jesus said again, "Go, and I will be with you."… I saw more in that vision than I could have learned in years of hard study…. I was to be God's mouthpiece.[150]

Anointing Encounter of Liquid Fire

In the midst of Maria's continuing struggle to step out in her calling, God met her with another vision. And when she called out to the Lord for the same power the disciples had as her seal of approval and qualification, He met her request with an encounter of liquid fire.

> Sometimes when the Spirit of God was striving and calling so plainly, I would yield and say, "Yes, Lord; I will go." The glory of God came upon me like a cloud, and I seemed to be carried away hundreds of miles and sat down in a field of wheat, where the sheaves were falling all around me. I was filled with zeal and

power, and felt as if I could stand before the whole world and plead with dying sinners. It seemed to me that I must leave all and go at once. Then Satan would come in like a flood…. Then I would be in darkness and despair. I wanted to run away from God, or I wished I could die; but when I began to look at the matter in this way, that God knew all about me, and was able and willing to qualify me for the work, I asked him to qualify me.

I want the reader to understand, that at this time I had a good experience, a pure heart, was full of the love of God, but was not qualified for God's work. I knew that I was but a worm. God would have to take a worm to thresh a mountain. Then I asked God to give me the power he gave the Galilean fisherman—to anoint me for service. I came like a child asking for bread. I looked for it. God did not disappoint me. The power of the Holy Ghost came down as a cloud. It was brighter than the sun. I was covered and wrapped up in it. My body was light as the Holy Ghost, and fire, and power which has never left me. Oh, Praise the Lord! There was liquid fire, and the angels were all around in the fire and glory. It is through the Lord Jesus Christ, and by this power that I have stood before hundreds of thousands of men and women, proclaiming the unsearchable riches of Christ.[151]

Just as Moses was not content to go anywhere without God's presence (see Exodus 33), Maria realized she needed God's power and anointing to step into her calling.

Activation

After receiving several visions, praying for the same power that the disciples had, and then receiving a "liquid-fire" encounter, in 1880, at the age of thirty-five, Maria activated her anointing when she stepped out to evangelize by holding a meeting. This was twenty-two years after she had first received her call. At first, it was hard for her to speak to people in her hometown, whom she had known for so long. However, many were impacted by her message; her sister-in-law even broke down in tears and had to leave the meeting. Maria continued to hold meetings for a few days, and over twenty people in the neighborhood were converted. Eventually, more and more people came to hear her preach.

There I was with several hundred people before me and no text—nothing to talk about. Everything was empty. I began to plead with Jesus. I told him he had called me to preach; that here was this starving multitude and I had no bread to give them. To verify his promise and to glorify himself in manifesting his power to this people, the words came to me, "What are you going to do with Jesus, that is called the Christ?" and also the place to find the text. Jesus seemed to whisper in my ear, "I am with you; be not afraid." I opened the meeting and repeated the text. As I did so the power came, and it seemed that all I had to do was to open my mouth. The people all through the house began to weep. I talked one hour and a quarter. The power came as it did when I received the anointing. It seemed as if the house was full of the glory of God. I felt as if I was drawn up over the people.[152]

Within a year and a half of first stepping out to evangelize, Maria held nine revivals, planted two churches, and preached over two hundred sermons for eight different denominations.[153] In a harsh place nearby called "The Devil's Den," she ministered for two weeks, and over seventy-five were converted. She also organized a Sabbath school for one hundred fifty scholars and appointed a man who had formerly been a notorious drunkard as superintendent. Additionally, she established two weekly prayer meetings and a Sunday service.[154]

Even though Maria's husband and others were opposed to her activities at first, they later became more sympathetic and supportive. A Friend's church even offered to pay all her expenses to travel and minister. In the early days of her ministry, while she had many offers to lead churches, to lead societies, and to be a part of various denominations, she felt God had called her to be an evangelist rather than be tied down to one church.

Increased Power and Anointing

As Maria continued to evangelize locally for a few years, several visiting ministers released prophetic words about how she needed to go West to save lost souls. She struggled with this idea because of feelings of inadequacy and because she could not take her seven-year-old son, Willie—her only living son—with her. A few days later, he passed away. Five of her six children had now died before their time.[155] Ironically, this tragedy freed Maria to step out and expand her ministry.

As she set out on her journey West, her stop in Fairview, Ohio, marked her ministry anew. There was conflict in the church there, but Maria believed that God would bring reconciliation. After meeting in the homes of several of the leaders and being successful in bringing resolution, on the third day, she saw something she had never seen before.

> All who were present came to the altar and made a full consecration and prayed for a baptism of the Holy Ghost and of fire, and that night it came. Fifteen came to the altar screaming for mercy. Men and women fell and lay like dead. I had never seen anything like this. I felt it was the work of God, but did not know how to explain it, or what to say.
>
> I was a little frightened, as I did not know what the people would think or what they might do to me, as I was the leader of the meeting. While the fear of God was on the people, and I was looking on, not knowing what to do, the Spirit of God brought before me the vision I had before I started out in the work of the Lord, and said: "Don't you remember when you was [sic] carried away, and saw a field of wheat and the sheaves falling? The large field of wheat was the multitudes of people you are to preach the gospel to; the falling sheaves is what you see here to-night, the slaying power of God. This is my power; I told you I would be with you and fight your battles; it is not the wisdom of men, but the power and wisdom of God that is needed to bring sinners from darkness to light." The Lord revealed wonderful things to me in a few moments; my fears were all gone. Those who were lying over the house as dead, after laying about two hours, all, one after another, sprang to their feet as quick as a flash, with shining faces, and shouted all over the house. I never had seen such bright conversations, nor such shouting.[156]

Notice how the increased signs and wonders in her ministry were released within the context of forgiveness, reconciliation, and unity within the body of Christ. While Maria had seen incredible results in a very short time before her travels West, she had not seen the power of God fall like it had when people were "slain in the Spirit" and taken up in trances and visions. Expanding the physical borders of her ministry had contributed to increasing her anointing to release God's power in greater measure. Unity within the church community provided a space for God to pour out His Spirit in this way. Building on her previous prayers to receive the same power the disciples had, as well as on her liquid-fire encounter, Maria's second major turning point came when she activated the anointing she had already received by taking her ministry from a local level to a national level.[157] She also ventured into the most spiritually dark places she could find, and God regularly backed up her boldness with signs and wonders.

Healing Introduced

Another shift in Maria's ministry came a few years after her increased anointing when she began to embrace healing. Maria originally struggled with the idea of integrating prayer for healing into her meetings, fearing it would take away from God's call on her life to evangelize.[158] She soon acquiesced when she came to realize that even more souls could be won that way. It was not until 1885 that Maria believed God had called her to pray for the sick.[159] After she integrated prayer for healing into her ministry, she began to see blind eyes opened, cancer removed, tumors disappear, the lame walk, the deaf hear, and the mute speak. She also saw dropsy, spinal meningitis, kidney failure, heart disease, and rheumatism fully healed.[160] Maria regularly prayed for those who were dying, as well as for resurrection for people who had died, and she saw God raise people from the dead.[161]

More Accounts of the "Slain in the Spirit"

Throughout the years, the "slain in the Spirit" became a mark of her ministry.[162] At one meeting,

> a woman fell, struck down, and lay until evening. They took her home, and she lay until next Sunday, eight days in all; then she came out shouting and preaching; and without taking any nourishment, she came straight to the meeting, and preached, and told the wonderful experience which she had had.[163]

Maria recalled another instance that occurred during a meeting in Warrensburg, Illinois, in the 1880s:

> One night the whole congregation was shaking under the power of God. Twenty-six were laid out at one time as dead men and women. Others were standing or sitting with their right hands raised towards heaven, pointing sinners to God. The largest man in the house was laid out as helpless as an infant for hours. Twelve men were laid out at once. Every time I went into the church the power of God came upon me like a cloud, I could not move or do anything, God was always preaching a wonderful sermon.[164]

Many times, the result of someone going "under the power of God" was salvation. After Maria later embraced healing, people would fall out in the power of the Spirit and wake up totally healed. She remembered, "One lady who came to the meeting to be healed fell in a trance while I was praying for her. She lay twelve hours, then came out of the trance and said she had been sick all her life, but God had healed her. She said she was going out into the field and would spend her life in his service."[165]

Many who were slain in the Spirit received a commissioning from God—even if they weren't present at Maria's meeting! In Summitville, Indiana, in February 1885, "for about twenty miles round men and women were struck down in their homes, in business places, and on the roads and streets. Some lay for hours, and had wonderful visions. Many went into the ministry, or became evangelists."[166] Maria saw that this activity of being slain in the Spirit not only tied to her earlier vision of the wheat falling but also that it was "the fire of the Holy Ghost."[167] In 1885, in Alexandria, Indiana, five hundred of the twenty-five thousand at the meeting fell to the ground under the power of God.[168]

Like a Statue

In addition to "slaying in the Spirit," there were other interesting signs and wonders in Maria's ministry. One of these was when she or others would be frozen like a statue.[169]

An infidel past seventy years of age was saved. He would never go to church or let his wife go. She managed in some way to get to our meeting, and was saved and healed of a terrible disease. One day the power of God fell upon her in her home; while she was walking across the room, the Lord took possession of her body, with her hand pointed to Heaven; her husband was in the house, and every place he moved, one of her hands followed him with her finger pointed at him. The fear of God fell upon him; he tried to hide, but that hand followed him. He laid down on the floor, but the finger pointed him out; he felt it was the hand of God calling him to repentance, and he trembled under the presence of God. He came to the meeting the next day and came like a little child and bowed at the altar, and was soon rejoicing in a Saviour's love.[170]

Fierce Determination

Choose Christ Now or Die

One thing that Maria intensely burned for throughout her whole ministry was the salvation of souls. She earnestly contended with people, begging them to yield to the Lord immediately. She believed the time was drawing near for them to make a decision for Christ or die. There are several accounts of individuals who refused to yield to her entreaty and died shortly thereafter.[171]

One night I was pleading with sinners to accept the invitation to be present at the Marriage Supper of God's Only Begotten Son. I felt that death was very near. Oh, how I pleaded with them to accept while there was mercy. One old man was so convicted he could not stand it. He would not yield. He left the house, cursing the Methodist church. He thought to run away from God. But swift judgment was on his track. In going out of town the train ran over him and killed him.... Reformation fire began to spread, till many were brightly converted.... When we closed we appointed cottage prayer-meetings from house to house. Sometimes there would be five or six a week.[172]

No Turning Back

Maria was not afraid to take a leap of faith to go where she felt the Lord was leading her, even if she had to embrace hardship or was not sure how things would work out. On a trip to California in October 1889, she was determined to release the kingdom of God to the point of no return. It was all or nothing for Maria. Either God was going to come in power and provide supernaturally or she would be stuck without provision. In today's terms, we might say she was unafraid to buy a one-way plane ticket to the other side of the country with no specific plan or connections, only an abiding trust that God would provide.

> Here we were in a strange land and our money about gone. No means to get back east…. We had not thought about going back till a great work had been done for the Master. We had no fear of suffering for want of means, we knew our God would supply all our needs, and his children should never be ashamed. The meeting was not advertised. The people did not know what was going to be done there. The first night twenty-three came. They felt that God was there. I told them that God had sent us there, and there would be a great work done; that hundreds would be saved. In a few days the tent would not hold the crowds that would come to hear the gospel.[173]

God also provided for Maria and her companions through donations of groceries as well as stoves so they could keep warm at night.

Not Afraid of Death

Maria was compelled to rescue people from hell even if she had to get as close to it as possible to lend a helping hand. She was willing to lay down her life so that others might be saved. She was attracted to the darkest of places, knowing that her light would shine even brighter there.

Accordingly, Maria was not afraid to face the spirit of intimidation head-on.[174] In the summer of 1890, Maria and her team set up their tents and camped in St. Louis, Missouri, in an extremely rough part of town called "Kerry Patch." They would minister there for five months.

Sometimes the stones went flying through the tent. They did not know what a camp-meeting was, but thought it was some kind of a show. Most of these people had never been to a church.... They would shoot off fire-crackers, and when we sang they sang louder; when we prayed they clapped their hands and cheered us. They had pistols and clubs, and were ready to kill us, and tear down the tent. It looked like we would all be killed. Several ministers tried to talk, but were stoned down, or their voice drowned out. It looked like surrender or death.... I said to my co-workers: "We will never give up, and if they are ready to go, they will take us out dead." I told them to lead in prayer one after the other, and the God of Elijah would answer.

A sister knelt on the pulpit pale as death, her hands and face raised to heaven, and in a clear ringing voice asked God to save and bless the judgment-bound multitude. A feeling of the awful presence of God began to fall on the people. Another sister followed in prayer, then I arose, and stood before them. I raised my hand in the name of the Lord, and commanded them to listen. I said the Lord had sent me there to do them good, and that I would not leave until the Lord told me to, when our work was done. I told them the Lord would strike dead the first one that tried to harm us, or to strike us with a dagger. If any tried to kill us the Lord would strike them dead.

The power of God fell, and the fear of God came upon all the multitude.... After that the hoodlum element always respected me. Many would take off their hats when they passed me; but they stoned the people coming and going to the meetings, and threw stones through and over the tent for some time, till we got them conquered in the name of the Lord, and the help of the police....[175]

Despite the opposition, people continued to be drawn to the presence God in this dark place. It was not long before many were saved and the area became transformed because of the power and glory of God there.

The tent held eight thousand. There were meetings every day and night for five months. There were thousands outside the tent, but they could see and hear....

Many were carried in, and got up and walked out. The blind shouted for joy, the lame threw away their crutches, and leaped and rejoiced, and said: "Oh, I am healed!" The deaf and dumb clapped their hands, while tears of joy ran down their faces. Children that had never walked ran about praising the Lord. Some, both young and old people who were perfectly helpless, received a shock from heaven's battery that sent life through their limbs: they clapped their hands and jumped and cried for joy....

Hundreds of men and women and children, of all classes, were struck down by the power of God, and lay as dead, some for hours, some for days, and all came out shouting the high praises of God. Many had wonderful visions of heaven, and told of the judgments to come, and the Soon Coming of the Lord, and of the Marriage Supper of the Lamb, and of the time of the Rapture, and Manifestation of the sons of God....

Many were baptized with the Holy Ghost, and received many gifts; all the gifts were manifested by the Holy Ghost. Many received the gifts of healing; the casting out of devils; some of miracles; of visions; of the gift of the Holy Ghost by the laying on of hands; some received the gift of new tongues, and spake very intelligently in other languages as the Spirit gave them utterance. He gave them to know what they were speaking.

The Lord called one man by name and told him he must go to many nations to give them the light....

The whole city was shaken. Missions started in many places. The different churches began to have street meetings and to visit the prisons and hospitals, as they had never done before we started this revival. The people were stirred; missionary work began all over the city, and revivals were started almost everywhere.

The man who owned the ground was a Catholic. He was so pleased with the change in the neighbourhood for the good he said he would let us have the ground free of charge. The interest of this five months' camp-meeting in "Kerry Patch" was wide-spread. It reached from the Atlantic to the Pacific and across the ocean.[176]

Impact and Strategy

City Transformation

"Kerry Patch" and the surrounding area was just one example of the transformation of a city that took place as a result of Maria's ministry. Hartford City, Indiana, was also greatly impacted by her ministry.

> The power of the Lord, like the wind, swept all over the city, up one street and down another, sweeping through the places of business, the workshops, saloons and dives, arresting sinners of all classes.... The fear of God fell upon the city. The police said they never saw such a change; that they had nothing to do. They said they made no arrest; and that the power of God seemed to preserve the city.... A spirit of love rested all over the city. There was no fighting, no swearing on the streets....[177]

City transformation would later become a defining factor of the Welsh Revival. But Maria was already contending for this and seeing it happen years before.

Planting Churches

Maria was not content to do evangelism without follow-up. Like Moody, she set up structures and strategies to help new converts continue in their faith. She was also a natural church planter. Many of her tent meetings would swell beyond the eight-thousand-person capacity and last for several weeks or months. After she felt her work was done and that the hard ground had been broken open, she would assign leaders or converts from the area to start a church or prayer meeting. After sowing seeds into one place for several months, she would go on to the next place. Many times, when she returned to visit the cities she had previously ministered in, she saw that the churches she had planted were alive and thriving. Other times, the churches had lost momentum, and she sought to re-spark the flame that had once been there.[178] Maria not only restarted these "fires" but also set up structures to contain them and keep them burning strong.

While she ministered ecumenically, in 1884 she became a licensed evangelist with the Churches of God Southern Assembly founded by John Winebrenner.[179] Many of the churches she planted in the early years became a part of the Church of God. However, after much controversy with her own denomination over trances and visions, by 1904, she was asked to give up her Church of God credentials. She continued to minister independently.[180]

Final Years

In 1891, Maria divorced her husband for infidelity. He died a year later after trying to discredit her ministry.[181] In 1902, she married Samuel Etter. They ministered together, and she found him to be a true gift from God. At some point in Maria's life, she received the gift of tongues.[182] After a few "hidden" years, Maria reemerged more openly on the public scene in 1912 in Dallas, Texas, to minister alongside F. F. Bosworth, Carrie Judd Montgomery, and many other prominent leaders, where thousands were saved.[183] When Maria was leaving one of these meetings, she raised her hands on her way out, and many were instantly healed.[184] The revival meetings in Texas expanded her popularity.

In 1914, after her second husband died, she nearly died as well but received a vision from the Lord about Him being the Conqueror. In 1918, she started a church in Indianapolis that is now called Lakeview Christian Center.[185] She used this as a base while she continued to minister. This is the church where Aimee Semple McPherson's dream of meeting Maria came true on October 31, 1918.[186] On September 16, 1924, just over a month after her daughter died in a streetcar accident, Maria died at the age of eighty.[187]

Legacy

Maria lived a commanding life of legacy as a forerunner and "grandmother" to the Pentecostal movement. Her relentless determination to go into the most spiritually dark places to release the kingdom of God without backing down is inspiring. Other leaders of her day recognized her strength, including John G. Lake, who regularly referred to her as "Mother Etter" in his sermons.[188] Her books were translated into several languages and, from 1912–1921, sold over twenty-five thousand copies.[189] Maria preached for over forty-five years, sometimes to crowds of up to twenty-five thousand.[190] Her preaching span was six years longer than that of Billy Sunday and Dwight L. Moody, who each preached for thirty-nine years.[191]

By 1894, she had gone coast-to-coast three times. She and Carrie Judd Montgomery, whom she met in 1890 at the Oakland meeting, were among the first women to preach itinerantly across the United States and to spread the divine healing message to the West Coast.[192] For up to fourteen years after she started ministering, she went "from one battlefield to another almost day and night." During this time, she traveled over thirty-five thousand miles and held meetings in thirteen states. She claimed to have stood before "hundreds of thousands" during that time. Thousands were saved and healed through her ministry, and over two-thirds of those were past middle-age. Many were also launched into ministry in the United States and around the world as a result of her ministry.[193] Maria paved the way for women in ministry and for signs and wonders to be released in increasing measure.

Prophetic Inheritance

Signs That Make You Wonder

I find it interesting that God chose to minister to Maria Woodworth-Etter in the same way He would often minister to those whom she served. God changed her life through visions and trances, and she was also known for unusual signs and wonders. The people who were ministered to by her were often transformed through the same kind of visions and trances that she had experienced. But the "signs that make you wonder" went beyond that, including sometimes the death of opponents of the gospel.

Maria became an example of great courage. This woman, who was small in stature, earned the respect of the most hardened criminals because of her unwavering passion to bring transformation to the most sin-filled parts of our nation. Because this courage was supernatural in nature, she outlasted the resistance; her determination to faithfully preach the gospel was greater than the sinners' determination to resist it. She presented the gospel with a power that brought miracles of healing, trances, visions, and a falling under God's power by believer and unbeliever alike, all of which brought people to God.

Perhaps the most impressive part of her miracle lifestyle was how God entrusted her with the actual atmosphere of heaven. It rested upon her. Oftentimes, people for miles around her meetings would fall under the power of God. The conviction of God would touch their hearts, and they would be saved. Think of the implications of this kind of anointing. When a bomb goes off, there is the damage from the impact, but there is also collateral damage. When the presence of God would fall upon Maria Woodworth-Etter, there was powerful blessing in the tent, and there was also collateral blessing. It literally transformed cities. God was not ashamed to be called her God, and He was delighted to be seen upon her. She truly was a friend of God.

The mandate to carry the presence of God into our cities is undeniable. It must be taken seriously. While the Holy Spirit is resident in every believer, it wouldn't be accurate to say that He rests *upon* every believer. However, that should be our goal. In the same way that the Dove, the Holy Spirit, remained upon Jesus after His water baptism, so the Spirit of God is to remain *upon* us. One way to describe this relationship with the Holy Spirit is this: "He is in me for my sake, but He is upon me for yours."

Spirit of Wisdom and Revelation

I consider the prayers of the apostle Paul in the book of Ephesians some of the most important prayers ever prayed. The church at Ephesus is the only church not to receive a word of correction from the apostle in a New Testament epistle. The Ephesians were honored in Scripture for their discernment and devotion to Christ, as well as for their unparalleled revival, which is recorded in the book of Acts. (See Acts 19:1–19.) So, what do you pray for the church who seems to have everything? Paul prayed that God would give *"a spirit of wisdom and of revelation in the knowledge of Him"* (Ephesians 1:17 NASB).

Interestingly, these two realms—wisdom and revelation—became of upmost importance for Maria Woodworth-Etter. She cried out for wisdom continuously. She knew that without divine reasoning, she could not accomplish all that she had been called to do. Additionally, in many ways, what launched her ministry was the spirit of revelation that came upon her, when, in a moment of time, she received a download of biblical insight that would have taken her years of study to obtain, if at all.

God's unusual graces are never to take the place of hard work and devotion. Instead, they often come to those whose faithfulness attracts these graces, bringing about a promotion in ministry that might not have come otherwise. Maria's ignorance of the Scriptures had kept her from having the courage to preach. However, when revelation came upon her, courage came too—to the point that she became a model of courage, not only for her day but also for ours.

I don't think it's possible to be overqualified for ministry. The problem isn't with how much knowledge or training we have. It's with the amount of trust in God we're willing to maintain in spite of our increased knowledge and experience. Sometimes, what appears to be over-qualification in ministry is actually a state of being bound to what we already know at the expense of our need to learn something new from the Lord. Putting it another way, what we know can keep us from what we need to know if we don't maintain the attitude of a novice, staying open and teachable.

God often moves among groups of people who know that they don't know what they're doing! That's because their awareness of their need increases their dependence on God. Revivals usually work best in such an environment, because people are at their greatest point of trust and flexibility. It's when we become more seasoned that we tend to become less flexible. Again, as God increases our understanding of Scripture and the ways of the Holy Spirit, the challenge for us is to remain dependent children of our loving Father. The problem isn't with being blessed. It's with staying humble while being blessed.

Power Encounter

Jesus commissioned His disciples to preach the gospel all over the world. (See Mark 16:15.) He also told them not to go until they had been clothed with power. (See Luke 24:49.) It's possible for us to know what we're to do, and even to have the open door to do it, but still not be qualified. Knowledge won't qualify us. College degrees won't, either. Only a life-changing encounter with the power of the Holy Spirit can truly qualify us to serve God. We are qualified by the anointing.

Maria Woodworth-Etter put it best in her description of her defining moment:

> I came like a child asking for bread. I looked for it. God did not disappoint me. The power of the Holy Ghost came down as a cloud. It was brighter than the sun. I was covered and wrapped up in it. My body was light as the Holy Ghost, and fire, and power, which has never left me. Oh, Praise the Lord! There was liquid fire, and the angels were all around in the fire and glory.[194]

What is most interesting to note is that even after visions, trances, and other wonderful divine experiences, Maria was not really ready for ministry until this moment of the Holy Spirit's power. As we seek additional encounters with the Holy Spirit, looking to be increasingly clothed with power from on high, it is important that we not try to hold God "hostage" to our receiving the same encounter as another. It should be increasingly clear that not everyone featured in this book had the same experience. That fact will become even clearer in the chapters that follow. Let us note that God is the One who clothes us with power, and it must be done His way. Spiritually hungry, humble people do not attempt to put demands upon God. They do not "command" Him to do something in a way that pleases them. They hunger with trust, knowing that if they ask for bread, He will not give them a stone. (See Matthew 7:9; Luke 11:11.)

Suffering and Brokenness

I once created quite a stir when I was asked a question in front of a couple of thousand leaders about my theology of suffering. I responded, "I refuse to have a theology for something that shouldn't exist." The context was suffering in sickness. While many people may struggle with health issues, I refuse to create a legal (theological) reason for sickness to remain. However, if we're talking about suffering for the cause of Christ, that is another matter altogether. The persecutions and death threats, the opposition from the criminal elements in city after city, and even the resistance within her own family that Maria Woodworth-Etter endured couldn't have been as difficult for her as losing five of her six children. That is something I can't imagine. I personally would never feel comfortable attributing that tragedy to God's will, as that pattern was never illustrated in Jesus' ministry, and Jesus Christ is perfect theology. Just because God can use something in our lives doesn't mean He designed it. It can be quite the opposite.

But God still uses broken people. And Maria not only lost five children, but she also went through a divorce. The personal anguish must have been overwhelming. Yet she continued to rescue the perishing and care for the dying, as Jesus had commissioned her to do. She never lost sight of the goodness of God. So many people alter their call according to their circumstances. This great woman of God stayed true in spite of seemingly impossible circumstances. I respect her because, in addition to this, she followed every transition that the Holy Spirit was making in the church in her day of service. In other words, she didn't become stuck in what God had done in the past but continued to listen to see what He was doing presently. Thus, she was a part of every move of God in her lifetime, and she missed nothing. She continued to listen, and she responded to every call that He presented her with. Such an example is very rare in all of church history.

In Luke 4, Jesus spoke of the Spirit of the Lord God that had come upon Him to *"heal the brokenhearted"* and to bring *"recovery of sight to the blind"* (Luke 4:18). This passage quotes Isaiah 61, which includes a statement that too often seems to be forgotten: *"They* [the broken ones mentioned in verses 1–2] *will rebuild the ancient ruins,…and they will repair the ruined cities"* (Isaiah 61:4 NASB). Maria Woodworth-Etter actually got to see a fulfillment of this Scripture. In spite of her own brokenness, she went to the worst parts of various cities so that people could be saved, healed, and delivered, and in turn became a rebuilder of cities. The testimony is very clear in the story of the rough part of St. Louis, Missouri, called "Kerry Patch." The end result was that other broken people joined with her and were used by God to rebuild the city into a place of great peace and blessing.

In Christ, suffering always leads to a positive result. It's not an end in itself. In Maria's case, it became the platform for supernatural courage, making her a rebuilder of cities.

Postscript

Maria Woodworth-Etter has become a hero to many. She deserves honor for her courage, her boldness, and her lifestyle of taking great risks for God. Her resolve to serve Him in spite of personal tragedy is legendary. Yet, in all of these things, she needed special grace to go beyond endurance into victory. That grace was found only in the *liquid fire of God*. That heavenly encounter stands as a summons from God for all who will do as this woman of God did and ask like a child, expectantly. His offer still stands.

6

The Power of the Testimony:
Carrie Judd Montgomery[195]

"Now, who is going to trust God for the winged life? You can crawl
instead if you wish. God will even bless you if you crawl; He will do
the best He can for you, but oh how much better to avail ourselves
of our wonderful privileges in Christ and to 'mount up with wings
as eagles, run and not be weary, walk and not faint.' O beloved
friends, there is a life on wings. I feel the streams of His life fill me
and permeate my mortal frame from my head to my feet, until no
words are adequate to describe it. I can only make a few bungling
attempts to tell you what it is like and ask the Lord to reveal to you
the rest. May He reveal to you your inheritance in Christ Jesus so
that you will press on and get all that He has for you."[196]
—*Carrie Judd Montgomery* (1910)

T
his great woman of God demonstrated the power and the beauty of holding to the testimony of God's activity in other people's

lives until it becomes one's own. She also used the stories of her own break-throughs to bring others into life-changing encounters with God. These stories contain revelations of the nature of God that have often been forgotten. *"Yes, again and again they tempted God, and limited the Holy One of Israel. They did not remember..."* (Psalm 78:41–42).

It takes believers who will press into the supernatural lifestyle made available for every follower of Jesus to reveal these aspects of God's nature again. Carrie Judd Montgomery was such a believer, and her example affected the lives of countless people, some of whom became generals of the faith in their own right. Her trait of *holding to the testimony of God* is one of the most prized characteristics of perhaps any believer in all of history. As such, it has become a mandate for this generation to follow if we want to fully accomplish all that the Father has given us to do.

Stewardship of Encounters

Carrie Judd Montgomery (1858–1946) is a lesser-known healing revivalist, but one who nevertheless made history with God. Her spiritual hunger led her on journeys where she experienced God's presence in profound ways. She was then able to steward those encounters to impact movements of the Spirit. Her testimony of healing shaped the North American divine healing movement in the late 1800s and also had an impact on A. B. Simpson, the founder of the Christian and Missionary Alliance. Her subsequent anointing experience immediately activated her into a ministry of evangelism and of teaching the Word with greater power. Years later, her hunger for God continued to increase and caused her to press in for a Pentecostal Spirit baptism. Carrie introduced apostolic leaders such as A. J. Tomlinson to divine healing, and still others like Francisco Olazábal to healing and Spirit baptism, making a significant impact on the foundations of Pentecostalism and its early formation.

Carrie also initiated some of the earliest healing homes in the country (1882), which preceded A. B. Simpson's (1883) and John Alexander Dowie's (1894) and came over twenty years before John G. Lake's Healing Rooms (1913).[197] Along with Maria Woodworth-Etter, Carrie paved the way for women in ministry. Before there was Aimee Semple McPherson or Kathryn Kuhlman, there was Carrie Judd Montgomery. Throughout the years, friends like Maria Woodworth-Etter, Aimee Semple McPherson, William J. Seymour, Alexander A. Boddy, Smith Wigglesworth, A. B. Simpson, and others visited her Home of Peace in Oakland, California. While Carrie had three major encounters—healing, anointing, and Spirit baptism—her entire life was marked by an intense hunger for God and love for the power of the testimony.

Healing Encounter

Carrie Frances Judd, the fourth of eight children, was born in Buffalo, New York, on April 8, 1858. She grew up in the Episcopal Church and had dreams of becoming a teacher and a writer. Her first major life-changing event occurred when she was seventeen. She claimed that God asked her to surrender all to Him—even the good things. She responded by saying, "I am going to hold [my talent for writing] tight in my clasped hands, but if Thou MUST have it, tear my hands apart."[198] Not long after this, in 1876, when she was walking to school, she slipped and fell hard on the icy ground. Her injuries from that fall turned into a disease called hyperesthesia, which later developed into tuberculosis of the spine and of the blood. This accident shattered her dreams and subjected her to severe, chronic pain. She was bedridden for most of two years. She couldn't handle touch, sound, or light; even a small pillow under her head felt "like a block of stone."[199] Two of Carrie's sisters had already died of sickness, and the outlook of her own life didn't look promising. In the midst of her struggle to stay alive, Carrie still believed she had heard from God with a "little prophetic hint of things to come" that she had an *active mission* to complete.[200] Her illness got so bad, however, that her mother invited some of Carrie's friends to say their last good-byes.

A glimmer of hope came in 1879 when Carrie's father was reading the newspaper and came across a testimony of someone who had been healed. The Judd family quickly sent a letter to the woman in the article and requested prayer. African-American healing evangelist Sarah Mix responded with a catalytic letter on February 24, 1879.

Miss CARRIE JUDD: I received a line from your sister Eva, stating your case, your disease and your faith. I can encourage you, by the Word of God, that "according to your faith" so be it unto you; and besides you have this promise, "The prayer of faith shall save the sick, and the Lord shall raise him up." Whether the person is present or absent, if it is a "prayer of faith," it is all the same, and God has promised to raise up the sick ones, and if they have committed sins to forgive them. Now this promise is to you, as if you were the only person living. Now if you can claim that promise, I have not the least doubt but what you will be healed. You will first have to lay aside all medicine of every description. Use no remedies of any kind for anything. Lay aside trusting in the "arm of flesh," and lean wholly upon God and His promises. When you receive this letter I want you to begin to pray for faith, and Wednesday afternoon the female prayer-meeting is at our house. We will make you a subject of prayer, between the hours of three and four. I want you to pray for yourself, and pray believing and then *act faith*. It makes no difference how you feel, but get right out of bed and begin to walk by faith. Strength will come, disease will depart and you will be made whole. We read in the Gospel, "Thy faith hath made thee whole." Write soon. Yours in faith, MRS. EDWARD Mix.[201]

Carrie followed the instructions in the letter, prayed the prayer of faith found in James 5, got up from her bed, and was healed.[202] This began a process of her being strengthened and recovering fully over the next few months. Less than six months later, she returned to teach her Sunday school class.

For Carrie, her illness—the point of her greatest loss—became an invitation to pursue and to obtain her greatest victory. While the enemy tried to kill, steal, and destroy, God turned the circumstances around to release life more abundantly in her. (See John 10:10.) Not long after her recovery, Carrie's testimony was printed in the newspapers, and news of her healing spread as far as England. This all happened during a time when the prevalent view in the church was that it was good to suffer even illness as unto the Lord. Not many people were praying and believing for healing at that time. Carrie's healing helped to introduce the evangelical Christian world to a God who longs to heal. God also used her testimony as a springboard to launch her into her destiny.

Foundations Laid

In the few years following her healing, several important foundations were laid that Carrie would build upon for the rest of her life. The first foundation was her writing and her publications. When she was only twenty-two years old, she released a catalytic book called *The Prayer of Faith* (1880), a testimony of her healing. This book spread beyond the United States and was even translated into French, Dutch, German, and Swedish.[203] Thousands of people in Carrie's time and in the present day were healed while reading her testimony. Her book also became one of the earlier works on healing in the atonement.[204] By 1893, its circulation had grown to forty thousand.[205] In 1881, shortly after she wrote this revolutionary book, Carrie stepped out in faith to produce a holiness and healing periodical called *Triumphs of Faith*, with only enough money to launch its first issue.[206] This monthly newsletter outlived Carrie and became a significant vehicle for spreading healing testimonies and revival fires around the world, as well as for empowering women in ministry.

Second, not long after her healing, Carrie embarked on her ecumenical preaching career when she shared her testimony at a local church outside of her Episcopalian denomination. By 1883, she had already initiated Thursday night prayer meetings, Tuesday afternoon Bible studies, and a once-a-month prayer meeting for missionaries.[207] The weekly meetings continued for many years. Carrie would later speak at conferences, conventions, and camp meetings, becoming one of the first women to preach itinerantly across North America.

In addition to her writing and her preaching, the third major thread in her ministry developed when she opened Faith Sanctuary in 1880. This was a room in her house that was set aside for prayer for the sick. Taking this one step further, on April 3, 1882, Carrie moved out in faith to open one of the earliest healing homes in the country, which she called Faith-Rest Cottage.[208] She did not have enough money beyond the first few months' rent, but she chose to believe that what God had initiated, He would complete. (See Philippians 1:6.)[209] Following George Müller's example, Carrie operated her cottage by faith and trusted in the Lord to meet her every need.[210] Because healing was such a controversial subject in the church at that time, many people had to go to healing homes where it was "safe" to learn about and to pray for healing.[211] Carrie became a forerunner for the healing home movement and later inspired many others to open similar homes.[212] These foundations of writing, preaching, and healing ministry were all laid before Carrie had celebrated her twenty-fifth birthday.

The Power of the Testimony

Carrie's passion for the power of the testimony contributed to the drastic acceleration and shift that occurred in her life. Divine healing was a radical and controversial message during Carrie's time. As she sought to steward her testimony well, Carrie and some of her friends, like A. B. Simpson, faced rejection and risked being associated with misleading movements such as "positive thinking" or "Christian Science." Despite this, her testimony catalyzed within people hope and faith for healing. Her personal breakthrough released a corporate breakthrough. It acted as a tipping point within the American evangelical church to shift mind-sets from believing that it was good to suffer illness as unto the Lord to believing that it was God's heart to heal.

God speaks to us through testimonies. Every testimony brings something of heaven into the atmosphere. It gives us a divine moment when things shift and are transformed because the record of God's activity is revealed. God does not show partiality. (See Acts 10:34.) He is *the same yesterday, today, and forever* (Hebrews 13:8). So, whether it is Carrie's testimony of being healed or a testimony of something that God did for someone last week, it makes no difference. It is a living, active element of what God is doing and saying. Testimonies are living stories that can literally change our life, our health, our family, or our business. It is important that we get our personal story down well and tell people what God has done for us. Throughout her life, Carrie regularly celebrated the anniversary of her healing in her newsletter. As we, too, are good stewards of our testimonies and write out the details of them, similar ripple effects from heaven to earth will take place.

Anointing Encounter

Even after her ministry success, Carrie's hunger for God continued to deepen. When we live in blessing, we need to remain in a posture of spiritual hunger, as Carrie did. Hunger is a sign of spiritual health. Carrie's hunger led her on a journey that brought her to an even deeper encounter with the Lord a few years later.

As I went on with the Lord I felt an unspeakable hunger springing up within me for more of God. I hardly knew how to pray.... It seemed to me it was more His desire to obtain full possession of me than my desire for Himself. Previously I have spoken of the great blessing I received when I was healed, and my consciousness that the Holy Spirit had come to abide with me. Now, it seemed that He was longing to get full control of me and to fill the temple although I scarcely knew how to put this into words.

While still feeling this great hunger after more of God, I heard of Christian people farther East who had had a great anointing from the Lord and my heart cried out for fellowship with these dear people.... I well remember how my hunger seemed to deepen more and more even while I was on the train journeying from Buffalo to this sister's place of residence.

When I arrived at the Home I was met in the most affectionate and motherly way by this dear saint, who informed me, after she had given me her welcome, that the evening meal was just about ready. My reply to her was as follows:

"Oh, I do not want anything to eat; I want God."

She left me alone in the upper room waiting on God, while she looked after some household duties, and then she returned to me. We knelt quietly together and I do not remember that there was much, if any, audible prayer by either of us, but the presence of the

Lord became more and more manifest as we continued our worship together.

All at once I experienced a blessing that is difficult to put into words. It seemed as though God manifested Himself in a cloud of Heavenly dew which descended gently upon my head and entered into my being, taking full possession of me. At the same time a sweet, restful feeling almost overpowered me so that my own strength somewhat left me and I leaned over and rested my head upon this sister's shoulder. No words were given me, but the dear one by my side seemed to be so one with me that she fully understood the cloud of glory into which I was entering, for His presence seemed to surround me, and at the same time to fill me.

While waiting on the Lord a few more days in this hallowed Home, the manifestation of the Lord's presence about me, and within me, became still more glorious until my whole being seemed to be filled with "rivers of living water" and Jesus Himself revealed as the One among ten thousand, the Lily of the Valley.

I was so conscious that my body, as well as my soul, became so hallowed with the Lord's presence that I was made to realize as never before that I was indeed a temple of the Holy Ghost.... I was held silent in adoration of the glorious Being who was thus revealed to me, conscious of great joy in His immediate presence, and especially delighting in the thought of entire yieldedness to His perfect will....

On my way home on the train I had occasion to speak to a lady about her soul and great anointing was upon me as I talked to her, such as I had never experienced before. When I reached my home I quietly confided to my dear mother my joyful experience, and she praised God with me. The power of God continued to rest upon me in my meetings so that it was told me by one of my friends that it was quite noticeable to others who attended the meetings that I had received an anointing which they had never discerned in me before. The Word of God became more and more precious and it was opened to me increasingly as I expounded it to others.[213]

Carrie immediately imparted what God had deposited. While not as dramatic in physical manifestation as her healing encounter, this encounter resulted in a greater anointing in Carrie's life. This came about after she had put everything to one side and gone on a journey with only one focus—God Himself.

Transitions and Ministry Expansion

In 1890, Carrie married businessman George Montgomery, who relocated her to Oakland, California.[214] George had previously been healed under the ministry of John Alexander Dowie.[215] In 1893, Carrie opened the first healing home on the West Coast, which was called The Home of Peace. This came over twenty years prior to John G. Lake's healing rooms and is still open today. Currently, the home functions as a historic site of revival history, a retreat center, and a bed and breakfast for missionaries, ministers, and others longing to encounter God in a place with deep spiritual "wells."[216]

As a spiritual "entrepreneur," Carrie also started healing and revival camp meetings, orphanages, missionary training schools, and homes for minorities. Additionally, she introduced many significant leaders, such as A. J. Tomlinson, the founder of The Church of God of Prophecy, to divine healing.[217]

Spirit Baptism Encounter

Nearly thirty years after her healing and anointing encounters, Carrie had another experience that she claimed brought her deeper into the rivers of living water than any of her previous experiences.[218]

Azusa Street Revival

The Azusa Street Revival in Los Angeles was ignited by William J. Seymour, an African-American, in early 1906. The major longing of people in this revival was to be baptized in the Holy Spirit, and the outbreak of speaking in tongues was one of the main signs manifested in this new move of God.[219] By the time the Azusa Street Revival broke out, Carrie was nearly fifty years old and already an established leader within the Holiness and divine healing movements.

In 1906, Carrie's husband went to investigate the revival. He returned home very optimistic about this "fresh fire" falling in Southern California. Carrie was so busy running her various ministries that she did not initially have the energy to explore the new signs at Azusa Street.[220] However, as a Pentecostal stream developed in Oakland, Carrie finally made it to a meeting. She was impacted when she saw a young Spirit-baptized girl "shining" in God's "glory," urging her friend to be born again. Carrie later reflected, "I had myself received marvelous anointings of the Holy Spirit in the past, but I felt if there were more for me I surely wanted it, as I could not afford to miss any blessing that the Lord was pouring out in these last days."[221] Then, in July 1907, one of Carrie's workers at The Home of Peace was baptized in the Spirit and spoke in tongues.[222] Not long after, a revival broke out among the children at her orphanage.[223] This caused Carrie to hunger for something she had never known existed at a personal level. Even though she had already experienced the Holy Spirit's presence powerfully in her healing and in her anointing encounter, she still felt there was something more.[224] Her experience demonstrates that it is important to be thankful for what God has already done while at the same time continuing to hunger for more of Him.

Embracing Journey

As a result of these stirrings, Carrie petitioned others for prayer. She recalled, "I wrote to a dear brother who was wonderfully filled and blessed to pray for me that I might be filled with the Spirit. He prayed, and I only seemed to get more hungry."[225] Carrie was finally so hungry for more of God that she took a trip back East to pray about the signs related to the Pentecostal revival. She met with some friends in Cleveland, Ohio, who spoke in tongues, and she urged them to pray with her. She later reflected on this prayer time:

> I grew still more thirsty for the rivers of living water. I knew I had tiny streams, but not rivers. I tried to go to meetings where people were tarrying for the enduement of power from on High,

but seemed again and again providentially hindered from going to them. I then prayed that if it were His will He would let me receive His fullness while waiting upon Him alone, or with some Christian friend. I asked Him also for quiet, sweet manifestations, which would reveal His majesty and dignity, and not such as might seem like excitement of the flesh....

As these dear ones prayed for me, the Spirit said, "Take." I waited and was afraid to do this, lest I should go back on this position of faith. The Spirit said again, and yet again, "Take," and finally I received the Spirit, by faith, to take complete possession of spirit, soul and body, and testified thus to the dear ones praying for me. I kept on tarrying at His feet for the manifestation of His gracious presence. I asked Him to teach me to "drink." Rom. 8:11 was vividly brought to me, and I saw in a most forcible way that my body, His temple, was to be filled with His resurrection Spirit. That same evening, in a measure, I began to experience His power, but He held me steadily to my position of faith, not letting me get my eyes on manifestations.[226]

Carrie did not speak in tongues at this time. She returned to Chicago to reunite with Lucy E. Simmons, a close friend who had received the "fullness of the Spirit, with the sign of speaking in tongues."[227] They spent some time "tarrying" in the Lord's presence. Then something new happened to Carrie. She recorded the following account:

On Monday, June 29th, less than a week from the time I first took my stand by faith, the mighty outpouring came upon me. I had said, "I am all under the blood and under the oil." I then began singing a little song, "He gives me joy instead of sorrow," etc. To my surprise, some of the words would stick in my throat, as though the muscles tightened and would not let me utter them. I tried several times with the same result. Mrs. Simmons remarked that she thought the Lord was taking away my English tongue, because He wanted me to speak in some other language. I replied, "Well, He says in Mark 16:17, 'They shall speak with new tongues,' so I take that, too, by faith." In a few moments I uttered a few scattered words in an unknown tongue and then burst into a language and came pouring out in great fluency and clearness. The brain seemed entirely passive, the words not coming from that source at all, but from an irresistible volume of power within, which seemed to possess my whole being, spirit, soul and body.

For nearly two hours I spoke and sang in unknown tongues (there seemed three or four distinct languages). Some of the tunes were beautiful, and most Oriental. I tried sometimes to say something in English, but the effort caused such distress in my throat and head, I had to stop after a few words and go back to the unknown tongues. I was filled with joy and praise to God with an inward depth of satisfaction in Him which cannot be described. To be thus controlled by the Spirit of God and to feel that He was speaking "heavenly mysteries" through me was most delightful. The rivers of living water flowed through me and divine ecstasy filled my soul. There was no shaking, and no contortions of the body. I felt that I drank and used up the life and power as fast as it was poured in. I became very weak physically under the greatness of the heavenly vision and staggered when I tried to walk across the floor. But when the exhaustion became very great, dear Mrs. Simmons asked the Lord to strengthen me, which He did so sweetly, letting His rest and healing life possess my weary frame. Passages from the Word of God came to me with precious new meanings. Not long after this I had a vision of the work of His Cross as never before.[228]

Like D. L. Moody, regardless of her previous encounters or ministry successes, Carrie went after more of the Spirit, which was freely available to her. By faith, she learned to possess what was already in her spiritual account. It is important to realize that by covenant in Christ, everything is already given to us. We simply need to take hold of what has already been given. In Carrie's time, speaking in tongues was a newer phenomenon and was controversial within the church. But when we want Him more than anything else, it doesn't matter what His manifest presence might look like. Knowing that there is more and being hungry for full immersion in God changes everything.

After Spirit Baptism

Carrie's Spirit baptism encounter touched her deeply. Her experience brought her satisfaction in ways she had not previously experienced. She observed a multiplication of joy, power to witness, "teachableness," a hunger for the Word of God, and "freedom of the mind from all care," which had not been settled in her up to that point. She also said that "the precious reality of His grace, the perfection of His love in my spirit, the absolute rest and quietness of my mind (having the mind of Christ) and the indescribable quickening of my mortal body by His life-giving Spirit (Rom. 8:11), seem infinitely beyond any experience I have had in the past, freighted as the past has been with His blessing."[229]

Carrie sought to impart her encounter so that it would bless others. Shortly after, she transitioned from her orphanage work to give more time to the ministry of the Word.[230] She no longer wanted to succeed at anything besides her assignment for each season. She also went with her husband and her only child, Faith, on her first overseas ministry trip.[231] Upon hearing about her Spirit-baptism experience, many evangelical missionaries were baptized in the Spirit and spoke in tongues. Additionally, Carrie wrote about her encounter in her monthly newsletter and created space for others to share their testimonies of Spirit baptism. This released a widespread hunger for the Pentecostal Spirit baptism across denominations and around the world.[232] As a result of this shift in Carrie's life, The Home of Peace expanded its mission and became a place of prayer for Spirit baptism, as well. As Carrie released her testimony, her personal victory and breakthrough became a corporate blessing once again.

Influencing the Apostolic

Carrie's encounter especially impacted apostolic leaders. One such leader was Francisco Olazábal (1886–1937), whom Aimee Semple McPherson once referred to as the "Mexican Billy Sunday."[233] After Carrie's husband led Olazábal to the Lord, Carrie introduced him to divine healing and then prayed with him to receive Spirit baptism and to speak in tongues. Olazábal went on to preach to over two hundred fifty thousand people and to help plant over ten denominations (both Protestant and Pentecostal).[234] Further, Smith Wigglesworth, Alexander Boddy, and other significant Pentecostal leaders partnered with Carrie in her 1914 Cazadero World-Wide Camp Meeting, where they invited many to be "baptized with the Holy Spirit in Pentecostal Fullness (Acts 2:4)."[235] The camp meeting became an important event for the developing Pentecostal movement because many Christian leaders who had been seeking Spirit baptism finally received it during their time there. The fruits of her Cazadero Camp Meetings and of Olazábal's ministry provide just a few examples of the direct impact of Carrie's stewarding her testimony to release breakthrough to others.

Legacy

Carrie remained faithful to her husband and to the Lord all the days of her life. She finished her life on this earth well. In addition, thousands of key leaders have been significantly impacted by her faith, love, and impartations of her own breakthroughs. Carrie went to be with the Lord on July 26, 1946, at age eighty-eight, outliving both Maria Woodworth-Etter and Aimee Semple McPherson. Because Carrie was so young when she entered the divine healing movement, she is one of the best examples of what early Holiness and divine healing roots lived out within Pentecostalism look like.[236] Since Carrie lived effectively within two major moves of God, her life also provides us with a model for how to embrace, sustain, and carry forward revival.

Unity in Love

Carrie grew up in the Episcopal Church and was a founding member of the Christian and Missionary Alliance, an honorary officer of the Salvation Army, and an early member of the Assemblies of God; she was passionate about cultivating unity in love, regardless of denominational label. This allowed her to supersede sectarian barriers and influence the foundations of several movements. As a result of the covenant friendships she nurtured and her passion to love the whole church, Carrie was a bridge between evangelicals and Pentecostals. By remaining in a place of humility, she was able to influence many leaders to encounter God in a greater measure. Her hunger for God caused her to venture outside of what was safe and to invite others to enter in.

Women in Ministry

Like Maria Woodworth-Etter, Carrie pioneered new territory and paved the way not only for healing and for early Pentecostalism but also for women in ministry. In Carrie's early days, A. B. Simpson regularly created space for her to preach in his meetings. At times, he even scheduled extra sessions for her at his conferences when she made surprise visits. Simpson's willingness to share his platform with Carrie helped to launch her further into her own destiny, which had great ripple effects on the church. Carrie's "impact on the divine healing movement, though strong in its own right, was undoubtedly magnified by her association with people like Simpson, who opened doors and nurtured her early steps of faith into the arena of public speaking."[237]

Further, Carrie never taught about or tried to defend being a woman in ministry; she simply did the things God had called her to do.[238] She resisted the temptation to pick up the debate about women in ministry. She also chose not to live in reaction to others. The gospel was her message, not women in ministry. Yet, with Carrie's life as an example, many women were inspired to start healing homes; still others were inspired to preach. Carrie also gave women a voice by inviting them to publish articles in her periodical. This provided them with a platform to be heard. Additionally, Carrie regularly created space for women in her weekly meetings, church services, ministry training school, and camp meetings. Through her life and ministry, Carrie helped pave the way for future generations of women to be launched into their God-given destinies.

Patterns

Heart Set on Pilgrimage

In all of Carrie's significant encounters, she sought out others who had experienced a similar breakthrough or encounter and asked them for prayer. Worship, prayer, and waiting on God were consistent features of the process by which she reached out to God. She chose to yield, to surrender, and, by faith, to actively take hold of all that was available. As she freely received, she was quick to freely share her testimony and release the same blessing to others. With the exception of her healing, Carrie's encounters were also preceded by journey. Distractions were removed, time was set aside, and there was a cost.

It is time for us, also, to go on a journey with the Lord to a deeper place. Something special is released when we take a journey with God as our only destination. If our hearts are set on this one voyage, something happens that releases life into our entire bodies. Psalm 84:5 says, *"Blessed is the man whose strength is in You, whose heart is set on pilgrimage."* There is blessing for those whose hearts are set on this single pilgrimage. This is a lifestyle without other options. On such a journey, all of our other options need to be laid down. We must have one ambition: to know Him.

Destiny

Many times, encounters are keys that unlock deeper levels of our destiny. Each of Carrie's encounters propelled her further into her destiny. Her healing in 1879 was her most defining moment because it activated her writing in a powerful way, launched her into her healing ministry, and caused her to lay important foundations for the rest of her life. Led by an intense hunger for more of God, her next notable encounter resulted in a deeper understanding of the Word and a greater anointing. Her Spirit baptism in 1908 released a new heavenly language that increased her intimacy with God. It also caused her to refine her focus, expand the borders of her ministry, and position herself to impact the formation of early Pentecostalism. Even after these important experiences, Carrie continued to pursue more of the fullness of the Spirit and to encounter God in even profounder ways. She recounted one experience that she had two years after her Spirit baptism:

> Early this morning as the power of God was upon me, and I was recognizing, as I so often love to do, the presence of the indwelling Comforter, and worshipping Him in His temple, with the Father and the Son, was led out in prayer for different things, but all at

once He said to me, "I want you to recognize definitely that I am filling the temple." Of course, I know He always fills it, but this was something a little different and He wanted the recognition that every part of spirit, soul and body was pervaded with His presence, and that meant, as He revealed to me His meaning, that I should drop even prayer for the time and be occupied with the presence of His glory, and I said, "Oh, God, the Holy Ghost, Thou art filling Thy temple," and immediately, just as though a little vial of attar of roses had been broken in this room and every part of it would soon be filled with the perfume, so the presence of His glory, sensibly pervaded every part of my being and even love and prayer were lost in worship. Then I thought of the time in the Old Testament when the temple was so filled with God's glory that the priest could not even stand to minister.... There is, therefore, an experience beyond service and beyond prayer, and that is a revelation of His own personality to such an extent that there is nothing but adoring worship filling our being. Usually it is a blessed experience to be able to speak in tongues, to let the heavenly song flow out, but there are times when even tongues cease, when His presence is so all-pervading and the atmosphere so heavenly that I cannot talk at all in any language, but the power of His blessed Spirit upon me is so marvelous that it seems as though I were almost dwelling in heaven.[239]

Oceans of Living Waters

Each of Carrie's encounters allowed her to drink deeply from the river of life. Total surrender gripped her life, a life marked by a hunger to live in the deepest place possible with the Spirit. Carrie called for people to move beyond a single experience with God and to be "swept off their feet" into the limitless measures of the Spirit. (See Ezekiel 47.) She believed that it was possible to thrive where the living waters flooded, overwhelmed, and baptized one's life continuously.[240]

The Spirit of the living God is a river that we can freely dive into. It is impossible for us to stand in a place where we do not have access to the Spirit, to the springs of life. We have connections because the kingdom of

God is within us. There is no shortage in heaven. That realm is in our lives and is flowing through us. Carrie dove into the floods of God's Spirit, and we, also, have access all of the time to the same vast measures of His presence. We must contend for divine encounters in our lives. If we want to know Him more and be empowered to fulfill our destinies, we must pursue increasing breakthroughs, increasing baptisms of the Spirit. I know that I need a fresh encounter. Like Carrie, we cannot afford to settle for just one touch from twenty years ago. We must press forward for the ongoing fire that gets ignited in us day after day, year after year. We must come to Him as children because all things are new.

My cry is for explosions of God's power in our lives so that what is in us can transform the world around us. We must have a fresh Holy Spirit baptism today.

Prophetic Inheritance

Because God does not show partiality, and He really is the same yesterday, today, and forever, what we have seen Him do in the past creates a momentum for us to experience Him in the present day. It just takes someone to recognize the living reality that exists in a testimony and to put a demand on the power it carries. Carrie Judd Montgomery models this response very well. She not only benefited from the testimony of others, but she also became the source of testimonies of miracles that created faith in her hearers, positioning her to give away what God had given her.

Purpose for Authority

Our authority in God is not for self-promotion. It is to benefit the people we touch. Almost immediately after she was healed, Carrie shared her testimony and began to pray for the sick. Jesus gave the command, *"Freely you have received, freely give"* (Matthew 10:8). The key for Carrie was that she didn't think God's working a miracle in her life meant that she was more significant than others. For that reason, she lived with the realization that she was to give away all she received. She knew that others were as worthy of the supernatural interventions of God as she was. The wonderful power of the testimony is in the fact that a story about God carries the presence of God. He is powerfully released into the atmosphere in a way that is new and refreshing for all who hear—who truly hear.

Again, after she was baptized in the Holy Spirit and began to speak in tongues, Carrie immediately started to minister to others who were looking for the same outcome. Genuine experiences in God equip us to give away what we've received. This is the evidence of real biblical authority. Those called by God to serve the body of Christ are to do so to equip their fellow believers for service. In other words, to equip those around them with the grace they have received for ministry so that others might be able to do what they do. Those who protect their gift because they believe that they alone are qualified to use it miss the point altogether.

There will always be generals in the army of God. We need them. Their call, their experience, and their anointing in God will put them head and shoulders above everyone around them. But this is not so that everyone will merely receive and depend on their gift. The generals are made visible so that, as they equip others, what was once the high-water mark of the highly gifted one will become the new norm as people are equipped and released. This is the way Carrie Judd Montgomery was able to multiply herself over and over again throughout her lifetime. Many, many leaders benefited from the grace she carried. Their lives and ministries were forever changed because of the impact of this wonderful woman who lived so open-handedly. Perhaps this is why she is largely unknown today: she imparted to so many people that she no longer remained the focal point of her gift. Those whom she served became the faces that revival historians remember. But heaven remembers Carrie. Elijah's anointing is what John the Baptist operated in; as a result, he was called the greatest of all prophets. Why did John not walk in the spirit and power of *Elisha*, rather than Elijah? Elisha had twice the anointing and measure of breakthrough as Elijah. It was because Elisha walked in the momentum created by Elijah. Heaven gives honor to the ones who blaze the original trail and become a fountain of life for others to benefit from.

Bridge-Builder

I don't know a single leader in the body of Christ who doesn't want unity. We sing about it, we pray about it, and we even preach about it. But that usually means we expect others to move toward us, to honor our theological positions and our experience, and to adjust their lives to accommodate our ministry. Consequently, unity becomes possible to the degree that others show us respect. Randy Clark says it best: "Every stream thinks it is the river." Carrie lived differently. She moved toward others, looking for common ground, honoring other people's place in God. She actually understood the thought processes and values of other movements. When you know people's hearts, and you know that their hearts are good, it's much easier to celebrate who they are in God. My dad used to say, "When you wash someone's feet, you find out why they walk the way they do."

In her lifetime, Carrie belonged to at least four different denominational groups, all of which celebrated her, not just tolerated her. (She was even involved in the beginnings of some of them.) As a result, she was highly respected in both the evangelical and Pentecostal worlds. She was able to bring many evangelicals into a Pentecostal experience because of her position of great favor with them. She was a favorite of A. B. Simpson, the founder of the Christian and Missionary Alliance, who created space for her in his conferences. It is important to honor Simpson for his contribution, as well, since he created controversy for himself by promoting a woman in ministry, which was even less acceptable in that day than it is today. But he favored the anointing of the Holy Spirit on Carrie more than he feared the controversy such a move would create.

It must delight the heart of God immensely that Carrie's life was such a catalyst for true unity. She was a bridge-builder, not a divider.

Childlike Adventurer

In many ways, Carrie really lived outside the box—but not because she needed to be noticed as unique or different. She discovered a big God who wanted to be expressed in ways that many people had not considered. She also became an author at a very early age. In fact, her book on faith became a standard in the church, but she wrote it at the age of twenty-two. Then, at the age of twenty-three, she started a periodical that fanned the flames of revival by declaring the testimony of the Lord. These accomplishments would have been exceptional for anyone, but they were especially so for a young lady. She succeeded in ignoring what others might have thought was a strike against her (being a woman) and lived her life to the fullest, in spite of it all.

One of the most fascinating aspects of the history of divine healing in this nation is the raising up of healing homes where the sick and dying would come to stay for a period of time to be prayed for and to learn to pray in faith. John Alexander Dowie and John G. Lake are both known for using this incredible ministry tool. But Carrie experimented with this concept before they did, no doubt providing encouragement for it and, in some ways, a model to follow.

Many of us are good at following in someone else's shoes, taking their example of living life to the fullest. It's beautiful that this is even possible. But some people are childlike adventurers who, through prayer and risk-taking, want to find out for themselves if God would like to be represented in another way. This is what Carrie Judd Montgomery provides for us—childlike adventurousness. She gave God her all and her best, just waiting to see what the Father might breathe upon. His breath truly spread the effect of her *offering* all over the earth.

The Power of the Word

Carrie was part of a healing movement that had a tremendous impact on the church in the United States. The divine healing movement existed long before the Pentecostal movement, which started around 1900. Those who were in the healing movement took what they had learned about their salvation and applied it to healing. In order to bring assurance to young believers, for example, they taught them to believe what God said in His Word about salvation and then to confess it with their mouths. If they did this, according to Scripture, they would be saved. This was standard teaching for new believers who might question whether they were truly born again when a problem arose.

So, those involved in the healing movement successfully took this insight and applied it to healing, believing that God's Word is true and must be trusted in. Such faith should then be expressed through a confession. Many ran the risk of being associated with some of the New Age thought that was emerging in that day, but they were nothing like that hellish movement, except where the cultic leaders borrowed concepts from the

Scriptures. The devil has a counterfeit for everything valuable. However, in the same way that we don't throw away our money because there is the chance of running into counterfeit currency, we must not fear the wonderful things that God has planned to do in our lifetime. Instead, we must be aware that the devil is a liar, and stay away from any movement that draws our attention away from Jesus to exalt a human vessel.

Carrie Judd Montgomery is the first person I've read about who used the principle of the authority of God's Word and the importance of confession to bring herself into her defining moment with God. It's probably happened many times, but I don't recall any others. She knew that God did not show partiality and that what He had done for others, He would do for her. So, when she saw that others had had encounters with God that she had not experienced, she confessed what she knew to be the heart of God for her. It wasn't too long after this that she had her baptism in the Holy Spirit experience, which, once again, changed everything.

We learn to hear the voice of God through the Scriptures. He won't violate His own Word (although He has often violated my *understanding* of His Word). It's His voice that makes what we read on the page come alive in a way that heals the body, saves the soul, delivers from torment, and even leads to a defining moment. Live in the awareness that this is God's heart for you.

Staying Hungry When Filled

Carrie didn't allow what society—or even the church—thought she might be lacking to keep her from her destiny. Although she was young, a woman, and unmarried, her hunger for God was greater than every argument used against her. The Bible teaches that if the farmer waits for all the conditions to be right, he'll never plant his crops. (See Ecclesiastes 11:4.) If that warning ever described our life in God, it would have to be in this context. In other words, when He says *go, GO!*

The issue of women in ministry will probably be debated until Jesus returns. Yet the greatest argument in favor of women in ministry is their testimony when they encounter God and are used in His power. In Acts 15, the apostles recognized that the Holy Spirit ministered to the Gentiles in the same way that He had ministered to the Jews at the beginning. That recognition gave them the courage to accept the fact that the Gentiles were qualified for the touch of the Holy Spirit, too, and they didn't need to obey the Law in order to earn it. Rather, Jesus qualified them for it. The same can be said of women. If you are a woman, get filled to overflowing with the Holy Spirit and serve people. Let the debaters debate while each woman increases the evidence of the Holy Spirit's choice to flow through her.

Like every hero of church history that I've studied, Carrie maintained a continual hunger for more in God. But much like Maria Woodworth-Etter, she transitioned with every fresh wind of the Holy Spirit. That cannot be said about all our heroes. Some found it very difficult to leave the place where they had finally found great success with spiritual breakthroughs in God. Yet Carrie had a hunger for God that made it impossible for her to embrace the status quo or to live what others thought to be a normal life. Hunger moves people. It moves them to take great risks and to give no thought to what others might think. This just might be a prerequisite to entering into the greater things in God. Defining moments aren't usually given to the casual or the content. Only those who hunger for *what might be* can be entrusted with the reality of what might be.

Hunger and humility are often found in the same heart. Carrie models what hunger looks like for someone who is already established and successful in ministry and yet is ready for more: becoming the child again. I've never read about one of these generals in God's army who did not model great humility. "*God is opposed to the proud, but gives grace to the humble*" (James 4:6; 1 Peter 5:5 NASB). Grace is the empowering presence of God that enables us to do what only God can do. This reality is modeled in the lives of history's finest. And they create a momentum that we now inherit.

Postscript

God is the ultimate steward. He plants where He expects a great return. He finds people whom others would never trust or believe in and gives them His finest. When He takes His best and gives it to us, He knows that we are more than capable of stewarding that reality in God and planting it into others' lives. In God's kingdom, we often receive more when we've taken care of what He has already given us. Carrie Judd Montgomery illustrates just how possible it is to enter into a defining moment in God through giving honor to what He has already given us.

7

Prevailing Faith:
Smith Wigglesworth

"Fear looks; faith jumps. If I leave you as I found you, I am not
God's channel. I am not here to entertain you but to get you to
the place where you can laugh at the impossible, to believe and to
see the goodness of the Lord in the land of the living."[241]
—*Smith Wigglesworth*

Smith Wigglesworth had a great impact on my family. My grandparents sat under his ministry, and my aunt was baptized in the
Holy Spirit in one of his meetings. My grandfather told me that not everyone loved Wigglesworth. Of course, he is well loved by many people today,
much like Israel loved all of its dead prophets!

Smith Wigglesworth had great faith—and faith offends those who are
stationary. Faith is aggressive, looking for problems to solve and feeding on
opportunities for the good news of the gospel to become manifest for what
it really is. It's not that people with great faith always do things right. We

all have blind spots and need one another for balance and perspective. But those who exercise faith can move mountains. And while people who live cautiously, instead of by faith, may be called wise by all their friends, they won't move many mountains.

If anyone stirs me and provokes me to seek more in God, it is Smith Wigglesworth. He was truly a living offering unto the glory of God. His heart for the Lord is measurable in his passion for the lost. And his impact on his surroundings (whether or not he said a word) is truly legendary.

"All Things Are Possible"

Smith Wigglesworth (1859–1947) became a powerful voice at the turn of the twentieth century. As a man of faith, his main message was "All things are possible, only believe."[242] He burned within to see the lost come to know Jesus. The only book he read was the Bible, and he feasted on it continually.

Wigglesworth had several significant encounters with the Lord that impacted his life. Following his conversion and confirmation, he had a sanctification experience in which he returned to the Lord in greater holiness. Several years later, he embraced divine healing and saw many people healed. In 1907, he had a "baptism of fire" encounter during which he spoke in tongues. After that encounter, his stuttering tongue and weak oratory skills disappeared, and he became a powerful preacher with unique "signs and wonders following." (See Mark 16:20 KJV.) After the loss of his wife, whom he had previously raised from the dead, he took his ministry to the nations. Wigglesworth released God's presence in powerful, unique ways.

Conversion

Smith Wigglesworth was born on June 8, 1859, in Yorkshire, England. Because his family was very poor, he had to start working at the age of six. Though his parents were not believers, he remembered always longing for God, even as a child.[243] His grandmother was an "old-time Wesleyan Methodist" who regularly took him to church. While at a revival meeting when he was eight years old, Smith observed "simple folks dancing around a big stove in the centre of the church, clapping their hands" and singing songs to the "Lamb." As he joined in, "a clear knowledge of the New Birth came into [his] soul," and he was born again.[244] Shortly after, he led his mother to the Lord, and his passion to win souls was ignited.

Confirmation Encounter

When Wigglesworth was about ten years old, he was confirmed in the Episcopal Church. When the bishop laid hands on him, he had a powerful encounter with God. He said, "My whole body was filled with the consciousness of God's presence, a consciousness that remained in me for days. After the confirmation service, all the other boys were swearing and quarrelling, and I wondered what had made all the difference between them and me."[245]

When Wigglesworth later moved to Bradford, he encountered the newly formed Salvation Army and was baptized in water at the age of seventeen. A year later, he became a plumber. His business grew so much that by the age of twenty, he moved to Liverpool to get more clients. Like Moody, he used much of the money from his flourishing business to feed and clothe the poor. Smith fasted every Sunday and never remembered "seeing less than fifty souls saved by the power of God in the meetings with the children, in the hospitals, on the ships, and in the Salvation Army."[246] He would regularly be asked to speak in meetings but struggled to do so eloquently. He constantly broke down in tears because of his concern for the spiritual state of his listeners; many times, this led to his giving an altar call.

When he was twenty-three, he returned to Bradford, where he met a young lady named Mary Jane Featherstone, nicknamed "Polly," at a Salvation Army meeting. They soon married and planted a church together. Wigglesworth admitted that his wife "was the preacher," and he "encouraged her to do it all."[247] Over the years, the Wigglesworths had one daughter and four sons.

Turning Back to God

In 1884, Wigglesworth got many requests for plumbing work and spent most of his time away from church. While his wife continued to flourish in ministry, his heart grew cold toward the things of God, and this affected their marriage. One night, Wigglesworth commanded Polly to stop coming home so late from her ministry endeavors. She let him know that while she was still his wife, Christ was her only Master. At this, his temper flared, and he locked her outside of the house. She walked around to the front door, which was open, reentered the house, and couldn't stop laughing. Smith couldn't fight it anymore, and he laughed with her. At that moment, something shifted inside of him, and his heart was rekindled for the things of the Lord. As a result, he decided to give ten days to prayer and fasting to get his heart right. Following this time of deep sanctification and consecration unto the Lord, there was a marked change in him, to the extent that his temper and moodiness left.[248] His wife's steadfastness and ability not to take offense was catalytic in his turning point to reengage with God at a deeper level.

Nearly ten years later, in July 1893, after ten days of focused prayer, Smith had another epiphany and an even deeper sanctification experience. At that time, he believed this to be his baptism in the Spirit.[249] He continued his plumbing business and evangelized whenever he had the chance.

Healing Encounter

In the early 1900s, Wigglesworth was introduced to divine healing when he went to get some plumbing supplies in another town and came across the Leeds Healing Home. Later, both he and his wife returned and received healing there. When the leaders of the Leeds Healing Home wanted to attend the Keswick Convention (an annual Christian conference in Keswick, England), they asked Smith to stand in for them and preach at the Healing Home. During his first time preaching there, fifteen people came up for prayer. One man on crutches was instantly healed, and he jumped up and ran all around the room.

When Wigglesworth returned to Bradford, he started healing meetings there.[250] After he and Polly introduced divine healing into their church, the congregation grew so much that they had to move to a larger meetinghouse on Bowland Street. Later, Wigglesworth almost died of appendicitis, but an elderly lady and a young man prayed and commanded the "devil" to come out in Jesus' name. Wigglesworth was healed and went to work that same day. Following this miracle, over the years, he fiercely released healing over appendicitis in people around the world. It is believed that every single person he prayed for with this condition was instantly healed.[251]

Spirit-Baptism Encounter

Journey to Sunderland

One day, a man came to Wigglesworth's home to ask for prayer for healing. Smith directed him to pray and fast for seven days to be healed. The man returned on the fourth day to share the news that he had been healed. He also said that he would finish off his seven-day fast. This same man later encouraged Wigglesworth to explore what God was doing in Sunderland, where people were being baptized in the Spirit and speaking in tongues (at that time, this was still a newer manifestation of the Spirit). The man invited Wigglesworth to Sunderland with him and offered to pay for all his expenses.

Because of his earlier sanctification experience, Wigglesworth believed that he was already baptized in the Spirit. When he attended the Sunderland Convention, organized under the leadership of Anglican Alexander Boddy, he was not satisfied with what he saw. It was spiritually dry compared to what he was used to. He disrupted the meetings by challenging the people and asking more about the experience of speaking in tongues.

> I was continuously in those meetings causing disturbances, until the people wished I had never come. They said that I was disrupting the conditions for people to receive the baptism. But I was hungry and thirsty for God, and I had gone to Sunderland because I had heard that God was pouring out His Spirit in a new way. I had heard that God had now visited His people and manifested His power, and that people were speaking in tongues as on the Day of Pentecost.
>
> Thus, when I first got to Sunderland, I said to the people, "I cannot understand this meeting. I have left a meeting in Bradford

all on fire for God. The fire fell last night, and we were all laid out under the power of God. I have come here for tongues, and I don't hear them—I don't hear anything."

"Oh!" they said. "When you get baptized with the Holy Spirit, you will speak in tongues."

"Oh, is that it?" I said. "When the presence of God came upon me, my tongue was loosened, and when I went in the open air to preach, I really felt that I had a new tongue."

"Ah, no," they said, "that is not it."

"What is it, then?" I asked.

"When you get baptized in the Holy Spirit—"

"I am baptized," I interjected, "and there is no one here who can persuade me that I am not baptized."

So I was up against them, and they were up against me.

I remember a man getting up and saying, "You know, brothers and sisters, I was here three weeks and then the Lord baptized me with the Holy Spirit, and I began to speak with other tongues."

I said, "Let us hear it. That's what I'm here for."

But he could not speak in tongues.[252]

During his time of frustration in Sunderland, Wigglesworth went on Sunday to the local Salvation Army to pray. Three times, he was "smitten to the floor by the mighty power of God."[253] The group asked him to preach that evening. The Salvationists were not supportive of speaking in tongues at that time, and they warned him against it, as did others.

Alexander Boddy called an all night "waiting meeting" at the Sunderland Convention for the next Tuesday night. Smith recalled that "it was a very precious time and the presence of the Lord was very wonderful, but I did not hear anyone speaking in tongues." At 2:30 a.m., the meeting closed, but Wigglesworth had forgotten his key in his hotel room, so a missionary from India invited him to stay with him. They prayed for the rest of the night and "received great blessing."[254]

The Fire Falls

Wigglesworth recalled that "for four days I wanted nothing but God."[255] Before heading back on Wednesday, he went to say good-bye to the vicar's wife, Mary Boddy.

> As the days passed, I became more and more hungry for God. I had opposed the meetings so much, but the Lord was gracious, and I will always remember that last day—the day I was to leave. God was with me so much. They were to have a meeting, and I went, but I could not be still. This revival was taking place at an Episcopal church. I went to the rectory to say good-bye, and there in the library, I said to Mrs. Boddy, the rector's wife, "I cannot rest any longer; I must have these tongues now."
>
> She replied, "Brother Wigglesworth, it is not the tongues you need but the baptism. If you will allow God to baptize you, the other will be all right."
>
> I answered, "My dear sister, I know I am baptized. You know that I have to leave here at four o'clock. Please lay hands on me so that I may receive the tongues."
>
> She stood up and laid her hands on me, and the fire fell on me.
>
> I said, "The fire's falling." There came a persistent knock at the door, and she had to go out. That was the best thing that could have happened, for I was alone with God.
>
> Then He gave me a revelation. Oh, it was wonderful! He showed me an empty cross and Jesus glorified....
>
> Then I saw that God had purified me. It seemed that God gave me a new vision, and I saw a perfect being within me, with mouth open, saying, "Clean! Clean! Clean!" When I began to repeat it, I found myself speaking in other tongues. The joy was so great that, when I went to utter it, my tongue failed, and I began to worship God in other tongues *"as the Spirit gave* [me] *utterance"* (Acts 2:4).
>
> It was all as beautiful and peaceful as when Jesus said, *"Peace, be still!"* (Mark 4:39). The tranquillity and the joy of that moment

surpassed anything I had ever known up to that time. But, hallelujah, these days have grown with greater, mightier, more wonderful divine manifestations and power! That was only the beginning.
There is no end to this kind of beginning. You will never come to
the end of the Holy Spirit until you have arrived in glory—until
you are right in the presence of God forever—and even then we
will always be conscious of His presence.[256]

After his encounter, Wigglesworth went straight to the church where
Alexander Boddy was in mid-service and asked to share about his experience. Boddy had not yet received the Pentecostal baptism, and many others had been waiting for months there and had not yet come all the way
"through" to speaking in tongues.

The place was full of people. I can't remember what I said, but I
know I made all those people extremely dissatisfied and discon-
tented with their position. They said, "We have been rebuking this
man because he was so intensely hungry, but he has come in for a
few days and has received the Baptism and some of us have been
waiting here for months and have not yet received it." A great hunger came upon them all. From that day God began to pour out His
Spirit until in a very short while fifty had received the Baptism.[257]

Like John Wesley after his "strangely warmed heart" encounter,
Wigglesworth was flooded with doubt and spiritual attack immediately
following his encounter.

On the train to my home town, the Devil began questioning, "Are
you going to take this to Bradford?" As regards my feelings at the
moment, I had nothing to take, but the just do not live by feelings but by faith. So I shouted on the railroad coach to everyone's
amazement, "Yes, I'm taking it!" A great joy filled me as I made
this declaration, but somehow I knew that from that moment it
would be a great fight all the time.[258]

I was so full of joy that I wired home to say that I had received the
Holy Spirit.

As soon as I got home, my boy came running up to me and said, "Father, have you received the Holy Spirit?"

I said, "Yes, my boy."

He said, "Let's hear you speak in tongues."

But I could not.[259]

While those he prayed for received the gift of tongues, it was not until nine months later that Wigglesworth was able to speak in tongues again.

Results of Spirit-Baptism Encounter

Greater Anointing for Preaching

Immediately after Wigglesworth's encounter, his wife, Polly, and others were skeptical. Polly said the true test would be the manner in which he preached on Sunday. By watching him, she would be able to tell if he had a different sort of baptism than the one she claimed to have already had. Wigglesworth preached on Isaiah 61:1–3 that morning with such assurance that Polly could barely believe it was her husband speaking! Revival immediately broke out. Wigglesworth recalled:

As soon as I had finished, the secretary of the mission got up and said, "Brethren, I want what the leader of our mission has got." He tried to sit down but missed his seat and fell on the floor. There were soon fourteen of them on the floor, my own wife included. We did not know what to do, but the Holy Ghost got a hold of the situation and the fire fell. A revival started and the crowds came. It was only the beginning of the flood-tide of blessing. We had touched the reservoir of the Lord's life and power.[260]

Full-Time Ministry

Wigglesworth was so passionate about releasing the kingdom of God that he responded to many requests for ministry; he would travel for miles just to pray for one person. When he returned from his ministry adventures, there would be fewer and fewer plumbing jobs due to his absence.

Soon, he watched his customers and his business dwindle away. One woman called on him for a plumbing job, and after he did all the work, she asked how much she owed. He told her it would be his gift to her and an offering unto the Lord as his last plumbing job. Following this, he left his plumbing tool belt behind and went into full-time ministry.[261] He and his wife regularly prayed every Saturday night, claiming a minimum of fifty souls to be won on Sunday. Many times, God answered their cries, and fifty or more people stepped into the kingdom the next day.[262]

Further Calls to Ministry

One of his early calls for ministry after his Spirit baptism was from a man who had a factory in Lancashire that employed over one thousand people. He shut down the factory so that Wigglesworth could conduct meetings for his employees. Many people fell under the conviction of the Holy Spirit in Wigglesworth's presence and got saved.[263] Not long after, Polly got baptized in the Spirit and also spoke in tongues. This new element of their ministry radically changed their Bowland Street Mission in Bradford.[264] And when they traveled together, wherever they went, many were baptized in the Holy Spirit.[265]

Another time, Wigglesworth received several telegrams to pray for a seriously ill boy in Grantham, England. He traveled to Grantham, and once he arrived, he had to go by bicycle another nine miles to get to the farm where the boy lived. When he arrived, the mother told him that he was too late because her son was nearly dead. Smith answered, "God has never sent me anywhere too late." He prayed and fasted and then asked the parents to get the boy's clothes ready to wear. He went to the Sunday meeting at a Primitive Methodist chapel, where he was invited to take charge of the service. Everyone there knew the boy and also had faith for his healing. This led Smith to see that faith could arise in others as it had in him. He returned to the boy's house, where the parents had not followed his instructions to lay out the boy's clothes. After Wigglesworth got the clothes himself, he told someone in the house to put the boy's stockings on. Then he had everyone leave, and he shut the door behind him.

He prayed, and the moment he touched the boy's hand, the presence of God filled the room so powerfully that Wigglesworth hit the floor, and he lay in the glory for over fifteen minutes. The power of God shook the room. While Wigglesworth was down, the boy regained his strength and began shouting that he was well. After the boy got dressed, he ran to tell his parents, but they had fallen down in the kitchen from the glory that filled the house. The boy's sister, who had recently returned from a mental asylum, was totally healed that same day. Revival fire was released that impacted the whole town.[266]

A New Realm of Faith and a New Spiritual Dimension

Before Wigglesworth's Pentecostal Spirit baptism in 1907, he had struggled to preach; he had stuttered, ended his sermons early, and regularly deferred to Polly as the primary speaker in the pulpit. He had not traveled internationally to minister. He had just been a successful plumber who also evangelized (many times not even going to bed at night until he had led at least one person to the Lord).

Although he had experienced healing, and regularly saw people healed instantly when he prayed for them, Wigglesworth's Spirit baptism shifted him into a new realm of faith and a new spiritual dimension.[267] Biographer Stanley Frodsham claimed that before Wigglesworth's Spirit baptism, "the Holy Spirit figured constantly in his experience and teaching, but from that time forward a new epoch began in his life. He relied implicitly upon the Holy Spirit for every phase of his ministry. He certainly sought to live in the Spirit and to be led by the Spirit."[268] Wigglesworth recalled, "When I was baptized in the Holy Ghost there was the unfolding of a new era of my life, and I passed into that and rejoiced in the fact of it, and others with me. But the moment I reached that God had been ready with another ministry for me."[269]

Double-Portion Anointing

Several years after Wigglesworth's Spirit baptism, Polly died right after preaching a sermon. Smith rushed home and commanded her to come back to life. She was restored for a short while until the Lord told Smith that it was time to let her go. He released her to be with the Lord on January 1, 1913, and asked for a double portion of her spirit.[270] Following the impartation of her anointing, Wigglesworth began to travel internationally, where he was used as a catalyst to start revival fires in California, Canada, Switzerland, Norway, Sweden, Denmark, France, Sri Lanka, Australia, New Zealand, and elsewhere.

International Travel with Unique Signs and Wonders

If you do not venture, you remain ordinary as long as you live.
If you dare the impossible,
then God will abundantly do far above all you ask or think.[271]
—*Smith Wigglesworth*

In 1914, Wigglesworth felt led to go to Carrie Judd Montgomery's camp meeting in Cazadero, California. Carrie reported, "God used him as a channel of blessing to many who sought and received healing, and the baptism of the Holy Spirit."[272] Another trip that produced profound results occurred in 1922, when Wigglesworth traveled to New Zealand and was used as a catalyst for a great revival that birthed many Pentecostal churches.[273] Thousands were healed and baptized in the Holy Spirit during his few months of ministering there. Many believe that he was used to usher in one of the greatest revivals on the North Island in over a century.[274]

When Wigglesworth shared a testimony about raising someone from the dead, a most unique sign and wonder occurred, as told by an eyewitness:

One evening in the Town Hall, the Evangelist [Wigglesworth] was telling the story of a young woman being raised from the dead. The narrative was like a chapter out of the Bible. He said he was asked to pray for the dying consumptive. He told the parents to go off to bed, and he would look after the patient and pray. During the night the young woman died.

At this point, he said that Satan had appeared at the foot of the bed, laughed at him, and said "I've got her safely held." He then made a statement that produced a merekara. [Maori for a divine manifestation.] His words were: "I seemed to be in hell, and everything in the room turned to brass."

That Wellington audience witnessed the most weird thing that ever happened in a public hall. Everything in the Town Hall appeared to turn to brass. What the Evangelist experienced in that death chamber was precipitated into the meeting by the power of the Spirit. That vast crowd just felt it had been ushered into the portals of hell itself. It was an ineffacible [sic] and awful sensation. The lights, chairs, walls, the people, the grand organ all looked like solid brass. Then tension only broken when he told how his own faith had fled away in that leering, faith-sapping presence of Satan himself; but he cried to God for help and pleaded the blood; and as he cried, the faith of God filled his soul. He prayed through, and knew that another victory had been won in His Saviour's Name.

Two beams of light settled on the dead face. He looked up and traced their source and saw looking through a window the smiling face of His Lord. The colour came back into the young woman's face and she sat up in bed; raised by the mighty power of God. It was then that the brassy condition dissipated, and the hall seemed to be filled with a warm glow of sunshine and love. The sigh of relief from the audience was distinctly audible.

That night, fully five hundred souls made the great decision to accept the Saviour, and many known to us personally are standing today.[275]

When Wigglesworth went to Norway, revival broke out in that nation as well. One time, while he was in the car on his way to preach, the church was already full and the streets around it were packed with cars. Wigglesworth began to pray for people in their cars before heading into the church. After returning home that night, he got a call that the town hall was full and that there were also thousands of people waiting for him outside. As he made his way there, God told him if he would ask for every soul, they would be saved. Cries for mercy swept the place, and Wigglesworth believed that God gave him every soul that day.[276]

In Switzerland, Wigglesworth was jailed twice. One time, an officer said that he had found no fault in him and that he had been a blessing to them in Switzerland. Another time, an officer went to him in the middle of the night and said he could go. Smith replied, "No, I'll only go on one condition, that every officer in this place gets down on his knees and I'll pray for you."[277] They did, and he prayed for them. Wigglesworth also told about another time of ministry among the Swiss:

> When I was in a little room at Bern waiting for my passport, I found a lot of people, but I couldn't speak to them, so I got hold of three men and pulled them unto me. They stared, but I got them on their knees. Then we prayed, and the revival began. I couldn't talk to them, but I could show them the way to talk to Someone else.[278]

In an account of Wigglesworth's ministry in Switzerland in 1920, someone reported that "a child was brought to one meeting very ill. The doctors said the sickness had to do with the head. Bro. W. [Wigglesworth] was shown by the Spirit it was the stomach, and as he laid hands on the stomach and prayed, a worm, sixteen inches long, came out of the child's mouth."[279] That must have been an exciting meeting! Apostolic leader John G. Lake had a similar gift of discernment; many times, he could determine what part of someone's body was infirm. In Wigglesworth's ministry, many were also slain in the Spirit and taken up into trances, similar to what occurred in Maria Woodworth-Etter's ministry.[280]

In Sweden, Wigglesworth was forbidden to lay hands on people, so he decided to have the twenty thousand people in the crowd lay hands on each other. Many people were healed in the process, and he was able to keep the law at the same time.[281] Wigglesworth recalled that during his time in Sweden, "over 7,000 people [were] saved by the power of God."[282]

In 1926, he went to India and saw powerful healings and miracles take place. One person reported that "God worked mighty miracles; blind eyes were opened, deaf ears unstopped, stammering tongues spoke, men on crutches put them over their shoulder and went away, stiff joints were made supple, headaches and fevers vanished, asthma was treated as an evil power and cast out in the name of Jesus."[283] After Wigglesworth ministered in a place, a church would spring up there as a result of his impartation.[284]

Further Healings

Wigglesworth released healing wherever he went and encouraged people to respond in faith to receive this healing. Many times, when he commanded the lame to run, they were healed during the very act of moving their legs to run in faith.[285] In Fiji, Wigglesworth prayed for a man who had been bitten by a snake, and the man was instantly healed.[286] When Wigglesworth ministered in the streets of San Francisco, people came and laid out those who were sick on mattresses in front of him. When he walked by them and his shadow hit them, they were healed.[287] Another time, when he cursed cancer in a woman, she was totally healed. He advised people,

> When you deal with a cancer case, recognize that it is a living evil spirit that is destroying the body. I had to pray for a woman in Los Angeles one time who was suffering with cancer, and as soon as it was cursed it stopped bleeding. It was dead. The next thing that happened was that the natural body pressed it out, because the natural body had no room for dead matter.[288]

Wigglesworth also prayed for relational healing. A woman came to him requesting prayer for her son, who was having difficulties in his marriage. Wigglesworth prayed over a handkerchief and told the woman to put it under her son's pillow without telling him. When the son went to bed that night, heavy conviction fell upon him. He repented and got right with his wife that same night.[289]

Like Carrie Judd Montgomery and others, Wigglesworth saw the value in and the power of the testimony. His Bowland Street Mission community regularly held banquets to feed the poor and hungry. Wigglesworth's way of providing "entertainment" was to relate healing testimonies. Prayer for healing followed, and many people were radically healed and touched by the power of God.[290]

Cultivating the Presence

Smith Wigglesworth was sensitive to the leading of the Holy Spirit and knew when to speak up and when to wait patiently upon the Lord. Once, in London, he stood up in the front of a bus and preached to all the passengers. He then laid hands on the people; many of them wept and were radically touched by God. Another time, while sitting in a passenger compartment on a train, Smith took out his Bible and silently read and prayed. Even though he didn't say one word, the five strangers who were sitting in the compartment with him were gripped with a terrible fear. One of the men asked him what was going on, and Smith was able to explain the way of salvation. Then all five people sitting next to him knelt down on the floor and accepted Jesus.[291]

Wigglesworth would regularly sit on a bench in a park near his home to commune with God. Many times, someone would come and sit beside him. Without saying anything, he would impart life to that person. If he saw that they did not know Jesus, he would silently pray that the Holy Spirit would convict them and draw them to God. People could often sense God's presence in his life, and they would open up their hearts to him. Those who sat near him would go away blessed. Wigglesworth used to say, "If you don't minister life, you will minister death and leave folks worse off than when you found them."[292] And filling himself up with God was one of the ways Wigglesworth ministered life to people.

One time, after Wigglesworth rode in an elevator with several strangers, a friend who met him at the top assumed that he had witnessed to the others on his way up. But when asked if he had given a word to them, Wigglesworth replied, "No, I wasn't to pray for them. I wasn't to do anything at all. I was one with them in a way. But I left something behind for them—that was the presence of God. It was more real than a tract."[293] One of Wigglesworth's personal friends, William Hacking, recalled that "Brother Wigglesworth, like Charles Finney, believed that the presence of a man filled with God could bring conviction to sinners without even a word being spoken. As he sat opposite a man in a railway carriage, the man suddenly jumped up, exclaimed, 'You convict me of sin!', and went out into another carriage."[294] By simply cultivating God's presence in his life, Wigglesworth impacted those around him.

Final Days

In 1930, Wigglesworth developed kidney stones but refused medical help. He was in extreme pain but continued to minister anyway, living with this pain for six years. During a convention in 1932, he asked the Lord for fifteen more years of life. The Lord granted him this request, even to the week. On March 12, 1947, when he was eighty-seven years old, Wigglesworth was at the funeral of a friend (Wilfred Richardson) and saw the father of a girl he had prayed for a few weeks before. He asked him how she was doing, fully expecting to hear that she had been healed. However, the father told him that there had been no noticeable evidence of healing in her body. Upon hearing that, Wigglesworth let out a sigh and went to be with the Lord.[295]

Legacy

God's glory and presence manifested in unusual and powerful ways in Smith Wigglesworth's life. Never tied down to one particular denomination, he ministered under the anointing and call of God Himself.[296] As mentioned previously, without his having to say anything, the presence of God in his life brought conviction to those around him. And during the course of his life, he raised fourteen people from the dead.[297] Wigglesworth was a man of faith who moved in tremendous signs and wonders.[298] Below is an account, entitled "Power in Prayer," of one such manifestation:

> There were eleven leading Christians in prayer with our Brother [Wigglesworth] at a special afternoon meeting. Each had taken part. The Evangelist then began to pray for the Dominion, and as he continued, each, according to their measure of spirituality, got out. The power of God filled the room and they could not remain in an atmosphere supercharged by the power of God.
>
> The author on hearing of this from one who was present registered a vow that if the opportunity came, he at any rate would remain whoever else went out. During the stay in the Sounds a special meeting was called to pray for the other towns in New Zealand yet to be visited. A like position to the other meeting now arose. Here was the opportunity, the challenge, the contest was on. A number prayed. Then the old saint began to lift up his voice, and strange as it may seem, the exodus began. A Divine influence

began to fill the place. The room became holy. The power of God began to feel like a heavy weight. With set chin, and a definite decision not to budge, the only other one now left in the room hung on and hung on, until the pressure became too great, and he could stay no longer. With the flood gate of his soul pouring out a stream of tears, and with uncontrollable sobbing he had to get out or die; and a man who knew God as few do was left alone immersed in an atmosphere that few men would breathe in.[299]

Prophetic Inheritance

It would be so easy to look at the exploits of Smith Wigglesworth and be intimidated by his position in God. After all, who could possibly become like him in our day? But I remind you that he had humble beginnings. He began as a plumber, and an illiterate one at that. It is said that he learned to read only so that he could read the Bible. He was not educated or trained in any way to become a world changer. Yet he was yielded to God and available for whatever pleased Him. Such lives of continual surrender become the lives we admire the most.

Apostle of Faith

Wigglesworth is often called the "apostle of faith." He protected his faith from the world in a way that is rare even today. He went so far as to not allow a newspaper in his home. And while I don't propose that, I would suggest looking at his example for how to stay strong in faith. He protected his heart from anything that could draw his attention, his affection, and his hope away from his Lord and Savior, Jesus Christ.

Like Carrie Judd Montgomery, Wigglesworth exercised his faith according to the Word of God. He did not wait to feel the anointing or to sense God's presence but rather acted on God's truth and stood on his authority in Christ. He wanted people to recognize the power that was already inside them and to step out in faith. Here are some of his exhortations:

We are a back number if we have to pray for power, if we have to wait until we feel a sense of His presence. "Ye shall have power after that the Holy Ghost is come upon you." Within you there is a greater power than there is in the world. Oh, to be awakened out of our unbelief into a place of daring for God!... "In season and out of season." God has authority over the powers of the devil—over all the power of the enemy. Oh, that we may live in the place where the glory dwelleth![300]

It is an insult to ask God for power after you have received the baptism of the Holy Ghost. You have power! You have to act![301]

Faith moves first; then God moves in answer to faith.[302]

Two things will cause you to leap out of yourselves into the great promises of God. One is purity, the other is faith. God has no room for the man who looks back, thinks back, or acts back.[303]

If the Spirit does not move me, I move the Spirit. As I start out in the natural, in faith, the Spirit of God always meets and anoints me, so that although I start in the natural I continue in the Spirit.[304]

Wigglesworth knew who he was in Christ, and who Christ was in him. He also knew the heart of God for people and even what God wanted to do in a given setting. Jesus modeled such a lifestyle perfectly for all of us. It is because of Christ's example that Wigglesworth was able to say he could "move the Spirit" of God. At first glance, his statement may sound like he thought he could get the Holy Spirit to do whatever he wanted. Of course, that's impossible. Wigglesworth just knew that fire always falls on sacrifice—and he was willing to be the offering that attracted the fire of heaven into a given setting. His lifestyle in the miraculous demonstrates how accurate his understanding of this reality was. His heart to see Jesus glorified and his compassion for people were the reasons for his boldness.

People who experience a defining moment gain such an overwhelming confidence in the God who is with them that it becomes unreasonable to them to ever question that reality. Boldness is a natural expression from a person who lives with an awareness that the Spirit of God is upon him or her.

There's Always More

So many people want to set limits on what's possible in our day. One of my favorite statements from my generation used to be "Kingdom now but not yet." I still like the phrase, but I find myself increasingly frustrated by the way it is used. When I first heard it, it freed me to long for things I had never thought possible. Now, almost every time I hear people use it, it's to set limits on what's available to us in Christ now.

Pastors often set such limits because they feel the pressure of shepherding people who are facing disappointment and pain. Theologians often set limits because so many of them are stuck in the classroom of theory; they haven't moved into experience. But people such as Smith Wigglesworth upset all our complacency and unbelief because they are unsatisfied with answers that suggest that affliction and torment are things we should live with, and they are unconvinced by answers that are merely academic. People like Wigglesworth have the heart of God for the impossible, *and* they immerse themselves in the lives of people who are facing intimidating situations. We need them. We need the discomfort. We need to come face-to-face with our own unbelief and be launched into our own defining moment. Only then will such boldness for healings and miracles make sense. And it does. It makes perfect sense.

Smith Wigglesworth left the following prophecy about a move of God to come after his death. It is about the "more" of God:

> For many years, the Lord has been moving me on and keeping me from spiritual stagnation. When I was in the Wesleyan Methodist Church, I was sure I was saved, and I was sure I was all right. The Lord said to me, "Come out," and I came out. When I was with the people known as the Brethren, I was sure I was all right then. But the Lord said, "Come out." Then I went into the Salvation Army. At that time, it was full of life, and there were revivals everywhere. But the Salvation Army went into natural things, and the great revivals that they had in those early days ceased. The Lord said to me, "Come out," and I came out. I have had to come out three times since.
>
> I believe that this Pentecostal revival that we are now in is the best thing that the Lord has on the earth today; and yet I believe that God will bring something out of this revival that is going to

be still better. God has no use for anyone who is not hungering and thirsting for even more of Himself and His righteousness.[305]

Wow, that's rather bold: "God has no use for any man who is not hungering and thirsting for yet more of Himself...." Wigglesworth demonstrated this idea well when he discussed who he would like to work with in ministry, saying, "I would rather have a man on my platform not filled with the Holy Ghost but hungry for God, than a man who has received the Holy Ghost but has become satisfied with his experience."[306] Impressive, yet intimidating, Wigglesworth seems to set a new high-water mark for faith, for spiritual hunger, and for the ability to spot similar passion in the lives of others. He said the following:

Do not rest satisfied with any lesser experience than the Baptism that the disciples received on the Day of Pentecost, then move on to a life of continuous receiving of more and more of the blessed Spirit of God.[307]

God wants to flow through you with measureless power of divine utterance and grace till your whole body is a flame of fire. God intends each soul in Pentecost to be a live wire. Not a monument, but a movement. So many people have been baptized with the Holy Ghost; there was a movement but they have become monuments and you cannot move them. God wake us up out of sleep lest we should become indifferent to the glorious truth and the breath of the Almighty power of God.

We must be the light and salt of the earth, with the whole armor of God upon us. It would be a serious thing if the enemies were about and we had to go back and get our sandals. It would be a serious thing if we had on no breastplate. How can we be furnished with the armor? Take it by faith. Jump in, stop in, and never come out, for this is a baptism to be lost in, where you only know one thing and that is the desire of God at all times. The baptism in the Spirit should be an ever-increasing endowment of power, an ever-increasing enlargement of grace.[308]

We owe the next generation a life of breakthrough, of discovering and displaying how real and tangible the "more" of God is.

The Presence

My favorite trait found in all of my heroes' lives is the ability to carry the presence of the Holy Spirit. Jesus did it perfectly, never grieving or quenching Him. The Dove remained upon Him always, never retreating or withdrawing, but revealing what the Father was saying and doing. For me, nothing is more attractive, costly, and powerful than hosting the presence of God. And few human beings have done it better than Smith Wigglesworth. That part of his life provokes me unlike any other.

Postscript

It would be hard to find many people who could equal Wigglesworth's life of faith and miracles. Yet none of the extraordinary things in his life happened before his defining moment. His encounter with God in his baptism of fire changed everything. His wife noticed. He noticed. And the devil noticed. And Smith did not sit on his experiences from the past but sought to continually grow in this wonderful life of the Holy Spirit that had been offered to him.

> Baptizing in water is an emblem of death and the moment a person is immersed in the water, he is lifted out. But not so with the baptism with the Holy Spirit. To be baptized in the Holy Ghost is every day to be deeper in, never lifted out, never coming out; in captivity, ready for gifts.[309]

One overwhelming encounter with God is meant to lead to countless others, each taking us from glory to glory—in this lifetime. Wigglesworth's example should be a picture of the normal life of a believer. I believe it will become the norm before the return of the Lord. Why not us, why not now?

8

Dominion: John G. Lake

"By the end of that year, I believe I was the hungriest man for God that ever lived.... It was the yearning passion of my soul, asking for God in a greater measure than I knew.... My soul was demanding a greater entrance into God, His love, presence, and power."[310]
—*John G. Lake*

In some ways, John G. Lake has had more of an impact on my life than any other historical figure. His understanding of the kingdom of God and the life of dominion over the powers of darkness is unparalleled. I have always felt that he was a hundred years ahead of his time.

Apostolic Call

John G. Lake (1870–1935) was a powerful apostolic leader greatly used by God, especially in the area of healing. He was introduced to divine healing when several of his family members were healed under John Alexander Dowie's ministry. After Lake prayed for his wife, who was near death, and she was completely healed, the word spread, and his own healing ministry took off. Although he had seen many people healed and had even raised the dead, his 1907 Spirit baptism, accompanied by an "electric" encounter, catapulted him to an even greater measure of power and anointing. Following this, he was called to Africa, where he had tremendous success in a short amount of time. He also began to build significant foundations and structures for his apostolic call, as well as to walk in greater, unique signs and wonders. He later returned to North America and founded Healing Rooms, which is still a viable ministry to this day. He continually emphasized total possession by the Holy Spirit and dominion over sickness.[311]

Conversion

John Graham Lake was born in Ontario, Canada, on March 18, 1870. He was the first of sixteen children, eight of whom died from illness while he was growing up. When he was sixteen years old, he moved with his family to Michigan, where he was first introduced to the gospel at a Salvation Army meeting. Shortly after, he knelt down by a tree and surrendered his life to the Lord.

In 1890, when he was about twenty years old, he had a sanctification experience that deepened his faith.[312] The following year, he moved to Chicago and studied to become a Methodist minister. However, rather than take a pastorate offered to him, he decided to start a newspaper called *The Harvey Citizen*.[313] In 1893, he married Jennie Stevens, with whom he would later have seven children. Because his wife became ill, they moved back to her hometown in Michigan, where he went into the real estate business.[314]

Healing Launches Ministry

Divine healing played a crucial role in activating Lake's ministry. When he was young, he suffered from rheumatism. Someone from John Alexander

Dowie's ministry prayed for him, and he was healed.[315] Later, when Lake was an adult, his family went to Dowie's healing home in Chicago to seek healing for his brother who was near death. His brother received prayer, got up from his cot, and was able to walk several miles to help in his father's business. Following this miracle, hope arose within the Lakes, and Lake was inspired to bring his thirty-four-year-old sister to Dowie's ministry for prayer, as well. After having already endured five surgeries to try to remove the lumps of cancer from her breast, she also was near death. While lying on her cot, she listened to the teaching about healing and was encouraged. When she received prayer, the swelling in her breast went down, and her pain disappeared. A few days later, the cancer turned black and fell out. The "mutilated breast" also began to be made whole again.[316]

Shortly after Lake's soul had been awakened to "Christ the Healer" through these miracles, Lake was summoned to visit his oldest sister, who was also on the verge of death. By the time he got there, it had been twenty-three minutes since his sister had stopped breathing and ceased to have a pulse. It broke his heart to see his parents in such distress after what would be the loss of their ninth child. And when Lake noticed his sister's baby in the crib, this stirred even deeper compassion within him. He telegraphed Dowie to partner in prayer with him. Within the hour, as they prayed for her, she arose from the dead. Five days later, she joined the family for Christmas dinner.[317]

Then, in 1898, after five years of sickness, Lake's wife was on her deathbed. Lake contended with the Lord and got so mad that he threw his Bible. When it landed on the table, it opened to Acts 10:38, which states how God anointed Jesus with the Holy Spirit and power, and how He went about doing good works and healing all who were oppressed by the devil. Lake cross-referenced this verse and found Luke 13:16, in which Jesus says that Satan had bound an afflicted woman. Reading these truths led Lake to discover that the battle against sickness was a battle against the devil. He concluded that because sickness was tied to the devil, that meant believers had authority and dominion over it.[318] He also came to see that God was not the author of illness, nor was it His will for people to be sick.

After these revelations, Lake declared that at 9:30 the next morning, April 28, 1898, his wife would be healed. He again invited Dowie to partner in prayer with him. The next day, at 9:30 a.m., he knelt down by his wife's bed and called out for God to do a miracle. The power of God fell upon her, "thrilling her from head to foot," and she was completely healed.[319] Many people who heard of Jennie Lake's healing were drawn to the Lakes' home to seek prayer for their own healing. The healing of his wife was a catalyst that launched Lake into the healing ministry. He remembered,

> A great new light had dawned in our soul. Our church had diligently taught us that the days of miracles were past. Believing thus, eight members of the family had been permitted to die. But now, with the light of the truth flashing in our hearts, we saw that such teaching was a lie, no doubt invented by the devil, and diligently heralded as truth by the church, thus robbing mankind of his rightful inheritance through the blood of Jesus. Others came to our home. They said, "Since God has healed you, surely He will heal us. Pray for us." We were forced into it. God answered, and many were healed.[320]

I love the fact that people like Lake and Carrie Judd Montgomery were "forced" into a healing ministry because of their own experience. We, too, can be launched into greater anointing as we have the privilege to freely give away what we have freely received.

Spirit Baptism

Hungering for More

In 1901, Lake and his family moved from Michigan to Zion, Illinois, to sit under Dowie's ministry. Lake worked for Dowie during the day as a building manager and also ministered in the evenings. In 1904, he moved to Chicago to remove himself from the financial problems associated with Dowie's ministry. After Dowie's death in 1907, the property investments Lake had made in the city of Zion depreciated, leaving him with nearly nothing. He eventually went back into the real estate business and became very successful.[321]

Lake attended a church service where the minister presented the need for the baptism of the Spirit. Lake recalled what he experienced when he knelt in prayer and reconsecrated himself to God:

An anointing of the Spirit came upon me. Waves of Holy Glory passed through my being, and I was lifted into a new realm of God's presence and power. After this, answers to prayer were frequent and miracles of healing occurred from time to time. I felt myself on the borderland of a great spiritual realm, but was unable to enter in fully, so my nature was not satisfied with the attainment. Finally I was led to set aside certain hours of the day that I dedicated to God, as times of meditation and prayer.[322]

At this time, he worked as a manager for life insurance agents during the day but preached nearly every night. Following the services, he regularly met with a circle of friends who were also hungry for more of God and "determined to pray through into God" to receive the baptism of the Holy Ghost as they believed the disciples had received it. Lake prayed, "God, if you will baptize me in the Holy Spirit, and give me the power of God, nothing shall be permitted to stand between me and a hundred-fold obedience."[323]

Lake's hunger for more of God continued to grow as he saw healing released in and through his life in greater measures. One day, when on a walk with F. F. Bosworth and Tom Hezmalhalch, Bosworth asked him when he was going to surrender all to Jesus. Lake was ready right then, so the three of them knelt right down on the sidewalk, and Lake surrendered all to the Lord.[324] He was still hungry for more of God.

By the end of that year, I believe I was the hungriest man for God that ever lived. There was such a hunger for God that as I left my offices in Chicago and walked down the street, my soul would break out, and I would cry, "Oh God!" I have had people stop and look at me in wonder. It was the yearning passion of my soul, asking for God in a greater measure than I knew. But my friends would say, "Mr. Lake, you have a beautiful baptism in the Holy Ghost." Yes, it was nice as far as it went, but it was not answering the cry of my heart…. My soul was demanding a greater entrance into God, His love, presence, and power.[325]

Lake prayed and fasted consistently over a nine-month period for the baptism of the Holy Spirit. After virtually giving up, he was invited by a friend to an all-night prayer meeting to receive the baptism of the Spirit. The group had been praying for a whole year for this but none there had received it, either. Lake recalled, "As we knelt to pray, my soul was in such anguish, I felt I must hear from heaven or die. Within a short time after kneeling to pray, I felt myself being overshadowed by the Holy Spirit. Then commenced the most vivid spiritual experience of my life."[326] He remembered,

> I was so hungry to pray, so I went with all the intentions of praying for the rest, but I had not been praying five minutes until the light of God began to shine around me. I found myself in a center of an arc of light ten feet in diameter—the whitest light in all the universe. O how it spoke of purity. The remembrance of that whiteness, that wonderful whiteness, has been the ideal that has stood before my soul, of the purity of the nature of God ever since.[327]

A voice came from the light and convicted him of something he had done in his childhood. He then began to be purified. He prayed on his knees for four hours straight, although he didn't notice the passage of time.

"Electric" Spirit-Baptism Encounter

Shortly after this experience, in October 1907, Hezmalhalch asked Lake to accompany him to pray for a woman in a wheelchair. Although Lake went with him to the woman's home, his mind was preoccupied with a deep yearning for God. He recalled,

> My soul was drawing out in a great silent heart cry to God. *O Jesus, I so long for the baptism of the Holy Ghost, but I feel so unworthy, so far from thee. O Christ, if it be possible to baptize such as me, please baptize me. I am so hungry, so tired of trying, so weary of doing things myself. I am sick of sin, sick of self, sick of trying, sick of working, etc. etc.* Presently a great quiet came upon me deepening rapidly into a peace as I had never before known or experienced—a quiet

of spirit, soul, and body. My being was soothed in a perfect calm, so deep, so quiet. My mind was perfectly still. I said, "O, Jesus, what is this—the calm of God? Is this the baptism of the Holy Ghost?" Presently, it seemed as if I had passed under a warm tropical rain that was falling not upon me, but through me. The realization of peace was such as I had never known. The rain continued to fall upon me.... The peace—I cannot describe—that passeth all understanding. This condition of peace was so great I feared to breathe. It was the silence of heaven. The saving rain continued to fall upon me. It soothed my brain. It soothed my body. It soothed my spirit. Would it ever stop? I feared it might. I said, "O, God, I did not know there was such a place of rest as this."

Then I became conscious of a change coming over me. Instead of the rain, currents of power were running through me from my head to my feet, seemingly into the floor. These shocks of power came intermittently, possibly ten seconds apart. They increased in voltage until, after a few minutes, my frame shook and vibrated under these mighty shocks of power. Then as I shook and trembled, the shocks of power followed each other with more apparent rapidity and intensity. My forehead became sealed. My brain in the front portion of my head became inactive, and I realized the spirit speaking of His seal in their foreheads. I could have fallen on the floor except for the depth of the chair in which I sat.

Again a change. The shocks of power lessened in intensity and now have taken hold of my lower jaw. It moved up and down and sidewise in a manner new to me. My tongue and throat began to move in a manner I could not control. Presently, I realized I was speaking in another tongue, a language I had never learned. O, the sense of power. The mighty moving of the Spirit in me. The consciousness it was God who had come.[328]

Lake's friend had not noticed that Lake was having this experience when he gestured for him to join in praying for the woman in the wheelchair. Lake got up "trembling so violently" and put his fingertips on her head. He "could feel the currents of power shoot" through him into her. Lake said that when his friend went to pray for her, at the instant their hands touched, a flash of dynamic power went through my person and through the sick woman, and as my friend held her hand the shock and power went through her hand into him. The rush of power into his person was so great that it caused him to fall on the floor. He looked up at me with joy and surprise and springing to his feet said, "Praise the Lord, John, Jesus has baptized you in the Holy Ghost!"[329]

After this, Lake began to pray in tongues for the woman.[330]

After Spirit Baptism

In the six months immediately following this encounter, Lake experienced "the most terrible fightings, sometimes victory, sometimes defeat, sometimes awful chords and soul storms, with glimpses of God's sunshine."[331] His enthusiasm for business quickly faded away; instead, he began to lead everyone who came to him for business to Jesus. He spoke to his boss about his change in passion and was given three months off to explore the idea of going into ministry full-time. If he then returned to his job, he was promised fifty thousand dollars a year, which was the equivalent of nearly one million dollars today. During those three months, Lake preached every day to large congregations and saw many people saved, healed, and baptized in the Holy Spirit. He quit his job permanently. He even sold his estate and gave his money away for the kingdom of God, relying totally on the Lord for all support.[332]

Additionally, Lake claimed that "a love for mankind such as [he] had never comprehended took possession of [his] life." He also experienced a "renewed, energized power for healing the sick," power as never before "to preach the Word of God in demonstration of the Spirit," and a "strong, forceful exercise of dominion over devils, to cast them out." He realized that his "own ministry multiplied a hundredfold in the very lives of others to whom God committed this same ministry."[333] Lake recognized that the Spirit flowed through him "with a new force" and that "healings were of a more powerful order."[334] He ministered to the sick similar to the way Smith Wigglesworth moved in healing, saying,

My nature became so sensitized that I could lay my hands on any man or woman and tell what organ was diseased, and to what extent, and all about it. I tested it. I went to hospitals where physicians could not diagnose a case, touched a patient and I knew the organ that was diseased, its extent and condition and location.[335]

While he had previously raised people from the dead and seen many healings, Lake believed that speaking in tongues had been to him the making of his ministry.[336] (It is amazing that even among Pentecostals today, speaking in tongues is reduced to a "nice, personal gift." But for Lake, it represented his life in God.)

When Lake was in Illinois for ministry, one of the workers at his hotel needed help cutting down a tree. He volunteered to lend a helping hand. During the very act of cutting down the tree, he clearly heard the Lord speak to him and tell him to go to Indianapolis to set up a winter campaign; the Lord also told him that he would go to Africa in the spring. Lake obeyed and went to Indianapolis, where he ministered alongside Hezmalhalch, leading people into the baptism in the Holy Spirit. During this season, both men had been "praying for greater power for the healing of the sick and casting out of demons." As a result, an intense desire to pray fell upon Lake; the desire was so strong that he couldn't even eat. During a six-day fast, he heard from God that he would be able to cast out demons. That same week, he acted on what the Lord had said and cast out a demon from a man who was insane. Three days later, the man was released from the asylum.[337]

Africa

On April 1, 1908, during a visit with someone he called Brother Osborne, Lake was caught up in a vision in which he was transported to South Africa and preached.[338] Several times, he "visited" Africa in visions before he ever went there.[339] Like D. L. Moody, Carrie Judd Montgomery, and others, Lake adopted George Müller's Philippians 4:19 philosophy of asking God alone to meet his needs.[340] Another similarity with these other revivalists is that Lake traveled internationally not long after his encounter.

On April 19, 1908, after a series of financial miracles, the Lakes and the Hezmalhalchs headed to South Africa.[341]

Lake and his family set sail with only one dollar and fifty cents to their name. Throughout the trip, Lake was aware that when they arrived, they would have to go through immigration and pay the required one hundred twenty-five dollars to get off the ship. When the time came, Lake stood by faith in the immigration line and trusted that the Lord would make a way. All of a sudden, someone tapped him on the shoulder, pulled him aside, and gave him two hundred dollars.[342] Lake and his family were able to exit the ship, go to Cape Town, and board the train to Johannesburg. Because they had no place to stay upon their arrival, many times during that train ride, Lake, his wife, and their seven children bowed their heads and reminded God of their need for a home.

When they arrived, a little woman came up to them and asked if they were the missionary family from America. Mrs. C. L. Goodenough told them that the Lord had sent her to meet them and to give them a home. Later the same day, they moved into a fully furnished cottage.[343] When we step out in faith toward the impossible where God and the body of Christ are our only options for help, something beautiful is bound to happen, as it did for Lake and his family.

A few days after their arrival, a pastor who was leaving for several weeks asked Lake to lead meetings for him. In his first service in South Africa, Lake prayed for the Holy Spirit to be released to over five hundred Zulus. Revival immediately broke out. The church where he had been asked to fill in was the same church he had been transported to in his vision before he left for Africa. He remembered,

> One night as I prayed I was overshadowed by the Spirit of the Lord. The Lord showed me various places in which I would labor for five years, and by the illumination that would appear in the heavens, I knew the extent of the work in each place. That night as I knelt on the floor, I was present in a church in Johannesburg, South Africa. I walked in at the front door of the church and walked to the front, and into the vestry.... In less than one year I was in that church, and pastor of that church. God did the whole thing, and I had

nothing to do with it. God showed me by illumination all over the land the marvellous extent and character of the work that He was going to do.[344]

Lake recognized that the power of God moved through him like electricity in this new land.

In 1908, I preached at Pretoria, South Africa, when one night God came over my life in such power, in such streams of liquid glory and power, that it flowed consciously off my hands like streams of electricity. I would point my finger at a man, and that stream would strike him. When a man interrupted the meeting, I would point my finger at him and say: "Sit down!" He fell as if struck, and lay for three hours. When he became normal they asked him what happened, and he said, "Something struck me that went straight through me. I thought I was shot."[345]

The similarities in ministry between Lake and Maria Woodworth-Etter are quite noticeable. Lake regularly referred to Woodworth-Etter in his sermons and spoke about her lightning-like faith, her union with God, and God's power through her to release instant healing.[346] Both of them walked in great authority and left people slain in the Spirit in their path. Continuing to describe the meeting in Pretoria, Lake recalled,

At two o'clock in the morning I ministered to sixty-five sick who were present, and the streams of God that were pouring through my hands were so powerful the people would fall as though they were hit. I was troubled because they fell with such violence. And the Spirit said: "You do not need to put your hands on them. Keep your hands a distance away." And when I held my hands a foot from their heads they would crumble and fall in a heap on the floor. They were healed almost every one.

That was the outer manifestation. That was what the people saw. But beloved, something transpired in my heart that made my soul like the soul of Jesus Christ. Oh, there was such tenderness, a newborn tenderness of God, that was so wonderful that my heart reached out and cried and wept over men in sin. I could gather them in my arms and love them, and Jesus Christ flowed out of me and delivered them. Drunkards were saved and healed as they stood transfixed looking at me.[347]

As Lake continued to minister in Africa, he saw great success. However, that only made him hungrier for God.

I continued in the ministry of healing until I saw hundreds of thousands healed. At last I became tired. I went on healing people day after day, as though I were a machine. And all the time my heart kept asking: "Oh, God, let me know Yourself [sic] better. I want You, my heart wants YOU, God." Seeing men saved and healed and baptized in the Holy Ghost did not satisfy my growing soul. It was crying out for a greater consciousness of God, the withinness [sic] of me was yearning for Christ's own life and love. After a while my soul reached the place where I said: "If I cannot get God into my soul to satisfy the soul of me, all the rest of this is empty." I had lost interest in it, but if I put my hands on the sick they continued to be healed by the power of God.[348]

Sometimes there is a holy dissatisfaction with anything less than capturing the heart of God. Regardless of the number of signs, miracles, and wonders he had seen, Lake was still hungry for more of God and desperate for Him.

In 1908, Lake's wife, Jennie, died while he was away on a trip to the Kalahari Desert. Although at least one account said she died as a result of a stroke,[349] her tragic, premature death may have had a different cause:

Most accounts of Jennie Lake's death attribute it to malnutrition and physical exhaustion. When John was away, scores of sick people would wait on his lawn until he returned. So Jennie would feed them while they waited with what little food she could spare. And she tried to make their stay as comfortable as possible until Lake returned. But in doing so, she physically neglected herself.[350]

Lake was devastated by Jennie's death, but he continued to minister. The following year, he went back to America to raise support and to recruit workers before returning to Africa. In America, he ministered with Hezmalhalch, and they released healing and revival wherever they went. In 1910, Hezmalhalch left their ministry partnership to branch out on his own.

Dominion over Deadly Germs

With a handful of recruits and some financial support, Lake returned to Africa in 1910 in the midst of a deadly plague. While Lake was busy ministering to the sick and dying, a visiting doctor asked him what he used to protect himself from the disease. Lake replied that it was the "'law of the Spirit of life in Christ Jesus.' I believe that just as long as I keep my soul in contact with the living God so that His Spirit is flowing into my soul and body, that no germ will ever attach itself to me, for the Spirit of God will kill it."[351] To prove this, he told a doctor to experiment on him.

> If you will go over to one of these dead people and take the foam that comes out of their lungs after death, then put it under the microscope you will see masses of living germs. You will find they are alive until a reasonable time after a man is dead. You can fill my hand with them and I will keep it under the microscope, and instead of these germs remaining alive, they will die instantly.[352]

They tried this and saw that what he had said was true. Again, Lake told the doctors that it was "'the law of the Spirit of life in Christ Jesus.' When a man's spirit and a man's body are filled with the blessed presence of God, it oozes out of the pores of your flesh and kills the germs." Lake reflected that if his "soul had been under the law of death" or if he was in "fear and darkness," then there would have been an opposite result. He believed that "the result would have been that my body would have absorbed the germs, these would have generated disease and I would have died."[353]

Transported Again

While Lake was ministering at his church in Johannesburg, a friend spoke up during a prayer time. He shared how he felt convicted that he had seen so many lame, blind, deaf, insane, and other sick people healed but had never spent time praying for his cousin who was in an insane asylum in

Wales. This confession stirred Lake to invite the congregation to call out in prayer on behalf of the insane woman. During this prayer time, Lake felt his spirit transport him through Cape Town and through Spain on his way to the asylum in Wales. He remembered,

> I went into that place, walked straight into the room where a woman was strapped to the sides of a cot, and as consciously as I stand here now I put my hands on the woman's head and in the name of the Lord Jesus Christ rebuked the insane spirit that possessed her and cast it out. Her face became calm, and she smiled up into my face. I recognized in the look of her eyes the awakened consciousness. At the time I had been kneeling on the platform at Johannesburg, and my heart and my voice had been expressing my desire to God.[354]

Not many days later, Lake's friend received a letter from Wales saying that on the previous Sunday, his cousin had been instantly healed.

During the time Lake was in Africa (1908–1912), he planted the Apostolic Faith Mission and the Zion Christian Church. He released 1,250 preachers and established 625 churches (125 white congregations and 500 black congregations). Over 100,000 people were saved through his ministry there.[355] Lake also raised up a national, Pastor Elias Letwaba, who continued in the ministry in South Africa as well as opened up Patmos Bible School. In just two years, Letwaba evangelized in remote places and saw more than 10,000 healed and over 100,000 led to Christ.[356]

Healing Rooms Launched in Spokane, Washington

In 1912, Lake returned to North America permanently. In 1913, he married Florence Switzer, who was a stenographer. Florence's diligence and stenography skills are one of the main reasons why so many of Lake's sermons are available today. He had five more children with her.

Later, a friend who worked at the railway blessed Lake with an unlimited train pass. This gift enabled him to go to Spokane, Washington, for the first time.[357] Even after all his success, Lake's hunger for God continued to increase. In Spokane, God met him yet again.

I will never forget Spokane, Washington, for during the first six months I was there God satisfied the cry of my heart, and God came in and my mind opened and my spirit understood afresh, and I was able to tell God, and talk out the heart of me like I never had been able to before. God reached a new depth in my spirit, and revealed new possibilities in God.[358]

In Spokane, Lake set up healing rooms and trained "healing technicians." Largely as a result of Lake's ministry, "Dr. Ruthlidge of Washington, D.C. declared, 'Rev. Lake through divine healing has made Spokane the healthiest city in the world, according to United States statistics.'"[359] During a period of five to six years, there were over one hundred thousand documented healings there. In 1919, Lake's team ministered to an average of two hundred people a day, with an estimated sixty thousand people having received prayer by the laying on of hands that year.[360] Lake also founded the Apostolic church in Spokane.

Queen Wilhelmina of Holland requested prayer from Lake after suffering six miscarriages. Lake brought her written request before his congregation during a Sunday service, and they all went to their knees in prayer. He then sent a response to the queen that the Lord had heard her prayer, and she would have a baby. Less than a year later, she had a daughter.[361]

In 1920, Lake moved to Oregon, where he started another church and set up healing rooms. He had a vision in which an angel opened the Bible and pointed to the day of Pentecost. The angel called him to inspire people to hunger for Pentecost.[362] For the next several years, he traveled and ministered in Oregon, California, and Texas with even greater intensity in his preaching.

Final Years and Legacy

Even in his later years, Lake traveled and continued to train and equip leaders. By 1924, he had planted forty churches throughout America. In 1931, he returned to Spokane and contended with God to be healed from impending blindness. The Lord answered his request. A few years later, on September 16, 1935, not long after he had a stroke, Lake died at age sixty-five.

Lake left a legacy of healing ministry. Gordon Lindsay, who was raised up in Lake's ministry, founded Christ for the Nations, which is now in over one hundred twenty countries. There is also a Christ for the Nations Institute, where over forty thousand students have been trained.[363] Cal Pierce has taken up the torch to continue the healing room ministry that Lake pioneered.[364] Currently, there are over three thousand healing rooms in more than seventy-three countries.[365]

Reflection

Before Lake's "electric" Spirit-baptism encounter in 1907, he had already raised his sister and his wife from the dead, seen hundreds of powerful healings, realized his authority over Satan, and been successful in business. But an important component to his ministry was still missing. He had not laid any major foundations nor set up any structures. He had not been called to preach, nor had he planted any churches.

But while he was praying over someone for healing, he encountered God in a life-changing way. After this 1907 encounter, during which he spoke in tongues, everything that he was already doing was multiplied, enhanced, or launched in a greater measure. Not long after his encounter, he was compelled to pray for dominion over the demonic. God answered his cries and gave him authority to cast out demons. Then, he took dominion over the power of material possessions to distract him from God when he quit his business and gave everything away. He also stepped out in greater faith than ever before when he went to Africa with practically nothing in his pocket. His healing ministry expanded, and more power was released. In only a few years, he raised up 1,250 preachers, planted 625 churches, and saw over 100,000 conversions. Even Mahatma Gandhi noticed Lake's leadership, saying, "Dr. Lake's teachings will eventually be accepted by the entire world."[366] Upon Lake's return to North America, he laid the foundation for the healing room movement, which continues today. Thus, after his 1907 encounter, Lake's apostolic anointing was realized, synergized, and released in great measures, evidenced by the number of churches he planted and by the healing room movement he started. And throughout all his ministry successes, Lake's hunger to go deeper with God only increased.

Prophetic Inheritance

Dominion and Divine Health

Few people have demonstrated an understanding of the ways of the Holy Spirit as did John G. Lake. He knew that as long as he stayed connected to the Holy Spirit (truly abiding in Christ), the presence and power of God would continuously flow through him to destroy the diseases in the people he was praying for. That really is the purpose of the laying on of hands—to release resurrection life. I believe this to be the reality that Paul spoke of in Romans 8:11: *"He who raised Christ from the dead will also give life to your mortal bodies through His Spirit who dwells in you."* The fact that doctors could test this resurrection life is astonishing to me. Not that realities in God shouldn't be measurable. Many should. It's just that Lake understood the unseen realm before there were any tests to verify what he claimed. He discovered and knew the ways of the Spirit and the kingdom of God.

To some people, Lake's death from the effects of a stroke proves that it's not always God's will to heal, and it gives them an explanation when a miracle doesn't occur. That view could have been theological shelter for the disciples when they weren't able to cast out a demon from a child, as recorded in Mark 9. Instead, Jesus delivered the boy and then taught His disciples why they hadn't succeeded. I'm not sure why some people are looking for the "fine print" saying that sickness is okay. The fine print doesn't exist. God's will is written in the bold letters of Jesus' life for all to see. It's best to leave Lake's early death from stroke, and the untimely deaths of countless others, as a mystery, and not as the basis for a doctrine. It's wisest to use as our example Jesus, who healed all who came to Him, and then to take people like John G. Lake as inspirational examples of those who were privileged to taste realms in God that few others in history have been able to. Lake's breakthroughs are legendary and have become spiritual, legal territory to pursue, providing us with inherited land to reinhabit.

Not everyone needs to die of disease. That lie must be exposed because it invites infirmity into people's lives as they get older. Remember the power of the testimony. Caleb was as strong at the age of eighty-five as he was at forty. (See Joshua 14:9–11.) If it happened once, it's available again.

It would be tragic to come to the end of time and see that the only genera-tion to live in divine health was Israel in the wilderness, neither born again nor filled with the Spirit, living in rebellion against God. It doesn't make sense. I know that in that case, God gave His people divine health as a special grace, but once again, the power of the testimony applies. I would challenge the reader to ask the Lord about His purposes in regard to health and longevity.

Divine health remains available. As much as anyone I've read about, Lake began to touch on insights for divine health by discovering the power of the resurrected Spirit of God, who lived in him and destroyed the power of any disease he touched. For us, confronting the lie that God designed us to die by sickness is the place to start. I would suggest that the next step is discovering the power of the Holy Spirit who lives in us, who has purposed to bring "life to our mortal bodies."

The Rich Get Richer

As we have seen, before his Spirit-baptism encounter, Lake had al-ready raised the dead twice. He had seen great breakthrough in the miracle realm. He was rich in the things of God and, in fact, had what all those around him said was the baptism in the Holy Spirit. Many people stop short of a divine encounter because they're satisfied with good theology. Not so with Lake; he knew there was more in God. And he had more of the power of the Spirit of God working in his life than probably 99 percent of everyone else around him who confessed Christ. But it was his hunger for more, a hunger to become richer in the things of the Spirit, that took him into a place of extraordinary breakthrough.

Lake's baptism in the Spirit manifested like electricity shooting through his body. Such an encounter is hard to forget! When someone has an experience like this, whether it happens only once in his lifetime or a thousand times more, he is responsible to be a steward of it—responsible to release into the earth what God has imparted to him. Such experiences are costly, as they never come to "excite" the seeker. They come to introduce us to places in God from which we can never retreat. And these experiences endear to us the One who works the wonders.

God wants to give such extraordinary encounters to all, but not ev-eryone is ready to run with what's given in the encounter. Encounters that don't empower us harden us to the very call of being a transformational influence in the earth. The miracle realm is a gift from God. When we respond to Him, we become an unstoppable force in the earth. When we don't respond, we become like the Israelites in the wilderness who lost their wonder of receiving the miracle of manna on the ground every day. They exchanged their mantle of praise for the spirit of heaviness by complaining about their circumstances and by longing to return to slavery in Egypt. The very thing that was given to cause them to cherish the God who works wonders accomplished the opposite—they despised the miracle. The glory and miracle realm of God is the most exciting realm possible for the believer. But it is costly.

In some ways, Lake's story illustrates godly stewardship. He had anointing—the presence of the Holy Spirit upon him—and he had unique gifts through which God operated the supernatural to bring many people into the kingdom. But Lake's breakthroughs in God began to pull on him for more of God. Then, his quest for "more" became more about seeking the face of God than about receiving His gifts. It became about *God Himself*. Lake's spiritual hunger was, in effect, crippling: it seriously impaired the normal function of his life until it was fully met by God. In Spokane, when God met Lake, who already had so much of the power of the Spirit flowing through his life, He gave to him a measure of power that was used to shape the culture around him, making Spokane the healthiest city in the world. The spiritually rich became spiritually richer!

I've heard people say that we're not to seek the hand of God; we're to seek His face. I like that statement, but it's not totally true. Jesus never scolded or corrected anyone for seeking a gift—including a healing or a miracle. The same applies to us. Paul commanded us to *"desire earnestly spiritual gifts"* (1 Corinthians 14:1 NASB). We are commanded to seek gifts! So, seek God's gifts. Then, when you find His hand, look up—His face is not far away.

Missionary Role

I love to see people involved in worldwide missions. My wife and I have each supported missions since before we were married and have continued to do so with great joy. We have also been on countless short-term missions trips all over the world. There's something to be said for going outside the familiar to discover what God has given you.

The ministries of D. L. Moody and John G. Lake exploded when they went to another country. For Lake, it was Africa. Again, getting outside our comfort zones sometimes helps us to discover for ourselves what we are carrying in God.

Raw Faith

The disciples left everything to follow Jesus. (See, for example, Mark 10:28–30.) But they learned that as long as they walked with Him, everything was taken care of. They saw the provision of the coin found in the fish's mouth (see Matthew 17:24–27), and they watched the food multiply (see, for example, Mark 6:33–44). They learned how to possess well by owning little to nothing. Lake was a wealthy man, and he left everything to follow Jesus. Sometimes, learning to trust God in the midst of impossible situations gives us the spiritual "real estate" to live from our life's call.

Giving everything away is not necessarily the prerequisite to following Jesus. However, a life of absolute trust in Him is vital for one who confesses Christ. We were designed by God for more than merely waiting quietly for Jesus to return. Jesus didn't accomplish everything just so that we would accomplish nothing. It should be normal for us to believe God. Having faith is part of our nature in Christ. That nature must be tapped into and expressed, for it is who we really are—we are *believers*.

Being Fully Full

The following quote from John G. Lake is rather astonishing when you consider that it came from a man filled with God's power who had seen extraordinary wonders and had lived in a realm of the Spirit where the supernatural worked through his life to impact the shape of the culture.

The greatest manifestation of the Holy Ghost-baptized life ever given to the world was not in the preaching of the apostles; it was not in the wonderful manifestation of God that took place at their hands. It was in the *unselfishness* manifested by the Church. Think of it! Three thousand Holy-Ghost baptized Christians in Jerusalem from the Day of Pentecost onward, who love their neighbor's children as much as their own.... That would be a greater manifestation than healing, greater than conversion, greater than baptism in the Holy Ghost, greater than tongues. It would be a manifestation of the love of First Corinthians 13 that so many preach about and do not possess.[367]

"The greatest of these is love" is the profound statement of the apostle Paul found at the conclusion of 1 Corinthians 13. The Bible declares it, so we know it's true. But when the statement is made by someone who has displayed unusual measures of spiritual power, who has been involved in a regular stream of miracles of biblical proportion, and has seen every manifestation and blessing that most of us long for, it screams truth. Here it is again: the greatest of all manifestations of God is *love*!

Postscript

The testimony of John G. Lake stirs me and provokes me in ways that few others do. My driving passion is to wade in the pool of his insights and testimonies until I think and see differently. For sure, that alone would be a perfectly good use of my time. But we must remember that Lake's spiritual breakthroughs, ministries, and manifestations came about because he was desperately hungry for God. As he said, "I believe I was the hungriest man for God that ever lived." He did not reduce his pursuit of "more" to a fun experience at the end of a meeting. He actually ached in his heart to live out what was modeled by the apostles of the first century. Nothing else would satisfy him. He knew that their experience was the testimony that summoned him to his own breakthrough. His experience now speaks to us—calling us, inviting us, into a place in God that few have ever known was available. Lake shows us that it is available for all.

Led by the Spirit:
Evan Roberts and the Welsh Revival

"The Church has been sleeping, but she is awake and putting on her armour now, and marching triumphantly. But do not make a mistake: God cannot do a great work through you without doing a great work in you first."[368]
—*Evan Roberts* (1904)

At times a wave of power, without any human instrumentality, or anything external to cause it, would sweep over the mass of the people, and spontaneously almost the whole company would pray aloud, no one heeding the other, and without the slightest confusion. Everyone was absorbed with God.... As the people gathered, the prayers and hymns burst forth—no one led but the Spirit Himself. One and another entered the place, knelt down, and in a few minutes an intense prayer, or as intense a chorus or verse of a hymn was sung, or a text of Scripture or a chapter read—but all in the most perfect harmony and intensity.[369]

—*Mary Baxter*, firsthand account of the Welsh Revival (1904)

I n some ways, the Welsh Revival stands out as the rarest of all revivals. The elements of this move of God were so diverse compared to historic revivals that probably few people could have predicted their success ahead of time. God honored Evan Roberts and his team for their simplicity of devotion to Christ, their absolute hunger for more, and the profound purity they brought to the equation.

Mass Conversions and Major Social Change

The Welsh Revival (1904–1905) was a remarkable, unique outpouring of the Holy Spirit marked by rapid mass conversions and significant social change. In only a few months, a spiritual awakening sparked city transformation, major social change, and Holy Spirit fires that spread to, or were a forerunner to, other great moves of God. Meetings where song, testimony, and prayer occurred spontaneously as congregants followed the leading of the Holy Spirit characterized this revival. As large numbers of people yielded to the lordship and direction of the Holy Spirit, a whole country was turned upside down.

One man who had been praying for revival for over ten years had the privilege of helping to ignite this flame.[370] Evan Roberts (1878–1951) spent much of his early life building a personal history with God. In his mid-twenties, he had several encounters with the Lord that positioned him to step into his calling. During the spring of 1904, God awakened him in the early mornings for three months straight. After journeying to attend ministerial school in the fall of 1904, he was "bent" before the Lord during a meeting in Blaenannerch. While this signifies his defining moment, he was not fully "activated" until a month later when he immediately responded to the leading of the Holy Spirit and returned home. Stepping out in faith activated his anointing in a new way.

A Prophet with Honor in His Hometown

Evan John Roberts was born in the small town of Loughor, Wales, on June 8, 1878. He and his fourteen siblings were raised by Calvinistic

Methodist parents. By the age of twelve, after his father had an accident and needed his assistance, he began working as a coal miner. At thirteen, while attending his home church, Moriah Chapel, he made a commitment to serve the Lord. Shortly after this, he initiated a Sunday school for the children of the miners.

Sometime during 1893–94, in the midst of hearing a teaching at Moriah Chapel, Evan decided to put his trust in God wholeheartedly. He made a vow that he would serve the Lord his entire life.[371] Following this, he regularly walked a mile to Moriah Chapel after work. At a service there one night, he heard deacon William Davies say, "Remember to be faithful. What if the Spirit descended and you were absent? Remember Thomas! What a loss he had!" Evan responded by saying to himself that day, "I will have the Spirit."[372] From the time he made that declaration, through all weather conditions and despite all competing circumstances, he set his heart on going after all that God had for him in his generation. He went to prayer meetings and church services nearly every night of the week. He was also drawn to study revival history in order to learn how to tap into the power of the testimony. He remembered that "for ten or eleven years I [had] prayed for a revival. I could sit up all night to read or talk about revivals. It was the Spirit that moved me to think about a revival."[373]

Roberts was a devout young man determined to live in the secret place in God and to cultivate God's presence in his life. He readied himself for any move of God that might come his way. He wanted to make sure his lamp was always full of oil so he could step into all that God had at any moment. (See Matthew 25:1–13.) He memorized Scripture in shorthand, prayed often, and regularly carried his Bible with him, even to his work in the coal mines.[374] Additionally, he sought to facilitate environments where others could encounter God. For example, in 1900, he formed prayer gatherings with the purpose of training young men to participate in public worship and service. It was decided from the very beginning that "no one is to lead the meeting, but each one is to take part as moved by the Spirit."[375] This conviction became foundational for the way he conducted ministry.

Encountering God for Three Months

In early 1904, spiritual hunger was being awakened once again in Wales. Joseph Jenkins led a conference in 1903 focused on cultivating a deeper life in Christ. In February 1904, during a meeting at Jenkins's Calvinistic Methodist Church in New Quay, a young woman stood up and "ignited a fire" that would sweep across Wales and beyond:

> On the following Sunday morning Florrie Evans was present in the young peoples prayer meeting, when Mr. Jenkins asked them to give their spiritual experience. Several attempted to on different subjects, but the Minister would not allow that. At last Florrie Evans got up, and with a tremor in her voice said — "I love Jesus Christ — with all my heart." This sentence was the means of breaking the ice, they say, at New Quay. Florrie's words sent a thrill through all those present. The fire was ignited, and the flame soon spread to Blaenanerch [sic], Newcastle-Emlyn, Capel Drindod, and Twrgwyn.[376]

While he was still in his hometown of Loughor, Roberts, at age twenty-five, had a series of encounters with God over a period of three months. He later recalled this season:

> One Friday night last spring [1904], when praying by my bedside before retiring, I was taken up to a great expanse—without time and space. It was communion with God. Before this a far-off God I had. I was frightened that night, but never since. So was my shivering that I rocked the bed, and my brother, being awakened, took hold of me thinking I was ill.
>
> After that experience I was awakened every night a little after one o'clock. This was most strange, for through the years I slept like a rock, and no disturbance in my room would awaken me. From that hour I was taken up into the divine fellowship for about four hours. What it was I can not tell you, except that it was Divine. About five o'clock I was again allowed to sleep on till about nine. At this time I was again taken up into the same experience as in the earlier hours of the morning until about twelve or one o'clock.

They questioned me at home. Why not get up earlier.... But it was too Divine to say anything about it. This went on for three months.[377]

Around the time of this experience, Roberts was moved after hearing a message about the Spirit of God for service, and he decided to apply to the Ministers' Training College at Newcastle-Emlyn.[378] In September 1904, he left home to attend school. Once there, he struggled to read any other book besides the Bible. The thought of souls being lost also continued to plague him.[379] After the first few weeks of school, he felt increasingly restless and became ill.

"Bend Me!" Encounter at Blaenannerch

The bending of the spirit will cost dearly perhaps—bending the will, the heart, the mind, the self. But what did it cost Him?[380]
—*Evan Roberts*

At the beginning of the school year, the community of students at Newcastle-Emlyn discovered revival stirrings nearby. They invited Roberts to come along to a meeting at Blaenannerch, Cardiganshire, which was about eight miles away. Even though he was still recovering from sickness, he was compelled to join them on their journey. At this point, Roberts was twenty-six years old and had prayed for revival for over eleven years, had prayed for increased fullness of the Holy Spirit for more than thirteen years, and had attended religious meetings nearly every night.[381] In his own words, he tells about his time at Blaenannerch:

On Wednesday I went to Blaenanerch [sic]. In the morning I met the (railway) guard in the Shop (the house of the Rev. Evan Phillips), and told him that I was like a flint—I was as if someone had swept me clean of every feeling. And my conviction was that I must either be cast on a bed of affliction or receive the Spirit mightily....

When returning Wednesday night the young women from New Quay tried to influence me, but nothing touched me. And they said: "We can do nothing for you?"

"No," said I. "I have only to wait for the fire. I have built the altar, and laid the wood in order, and have prepared the offering; I have only to wait for the fire."

About half-past nine next morning the fire fell, and it is burning ever since.

We started for Blaenannerch about six o'clock Thursday morning. Now joyful, now sad, now hard and cold—so my feelings varied on the journey that morning.

We sang in the break, and my feelings were very varied—now high, now low....

The seven o'clock meeting was devoted to asking and answering questions. The Rev. WW Lewis conducted. At the close the Rev. Seth Joshua prayed, and said, during his prayer, "Lord, do this, and this and this, &c., and bend us." He did not say, "O Lord, bend us." It was the Spirit that put the emphasis for me on "Bend us." "That is what you need," said the Spirit to me. And as I went out I prayed, "O Lord, bend me."

At the breakfast table at the Rev. MP Morgan's house, Mag Phillips offered me bread and butter. I refused, as I was satisfied. At the same moment, the Rev. Seth Joshua was putting out his hand to take the bread and butter, and the thought struck me: "Is it possible that God is offering me the Spirit, and that I am unprepared to receive him; that others are ready to receive, but are not offered?" Now my bosom was quite full—tight.

On the way to the nine o'clock meeting Rev. Seth Joshua remarked, "We are going to have a wonderful meeting today." To this I replied, "I feel myself almost bursting."

The meeting, having been opened, was handed over to the Spirit. I was conscious that I would have to pray. As one and the other prayed, I put the question to the Spirit, "Shall I pray now?" "Wait a while," said he. When others prayed I felt a living force come into my bosom. I held my breath, and my legs shivered, and after every prayer I asked, "Shall I now?" The living force grew and grew, and I was almost bursting. And instantly someone ended his prayer—

my bosom boiling. I would have burst if I had not prayed. What boiled me was the verse, "God commending his Love." I fell on my knees with my arms over the seat in front of me, and the tears and perspiration flowed freely. I thought blood was gushing forth. Mrs Davies, Mona, New Quay, came to wipe my face. On my right was Mag Phillips, and on my left Maud Davies. For about two minutes it was fearful. I cried, "Bend me! Bend me! Bend us!" Then, "Oh! oh! oh! oh!" and Mrs Davies said, "O wonderful Grace!" What bent me was God commending his Love [Rom. 5:8], and I not seeing anything in it to commend. After I was bent, a wave of peace came over me, and the audience sang, "I hear thy welcome voice." And as they sang, I thought of the bending at Judgment Day, and I was filled with compassion for those who would be bent on that day, and I wept.[382]

Roberts's encounter that day was an answered prayer for more than just himself. For four years, the Welsh minister and evangelist Seth Joshua had prayed that God would take some "lad from the coal mine or from the field, even as he took Elijah from the plough, to receive his work."[383] He had specifically prayed that it would not be a person from Cambridge or one of the other sophisticated universities so that pride and the praise of human intellectualism would not be lifted up. Little did Roberts know that he would become the fulfillment of Seth Joshua's prayer.

Immediate Effects of the Encounter

After this encounter, Roberts experienced several immediate changes. The next day, September 30, 1904, he wrote a poem reflecting his new state, mentioning how his heart had moved from being "like a stone" to being alive and thriving. He wrote how he felt that nothing could separate him any longer from union with God.[384] Roberts believed he had received three "great blessings" after he was "bent" at Blaenannerch. He claimed that he had "lost all nervousness," was able to sing all day unhindered, and was flooded with praise and thanksgiving like never before.[385] The nervousness he referred to was due to his extreme shyness. After his encounter, he was no longer afraid to stand in front of an audience. Depression and gloom were also lifted, and he was full of joy, singing, and laughter.

Shifting Paradigms

Roberts wrote to his sister Mary about the importance of seeing God as happy and full of joy.

> Before I came to Newcastle-Emlyn, I never met young ladies who could and were willing to speak of religious things. The old fashion was to draw a long face when speaking of religious things. But it was most part of it hypocrisy, and based on the fact and thought that God is a solemn and just God, and at the same time forgetting that God is a happy God and a joyful God. Therefore, we must be happy and joyful. Now, when we speak of religion we are full of joy, and our faces are lit up with joy. Shake off this death-like solemnity, and be joyful, ever joyful. We must show the world that we are happy, because of this blessed assurance of salvation. The old story was, "I hope I am saved," while we can say, "I know I am saved."[386]

Call to Evangelism

Roberts was also immediately stirred for evangelism in a new way. His desire to save souls grew in intensity and focus. His friend and biographer Daniel M. Phillips said that "this had existed in him for years...but now its intensity grew to such an extent as to conquer entirely all other desires."[387] The day after his "bending" in Blaenannerch, Roberts said,

> Henceforth the salvation of souls became the burden of my heart. From that time I was on fire with a desire to go through all Wales, and, if it were possible, I was willing to pay God for allowing me to go.[388]

Roberts drafted a list of people who could help him visit towns to preach the gospel. The team consisted of the ladies from New Quay, his friend Sidney Evans, and himself. Roberts was prepared to invest and finance the ministry trips with all of the two hundred pounds he had saved up. But as the team members continued to set these plans before the Lord, they did not feel led to move forward with them. Instead, they decided to spend the next few weeks reading the Word, praying, and ministering in nearby places.[389] In preparation for a meeting at Capel Drindod on October

28, 1904, Roberts wrote to his friend Miss Davies and encouraged her to be strong in prayer and dependent upon the Holy Spirit:

> Oh! that we could all feel that we can do nothing without the Holy Spirit, and in that feeling fall in lowliness before God with a broken heart, beseeching Him to show us His face, especially at Capel Drindod. It would be awful for us without God. Oh try to impress upon those who will be coming the importance of having the powerful influences of the Holy Spirit.[390]

Visions and Assignment

Throughout the month of October, God spoke powerfully to Roberts's community through several visions. One historian noted that their nights "were interrupted by visions which spoke of the advance of Christ's kingdom on an unprecedented scale, and seasons of unfettered communion with God."[391] On October 29, 1904, both Roberts and Sidney Evans had the same vision of an arm stretched out from the moon toward them. They believed this was a sign that revival was coming to Wales. Roberts was stirred to believe God for one hundred thousand souls to be saved.[392]

In late October 1904, Roberts spoke in a meeting on the importance of giving more glory to Jesus than to men. The Holy Spirit moved powerfully on the group, and people wept and repented. Roberts could not sleep that night because his room was so full of the presence of the Holy Spirit. God's presence was so powerful that he had to shout and beg God to stay His hand.[393]

Roberts attended a Sunday service on October 30, 1904, and while Evan Phillips spoke on the text "Father, the hour is come" (see John 17), Roberts was caught up in a vision. His body shook, and all he could see was the people of his hometown sitting and waiting for someone to speak to them. He felt this was God calling him to go to them. When he finally yielded, he felt the light of the glory of God fill the whole chapel in a marvelous way.[394]

Activation

On Monday, October 31, the day after Roberts received this vision from the Lord, he left Newcastle-Emlyn for Loughor by train. During his journey, he wrote Miss Evans a letter recounting what had happened the night before.

> Just a line to let you know that I am on my way home for a week to work with our young people. The reason for this is the command of the Holy Spirit. He gave the command last night at the meeting. I could not concentrate my thoughts on the work of the service. I prayed and prayed, so that I could follow the service, but of no avail. My thoughts were wandering, and my mind riveted on our young folk at Moriah. There seemed a voice, as if it said, You must go, you must go! I then told Mr. Phillips about it, and I asked whether it was the devil or the Spirit. He answered, No, no. The devil does not give such thoughts. It was the voice of the Holy Spirit. Therefore, I have decided to obey, and I feel as if the Spirit testifies of a blessed future.[395]

While on the train, he also wrote a sermon and practiced preaching it to the other passengers. By stepping out in faith, he began to activate what had been deposited in him from his earlier encounters.[396] He arrived home the same night, and he was able to arrange a small meeting following a main session. Seventeen people (sixteen adults and one little girl) were present at this first meeting in Loughor. After much encouragement from Roberts, the reserved Welsh all stood up and publically confessed Christ.[397] He continued to lead meetings in his hometown each night at nearby churches. He wrote to a friend about the results from the first week, "This is our success this week in public confession —Monday night, 16, Tuesday, 6, Wednesday, 4, Thursday, 20, Friday, 19 —Total, 65."[398] Roberts knew he was on the verge of something big. On November 4, 1904, he sent a letter to an editor of a newspaper saying, "We are on the eve of a great and grand Revival, the greatest Wales has ever seen. Do not think the writer is a madman."[399] A few days later, he sent another letter to a friend describing what he believed signified the coming revival:

> Last Thursday [November 3, 1904] I had a Vision. In front of me, some few yards ahead, I saw a candle burning, and away in front of me, I saw a sun rising majestically, throwing its rays in all directions; something divine in its aspect. Can you comprehend the meaning?

Yes, of course, you can. The grand revival is coming. Now, it is only as candlelight. But, ere long, we shall have the powerful light and heat of the sun. Now, if you think you can strengthen the young people's faith by relating this, you can do so. It was not a dream, but a vision.[400]

The Revival

Then, the revival broke out. Just one month after Roberts's significant encounter of total surrender to the Lord, he began leading hundreds from his hometown to Christ. This had a ripple effect, impacting cities and ushering his country deeper into its destiny. Some of the meetings in the early weeks started at 7:00 p.m. and continued without any breaks until 4:30 the next morning.[401]

Results of the Revival

It did not take long for the revival fire to spread. The timber had been prepared in the land through many years of prayer for awakening. It must be noted that even before Roberts held his first meeting in his hometown, there were already a few pockets of revival breaking out in Wales, especially in New Quay. However, by February 28, 1905, less than four months after Roberts released the Holy Spirit flame in Loughor, there were over eighty-four thousand conversions recorded.[402] That is an average of more than five thousand conversions a week!

From Wales, the revival spread to scattered cities in England (Cornwall, Hirst), Scotland (Glasgow), Ireland, and the Isle of Man. It also spread as far as New Zealand, Madagascar, India, the United States (Pennsylvania and New York), Mexico, Australia, and several other countries in Europe (Denmark, Sweden, Norway, Germany, France, and Belgium), Asia (China and Korea), and Africa (Algeria and South Africa).[403]

Cultural Transformation

The Welsh Revival was not merely a revival of souls saved; it included cultural transformation, as well. The reports of the revival in the press were positive. Shops closed down early so the owners could get a seat at the revival meetings.[404] Bibles flew off the shelves in bookstores. People with longstanding debts paid them in full, and relationships were reconciled. Drunkenness and crime drastically declined. Some people characterized the movement "by the most remarkable confession of sin, confessions that must be costly."[405] In Llanfair in Anglesey, every public house (bar) but one was closed. In Glamorgan, convictions for drunkenness went from 10,528 in 1903 to 5,490 in 1906.[406] The workhorses in the mines no longer knew how to respond to the commands of the workers; one manager said that the workers used to drive "their horses by obscenity and kicks. Now they can hardly persuade the horses to start working, because there is no obscenity and no kicks."[407] Below are a few more of the early reports and testimonies from the revival:

Truly God has visited His people in Wales. It is not a question of one town being awakened, but of the whole principality being on fire. Profanity silenced, public-houses deserted, theaters closed, betting books burned, football teams disbanded, police courts idle, family feuds pacified, old-standing debts paid, sectarianism and ecclesiasticism submerged, the family altar re-erected, and Bible study become a passion—it is certainly a wonderful record....[408]

In Cardiff alone, as yet only slightly moved by the revival, police reports show that drunkenness has diminished 60 percent.... The streets of Aberdare on Christmas Eve were almost entirely free from drunkenness, and on Christmas Day there were no prisoners at all in the cells.... At Abercarn Police Court, responsible for a population of 21,000 there was not a single summons on Thursday—a thing unknown since the court was formed fourteen years ago.[409]

A collier [worker in the mines], who has formerly spent his money on all kinds of sinful pleasure, has removed his younger brother from an orphanage, and has decided to support him with his savings till he is old enough to provide for himself.[410]

At one service a man with a tear-stained face rushed from the gallery to a pew downstairs, and, clutching passionately the hand of another man, entreated to be forgiven. It was evidently a request not easily granted, so the two repaired to the vestry, where the wrong was satisfactorily rectified, and then the two men newly-reconciled returned to take a happier part in the service.[411]

The revival even spilled into places of leisure. One night at a football game, the whole crowd broke out singing one of the revival worship songs.[412]

The revival was also a precursor and possible catalyst for future Holy Spirit movements. Frank Bartleman, who would later become a key figure in the Azusa Street Revival, corresponded with Roberts and urged him to pray that a similar move of God would break out in California. Joseph Smale, a pastor of the First Baptist Church in Los Angeles, visited the Welsh Revival and brought back an impartation that also impacted the Azusa Street Revival.[413] Additionally, George Jeffreys, who later founded the Elim Pentecostal Movement, was converted during the revival at Nantyffyllon.[414] Several Bible schools, as well as the Apostolic church in Wales, also emerged as a result of the revival.[415] Daniel Powell Williams, a miner who later founded the Apostolic church in Penygroes, was converted at one of Roberts's meetings in Loughor.

Leaving the Revival: Pressure and Seclusion

Many times, Evan Roberts would lead meetings and remain there into the early hours of the morning. This eventually wore him down. He would sometimes withdraw or not show up to meetings because He felt God had told him to stay home and pray. His absence disappointed people, and he received some criticism for his unpredictable leadership in the revival.[416]

Then, in 1905, Roberts had a mental, emotional, and physical breakdown. Shortly afterward, he met evangelist and author Jessie Penn-Lewis at a Keswick meeting and responded to her invitation to go to England to live with her family. She built a bedroom with a prayer room for him. While the revival died down shortly after Roberts left the scene, many people around the world were profoundly influenced and impacted by what had been released in that short amount of time.

Roberts stayed with Penn-Lewis and her family for eight years. During that time, he had little communication with the outside world. To many people, it appeared that Penn-Lewis overprotected him from all outside influence. Some saw their relationship as similar to that of Jezebel intimidating Elijah, although Roberts had showed signs of similar patterns of isolation before he met her.[417] In 1926, Roberts visited Wales again. After Penn-Lewis's death in 1927, he permanently moved back home. There was a brief period in which he preached again, and there were healings, deliverances, and conversions at his meetings. By 1931, he went into seclusion again, staying in a room provided by Mrs. Oswald Williams, writing poetry and letters to ministers. He died on September 29, 1951, at the age of seventy-three.

Results of Roberts's Life-Changing Year

For Roberts, 1904 was the year when everything changed. Before this, he had been an average workman, though he regularly prayed for revival and ministered to those in his circles. However, after his three months of communion with God (in the spring), his "Bend me!" encounter (September 29), and his obedience to the Holy Spirit to return home (October 31), he was used by God to help spark a significant revival that impacted not only his country but also other nations around the world. The anointing that had been deposited in Roberts's life through his years of prayer, through his time spent in God's Word, and through his 1904 encounters, was significantly activated when he immediately followed the leading of the Holy Spirit to return home. Obedience activates anointing. Many times, the quicker the obedience, the greater the power that is released.[418]

Journey also played a role in Roberts's activation. His encounter happened while he was away from home. Again, sometimes the anointings, giftings, and calls that God has already put inside of us are ignited when we go into a different environment. As was the experience of many of the visitors to the Welsh Revival, God may lead us to journey to a new place where we will catch a "fire" that we are called to carry back home.

Evan Roberts's Leadership During the Revival

Evan Roberts was only twenty-six years old when he emerged as the key leader in the Welsh Revival. He was passionate about giving space to the Holy Spirit to lead and never wanted to quench the Spirit in any way.

The great evangelist R. A. Torrey observed that Roberts "does not seem to try and run things in his own wisdom or strength.... Oftentimes, even when Evan Roberts is speaking, some man or woman will burst out into a song, and he immediately stops speaking and lets the meeting take its own course."[419] A woman from England named Mary Baxter visited Wales and reported that Roberts "has a real belief in the leading of the Holy Spirit, and knows how to wait *on* the Lord and wait *for* the Lord."[420] Well-known preacher and Bible teacher G. Campbell Morgan said that Roberts

> is the mouthpiece of the fact that there is no human guidance as to man or organization. The burden of what he says to the people is this: It is not me, do not wait for me, depend on God, obey the Spirit. But whenever moved to do so, he speaks under the guidance of the Spirit. His work is not that of appealing to men so much as that of creating an atmosphere by calling men to follow the guidance of the Spirit in whatever the Spirit shall say to them.[421]

Roberts believed that he had received directions from the Lord about how to cultivate an atmosphere where the Holy Spirit would be welcomed. He encouraged these instructions to be passed along:

> This is the plan—We begin by asking someone to read, another to give out a hymn, and another to pray. Then I say a few words. This is what is said every night:
>
> 1. We must confess before God every sin in our past life that has not been confessed.
>
> 2. We must remove anything that is doubtful in our lives.
>
> 3. Total Surrender. We must say and do all that the Spirit tells us.
>
> 4. Make a public confession of Christ.
>
> That is the plan that the Spirit revealed to me.[422]

Further, Roberts felt he had received a special "download" from heaven of a certain prayer to send on ahead of him to the people, and especially the children, to pray in the cities he was to visit. Many times, when they did this, by the time he arrived, revival had already broken out. In a letter to a friend, he explained these directions:

Continue to pray for us. The friends at Newcastle-Emlyn must be more fervent, and say that they will have the blessing. Establish revival meetings there. Call all the denominations together. Explain the "four ways" and at the close of the meeting, let those who have confessed Christ remain behind, and send this prayer around. All must see to it that they pray it:—

1. Send the Spirit now, for Jesus Christ's sake.

2. Send the Spirit now powerfully, for Jesus Christ's sake.

3. Send the Spirit now more powerfully, for Jesus Christ's sake.

4. Send the Spirit now still more powerfully, for Jesus Christ's sake.

Pray No. 1 again and again, all together or individually, according as you are prompted by the Holy Spirit, and in silence. Then No. 2 in the same way. No. 3 again. No. 4 afterwards. That is the simple instrument of the Holy Spirit. Remember to establish these meetings.[423]

Characteristics of the Revival

Throughout the Welsh Revival, the meetings had a few qualities in common. First of all, the Holy Spirit was the leader. After someone began the service, the meeting was turned over to the Holy Spirit. The meetings were also spontaneous in nature and mostly filled with prayer, worship, and testimonies.[424] While very little preaching was done by a minister, many common people had the opportunity to release testimonies.[425] Many times, after a meeting began, no one knew when it would finish because it "would not conclude until some definite point had been gained."[426] G. Campbell Morgan shared his perspective of the flow of the meetings:

The meetings open—after any amount of singing while the congregation is assembling—by the reading of a chapter or a psalm. Then it is go-as-you-please for two hours or more. And the amazing thing is that it does go, and does not entangle in what might seem to be inevitable confusion. Three-fourths of the meeting consists of singing. No one uses a hymn book. No one gives out a hymn. The last person to control the meetings in any way is Mr. Evan Roberts. People pray and sing, give testimony, exhort as the Spirit moves them. As a study of the psychology of crowds, I have seen nothing like it. You feel that the thousand or fifteen hundred persons before you have become merged into one myriad-headed but single-souled personality.[427]

Singing played a central role in the Welsh Revival. Whenever someone in the meeting confessed Christ, the crowd regularly broke out in singing the chorus of the popular Welsh revival song "Diolch Iddo," which is translated "Thanks be to Him."[428] William T. Stead noticed that "the revival has not strayed beyond the track of the singing people. It has followed the line of song, not of preaching. It has sung its way from one end of South Wales to the other."[429]

The people who were drawn to these meetings in Wales came from far and wide, and many of them wanted only to "meet God." They did not come to see a famous speaker or to hear an amazing worship band; they came because God was doing something powerful there. Mary Baxter was deeply moved during her visit to Wales, describing her experience in this way:

> I saw a large, deep gallery surrounding the chapel literally packed with men. They were manly, intensely earnest faces, not looking around or talking one to the other, but with one consent utterly taken up with God. The body of the chapel was also crowded with men and women of all classes, with but one purpose—TO MEET GOD.
>
> There was no opening to the meeting; the hearts were full, and burst with prayer and praise to a God felt to be in our midst....[430]

This was truly a revival founded on cultivating God's presence. Transformation was released as a result of people worshipping God. The spontaneous flow of the Holy Spirit in worship, testimony, and prayer were the rhythm of the Welsh Revival. It was a revival led by the Holy Spirit, the Conductor of a symphony of surrendered hearts.

Prophetic Inheritance

Enduring Faith

Only God knows how to prepare us for our future. He alone knows how to get us ready for the impossible lifestyle He has called us to. Yet some of this preparation is given only to those who are hungry. Evan Roberts spent ten years fiercely praying for revival. His heart's cry was anything but casual; it possessed him in every sense of the word.

Persistence in prayer is called for not so much to impact God as to change *us*. He hears the very first cry of our heart, but oftentimes the things that we pray for would destroy us if He released them in full the first time we prayed for them. For that reason, God also teaches us about *enduring faith*. That biblical concept implies that not every prayer is meant to be answered quickly. Quick answers are fun, for sure, but delayed answers increase one's interest in the matter that is being prayed over. Delayed answers also shape the character of those who are to receive them. It could be said that *faith brings answers, but enduring faith brings answers with character.*

Evan Roberts cried out for the salvation of his nation. It was a cry that came from a place so deep within him that it brought about serious adjustments in his life—affecting how he thought, lived, prayed, and dreamed. He was consumed with this mandate over his life. After ten years of prayer, the Lord gave him the very thing he had wept for. Earth had to invade heaven for ten years before heaven invaded earth. Such perseverance in prayer is the Lord's invitation to each one of us.

Thus, enduring faith and persevering prayers shape the life of the prayers until we are formed into the kind of vessel that wouldn't be destroyed by the answer. This is of great concern to God. Again, if given prematurely, some answers would literally kill the ones who are to receive them, because their strength, trust, and character are not broad enough to contain the glory ("weight") that is to be released in them. But persistence in prayer shapes us and matures us to receive what God has for us.

God also gives answers in seed form. Metaphorically speaking, we pray for an oak tree, and He gives us an acorn at first. Many people look with disgust at the acorn and say, "That's not an oak tree," as though their "gift of discernment" will produce the oak tree they've requested. Such an approach never works. But show me someone who can see the tree in the seed, and I'll show you someone who will give God thanks for the answer long before it comes. That person will treat the seed with the same respect they would show the full oak tree. And their gratefulness and vision will create the right environment for the acorn to grow.

We must realize that God is more committed to the process than we are committed to getting answers. Evan Roberts is an example for us of someone who knew how to persevere in prayer, and he prayed with great focus and intent. He was far from casual about it. Instead, his prayer life was all-consuming, impacting every area of his life. Right before the big breakthrough of revival, sixty-five people confessed Christ in five days. Roberts then wrote to the newspaper editor, announcing that they were on the eve of "a great and grand Revival." Think of it—Roberts was moved by the confession of sixty-five people and announced that revival was at the door! This was much like the prophet who ran for cover from impending rain because he saw a cloud the size of a man's hand. (See 1 Kings 18:44.)

I've watched many people announce that a move of the Holy Spirit is not really revival, or that it doesn't qualify to be recognized as one of the great moves of God. It's as if they think their ability to critique has the same value in the kingdom of God as it does in secular society. Again, God is looking for people who see the oak tree in the acorn, or the mighty outpouring in the cloud the size of a man's hand. Anyone who is given the "acorn" and does not treat it with the respect and honor that it deserves will never see it grow to become an "oak tree."

I wonder how many times God has given the Spirit of revival to a group of people, but because the manifestations and results did not seem to measure up to the historic record of a move of God, the spiritual seed was killed through neglect. I personally think that tragic scenario is common. In contrast, when Roberts announced that Wales was about to be transformed through revival because of the confession of only sixty-five people, that was brilliant, authentic faith. Possibly more than anyone else I am aware of in history, Evan Roberts treasured the seed until it became the outpouring that blessed his entire country. From there, it impacted many nations of the world. Moreover, the revival in Wales was used by God to ignite the coals of revival for the Azusa Street outpouring. The latter has brought more people into the kingdom than all other revivals in history combined.

Being Led by the Spirit

One of the most significant ways the Welsh revival was unique was the manner in which the meetings were conducted. According to many reports, it was as though the meetings weren't actually being led by anyone. Spontaneity was the norm as people came together to know God and to give themselves in worship to Him. As they did so, the presence of God became so pronounced that *anything that could possibly go wrong with spontaneity seemed to lose traction.* For example, those who might typically have craved attention, who might have been prone to spontaneous outbursts in the meetings, were apparently overwhelmed by the Holy Spirit in such a way that His peace made up for the self-control that was usually lacking in them. Those who might have felt a need to take charge of the meetings seemed to lose their appetite for such things after seeing what having the Holy Spirit in charge of a meeting looked like. A joyful, holy fear filled the chapels where the people met, and it spilled out into the daily affairs of their lives.

Few are the people in history who could be a catalyst to such a great move of God yet take an almost backward approach to their role of leadership. No one could ever rightfully claim that Evan Roberts was a control freak. He truly gave the Holy Spirit the supreme place, not just as a point of theology but in practice. This was the great beauty of the Welsh Revival; and it raised the high-water mark for all of us in learning to be led by the Spirit.

Another important factor of the revival is that being led by the Spirit was more than just a way to conduct meetings. Learning to trust God in the corporate gatherings no doubt trained people for how to live in Him on a day-to-day basis; the result was that their culture was transformed. Family life, the workplace, entertainment, politics, and more were changed by the prevailing presence of God over the nation. I have read the reports of spiritual leaders who recognized the presence of the Holy Spirit the moment they crossed the border into Wales. A desire for this to happen in every movement of the Spirit must be deeply rooted in the heart of God—He does not want to come to us just in visitation but to remain in habitation until every realm of life is affected by His glorious rule. If it can happen in Wales, it can happen anywhere. If it can last for a year, it can last for ten. If it can last for ten....

God in Music

Great moves of God are always represented by new music; many new songs are written and sung during revival. And while revival themes are often represented well in the newly inspired lyrics, the Welsh revival seemed to go a step further in that it was actually *led* through song and became known as "the singing revival." In part, this may be because the culture of the Welsh people is musically rich, and it is a singing nation. If you were to remove music from the Welsh revival, you would probably no longer have a revival—music was that central to it.

My wife went with a group of believers to tour the great revival sites in Wales for the purpose of prayer. At one point, they were taken into a cave where the tour guide told them many of the great voices of our day have visited to sing because of its amazing acoustics. Each of these gifted people has filled that place with beautiful songs and rich voices. This humble group of believers also began to sing, and the tour guide began to weep but didn't know why. The group leader informed him that this was his song and his inheritance because it was one of the great hymns born out of the Evan Roberts revival.

The Joy of God

An understanding of the goodness of God was the cornerstone of the theology connected to the Welsh revival. The revival was born from a revelation of God's love and joy. Evan Roberts's personal experiences with God were of such extreme joy that, at times, people questioned his sanity. As quoted earlier in this chapter, Roberts said,

> God is a happy God and a joyful God. Therefore, we must be happy and joyful. Now, when we speak of religion we are full of joy, and our faces are lit up with joy. Shake off this death-like solemnity, and be joyful, ever joyful. We must show the world that we are happy, because of this blessed assurance of salvation.[431]

Having an understanding of God as happy and joyful is not a small matter, nor is it a peripheral one. It is said that Jesus had more joy than everyone around Him. (See, for example, Hebrews 1:9.) Joy is also the commodity of heaven that was used to motivate Jesus to endure the cross. (See Hebrews 12:2.) To be Christlike is to be filled with joy. It is one of the evidences of being filled with the Spirit.

The nature of God really should define a move of God. In other words, a move of God must in some way reveal His nature. Our perception of our wonderful, perfect Father often affects how we expect Him to manifest in an outpouring of His Spirit. The Welsh Revival began with a person, and then a group of people, who knew that God was good and that joy was the only logical response to the gift of His grace. As a result, history is forever marked by a wonderful outpouring of the Spirit that maintained an awareness of the goodness of God.

Personal Disciplines

Evan Roberts practiced many personal disciplines. We will note two of them here. First, he was committed to attending the house of God because he was hungry for Him. He lived with the deep concern that he might miss a service where God would show up in an unusual way. In today's culture, there is so much to choose from in most churches that the average person approaches church as if they were eating at a smorgasbord; they take some of this and some of that but ignore anything that doesn't personally appeal to them. I've watched people leave a meeting simply because the subject of the message wasn't one they were interested in hearing. Complacent people always seem to have the luxury of picking and choosing. But Evan Roberts knew real spiritual hunger. Proverbs 27:7 (NASB) describes spiritual hunger well: "*To a famished man any bitter thing is sweet.*" Those who are really hungry will enjoy food that is far from perfect, thankful just for the privilege of eating. Hungry people who are given something to eat are usually thankful people, no matter what they are fed. And Roberts was always eager for spiritual nourishment.

Second, as we have seen, Evan Roberts was faithful and persistent in prayer. His prayer life was unstoppable. He didn't confine his worship and intercession to scheduled prayer meetings. I feel sorry for anyone who is limited in prayer to what is directed by another person. Prayers led by others are important, but they will never replace the need for our own heart-cry to be lifted up to the Lord. Prayers that are spontaneous, inconvenient, and costly seem to have the greatest impact—first on us, and then on our surroundings.

Postscript

In order to have the kind of revival that impacts the culture and truly becomes an awakening, we will have to learn how to sustain the revival apart from church meetings. If you think about it, the meetings are where the presence and power of God become manifest. But nowhere does the Bible tell us that that's the only place we can experience them. I think every reader would agree that Jesus *was* revival. And His life and ministry were primarily in public places, like the marketplace. His constant awareness of the heart of the Father through the presence of the Holy Spirit enabled Him to illustrate revival everywhere He went.

Let me conclude with a word of wisdom and caution for all who seek sustainable revival. Evan Roberts did not try to control the revival meetings, as some people would typically attempt to do, but allowed the Spirit to lead them. Nevertheless, he became unusually fatigued by them. A prophet once told me (as a warning) that spiritual laws are greater than natural laws, but if I disobey natural laws, the enemy will "take me out." We must remember that we are human beings with basic physical needs that must be met in order for us to function well. The anointing never leaves, but if we try to somehow "keep up" with the anointing in our own strength, we may violate the laws we've been made subject to in this lifetime.

Simply put, we have to make sure we are taking care of our physical needs. We must get plenty of rest. It's not spiritual to skip sleep. It's just foolish. History is filled with the nightmare stories of those who neglected this aspect of their lives. We must also eat healthy, nourishing food and drink plenty of water. Regular exercise is also greatly needed in this day and age. Even walking works—it just has to be done consistently. Observing these simple principles will help to make it possible for us to maintain a move of God for the long haul.

Evan Roberts continues to be an inspiration to us because he persistently called out to God, and God came upon him in answer to his cry. I've been in the little chapel where the "lightning" of God first struck him. That power is still present in the building after all these years. But neither the place, nor the person, is to be worshipped. The God who moved upon Evan Roberts and is now ready to move upon you and me. The time has come for another outpouring upon the hungry!

10

Prophetic Intercession:
Rees Howells

"Each day he cleansed and purged me so that I could never go back again to my former life, and finally he gave me one hour to decide whether I, myself, was to live on, or he was to live in me. My destiny for eternity depended on that hour."[432]
—*Rees Howells*

Early in my walk with the Lord, I devoured books on prayer. I had such a hunger to learn about this important ministry, and I remember one stretch of time where I read seven books on prayer in a row. Each book was a classic, written by the likes of R. A. Torrey, Andrew Murray, "Praying" Hyde, E. M. Bounds, and others. And each book had a big impact on how I thought about my relationship with God. Hearing the heartbeat of those who were light-years ahead of me in their walk with the Lord forever changed my approach to the duty of prayer. I can honestly say that since that time, I have rarely considered prayer to be a duty; I think of it instead as the greatest privilege.

It is not really fair to compare people, books, messages, or anointings. We seldom know enough or see clearly enough to make such judgments. Yet I must say that the book *Rees Howells, Intercessor* by Norman Grubb impacted me more than any other book at that time—and perhaps more than any book since. It shook me to my core. Howells's entire life prophesies what it means to be abandoned to Christ, creating an expectation of what should be the norm for those who follow Jesus.

Abandonment to Christ

Rees Howells (1879–1950) was drastically changed after an unusual encounter of complete surrender in which his final commitment came with only one minute to spare. Not long after this, he imparted the Welsh Revival throughout southeastern Africa, including Mozambique, where he saw revival break out with miracles, healings, and over ten thousand salvations. Upon returning to Wales with the equivalent of fifteen cents to his name, Howells stepped out in faith in 1924 to establish the Bible College of Wales—the ministry school that evangelist Reinhard Bonnke attended years later.[433] A revival centered on the presence of God and manifesting unique signs broke out in his Bible school.

Rather than travel the world evangelizing, Howells was led to a life of intercession. He also equipped others for a similar lifestyle of faith and prayer. He raised up an army of intercessors who prayed through major world crises in World War II, prepared the way for missionaries, and paved the way for revival.

Early Life in Wales

Rees Howells was born October 10, 1879, in the small town of Brynamman in Carmarthenshire, Wales.[434] He was the sixth of eleven children. By the age of twelve, he had already started working in a tin mill. When he was a boy, his father regularly read him Bible stories. Howells was also drawn to the home of his grandparents, who had been converted in the Revival of 1859, because he felt that "God was its atmosphere."[435]

As he grew up, he maintained a life set apart from the world. Even when he later worked in the mines, the miners would not use profanity around him. Sometimes, he "would walk miles to hear someone preach and bring him 'under the influence of God,' but he wouldn't cross the road to hear a concert."[436] When he was twenty-two years old, he attended a Sunday evening service where he heard the minister read Hebrews 12:1, about the *"cloud of witnesses."* This verse struck Howells in a powerful way, making the spiritual realm more real to him.[437]

Conversion in America

Not long afterward, Howells set sail for America, living with his cousin in western Pennsylvania and finding work in a tin mill. Despite a strong religious sensibility, Howells had not yet dedicated his life to Christ, and when his cousin challenged him to be born again, he eagerly searched for the way to God for five months. Then he contracted typhoid fever, causing him to cry out to God even more. He made a vow that he would live totally surrendered to God if given one more chance to live; he immediately began to recover and "was a changed man."[438]

Howells then moved to a different town in Pennsylvania where he met a Jewish man, Maurice Reuben, who had converted to Christianity. It was through Reuben's testimony and friendship that Howells's eyes were opened to see the impact of the cross and to understand that Jesus died for him personally. He responded to Christ's invitation to receive Him:

> Then [Jesus] spoke to me and said, "Behold, I stand at the door and knock. May I come in to you, as I came in to [Maurice] Reuben and took the place of his wife and son and home and store and world? Will you accept me?" "Yes," I replied, and He came in, and that moment I changed. I was born into another world....
>
> ...None of my old friends could understand what had happened. I had no fellowship with natural things. It wasn't a point of doctrine I saw; no, it was Calvary. It wasn't giving a mental assent; no, the veil was taken back, my eyes were opened, and I *saw* Him....

The love of the Savior was revealed to me.[439]

A few days after his conversion, Howells felt compelled to return to Wales to share what God had done for him. He arrived home in 1904—just at the beginning of the outbreak of the Welsh Revival.

The Welsh Revival

Howells's biographer Norman Grubb noted that in the Welsh Revival,

The presence and power of the Holy Ghost in the church has always been a fact recognized by true believers; so it was not so much a case of asking Him to come as acknowledging His presence, and very soon realizing his power…. But often they had to first pray out the hindrances to blessing: disobedience and unforgiving hearts were two sins that were constantly dealt with. On the other hand, obedience and promptings of the Spirit and open confessions of Christ brought down the blessing.[440]

Outside of his mining work, Howells spent most of his waking hours discipling the new converts from the Welsh Revival.[441] His biographer noted,

The real problem arose as the Revival proceeded and thousands were added to the churches. There were more children born than there were nurses to tend to them. The establishing of converts became the greatest need, which if not met would be the most dangerous weakness of the Revival.

As enthusiasm abated, there were bound to be many who had depended more on feelings and not yet learned to have their faith solidly based on the Word of God.[442]

Howells decided he needed more training to better support the move of God in his country. He enrolled in a theological college in Carmarthen and was eventually ordained with the Congregational church.[443]

"The Llandrindod Experience"

In the summer of 1906, Howells was twenty-six years old. He planned to go to the Llandrindod Wells Convention, which was influenced by England's Keswick Convention and based on the Higher Life holiness teaching. Two days before leaving, he listened to someone read Romans 8:26–30 and was struck by the truths in the passage. Up to that point, Howells had known that he was *"predestined"* and *"justified"* but was now unsure if he was also *"glorified."* On the train to the convention, a voice spoke to him saying that when he returned, he would be a new man.[444]

At the convention, Evan Hopkins (author of the classic book *The Law of Liberty in the Spiritual Life*), spoke on Ephesians 2:1–6 and the importance of being "quickened" by the Holy Spirit. Howells was stirred to respond, and he received a breakthrough: he not only saw the "Crucified Christ" and the "Risen Christ" but also the "Glorified Christ."[445] Additionally, he heard the same voice that he had heard on the train ask him if he wanted to come up higher. The next day, Hopkins spoke on being fully possessed by the Holy Spirit. This opened Howells's eyes even more.

> It never dawned on me before that the Holy Ghost was a Person exactly like the Savior, and that He must come and dwell in flesh and blood. In fact, the Church knows more about the Savior, who was only on the earth thirty-three years, than about the Holy Ghost who has been here two thousand years. I had only thought of Him as an Influence coming on meetings, and that was what most of us in the Revival thought. I had never seen that He must live in bodies, as the Savior lived in His on earth.[446]

During the meeting, Howells felt that God told him He needed a body for the Holy Spirit to dwell in and work through. He asked Howells to allow the Holy Spirit to come in and take full possession. He wanted "unconditional surrender." Straight from the meeting, Howells went into a field and cried out to the Lord. He knew that once he surrendered all to God, it would be for life. He spent the next five days alone with God, struggling over making this decision. He wept for days and lost seven pounds. During this time, he allowed the Lord to purge out all sin. He later recalled that God was not going to accept "any superficial surrender," saying,

> He put His finger on each part of my self-life, and I had to decide in cold blood.... It was a breaking, and the Holy Ghost taking control. Day by day the dealing went on. He was coming in as God, and I had lived as a man, and "what is permissible to an ordinary man," He told me, "will not be permissible to you."[447]

On the Friday of that week, Howells heard the Spirit say, "I have been dealing with you for five days; you must give Me your decision by six o'clock tonight and remember, your will must go. On no account will I allow you to bring in a crosscurrent. Where I send you, you will go; what I say to you, you will do." Feeling the pressure and also the weight of dying forever to self, Howells asked for more time but felt the Spirit say, "At six o'clock I will take your decision. After that you will never get another chance."[448]

> My will would have to go; I would never have another choice, and I was never to question him in thought, word or motive. Each day he cleansed and purged me so that I could never go back again to my former life, and finally he gave me one hour to decide whether I, myself, was to live on, or he was to live in me. My destiny for eternity depended on that hour.[449]

As six o'clock approached on the fifth day, it was time for Howells to give his answer. At 5:59 p.m., after intense struggle, he chose to bow and surrender all to the Lord, just in the nick of time. Immediately, the Holy Spirit rushed in, and Howells was "transported to another realm," where God spoke to him.[450]

> At last I said, "Lord, I am willing," and he came in. He did not force the decision on me: I had to decide. I was carried right into the presence of God and the verse he gave me was: "Having therefore, brethren, boldness to enter into the holiest by the blood of Jesus" (Hebrews 10:19). From that time on there was a line drawn between my old life and this new one. Like John the Baptist, I had to decrease and he had to increase.[451]

That same night, God's glory fell in a powerful way upon Howells and the small gathering of people who met with him. They sang "There's power in the Blood" for two hours straight. Then, from 9:00 p.m. to 2:30 a.m., the Holy Spirit spoke things to Howells that he "had never dreamed of" before, and the group spent time together "exalting the Savior."[452]

Immediate Changes

The very next day, the naturally quiet and reserved Howells experienced a new surge of courage and empowerment when he stood up to activate the anointing he had received during his encounter and spoke boldly to a crowd of one thousand.[453] He also experienced an outpouring of love for others that he had never known before.[454] Additionally, he was consumed with "floods of joy."[455] Following his encounter, Howells was also led to completely surrender his money to God and "learned the blessed truth that his extremity was indeed God's opportunity."[456]

The Llandrindod experience acted as a catalyst for Howells to dedicate himself to a life of intercession.[457] He decided to turn over his mission work to a friend so he could focus more on his calling. Shortly afterward, he committed to a Nazarite type of vow that consisted of fasting two meals each day. He also adopted certain behaviors that were like prophetic signs that he was set apart from the world. One of them was not wearing a hat. This act of consecration set him apart culturally since, at the time, it was an embarrassment for a man to be seen in public without a hat. He also let his beard grow without trimming it for six months, giving others no explanation for his action. In his day, this was also a mark of a social outcast.[458]

During the season immediately following his encounter, he set aside three hours every night, from six to nine, to be on his knees before God. He spent two of the three hours reading the Bible and one simply waiting on God. He recalled that "although we may be away from the presence of people, how hard it is to silence the voices of self. But after a time the Lord brought me to the place where the moment I shut the door at six o'clock, I left the world outside and had access into the presence of God."[459]

Like many of the other revivalists who transitioned into full-time ministry after their encounter, Howells eventually quit his job so he could work exclusively for the Lord. At one point, he was blessed with a month's holiday to spend time on a mountain alone with God. During this time, he did not intercede but rather lived in fellowship with the Lord, lost in His presence. Howells always remembered this period as one of the most special times of his life.[460] He cultivated God's presence in his life to such a degree that, at one point, someone came into town who did not know his name and "simply asked the ticket collector at the station where 'the man with the Holy Ghost' lived and was directed to Mr. Howells!"[461]

He also entered a season of extreme giving, to the point that he went without what he needed so he could give more. He recalled that he "started at the bottom and loved just one; and if you love one, you can love many; and if many, you can love all."[462] He had a profound encounter with God when he gave a man enough money to pay a full two years' worth of back rent. Giving this gift produced a radical transformation in Howells.

> That night I changed in the root of my nature. I changed towards the world, towards lost souls and towards giving. From that time I could not help but give to everyone in need. I lived to give.... Whoever would be in need, they had a claim on me and I found it more blessed to give than to receive, and the more I gave the more I wanted to give. I was tested on it for four years and never failed once. You would think the day would come when I should not be able to give, but there was the promise of the hundredfold for all that I gave, and I believed it. I had never once been without money for fifteen years, so could the Holy Spirit make the promises of God equal to current coin? When I got to the last pound the Lord said, "Cut the ropes and take the promises."[463]

Healing Through Intercession

Howells's calling of intercession seems unique. One of the reasons he gave away most of what he had was that he saw it as his responsibility to be an answer to those for whom he felt led to intercede. He distinguished between a "prayer warrior" and an "intercessor" by emphasizing ownership.

> A prayer warrior can pray for a thing to be done without necessarily being willing for the answer to come through himself; and he is not even bound to continue in the prayer until it is answered. But

an intercessor is responsible to gain his objective, and he can never be free till he has gained it. He will go to any lengths for the prayer to be answered through himself.[464]

Howells prayed not only for salvation for others but also for healing. When his friend Joe was dying, Howells heard the Lord say that within one month, he would be healed. Howells set his heart to intercede, even though Joe and the doctor were doubtful. He told Joe that in one month's time he would be healed and that after his healing, they would send a letter home to his family to share the good news. Then the Lord challenged Howells to send the letter in faith, declaring the victory based on God's word to him, even before its manifestation. He mailed the letter, and the "next day the Lord came down on Joe like a shower of rain and he was healed on the spot."[465]

Through the years, Howells developed specific principles for intercession.[466] His intercession was always focused, always led by the Spirit, and many times prophetic in nature.[467] He studied the powerful intercessors in the Bible, such as Moses, Hosea, Isaiah, Daniel, Queen Esther, Ezekiel, and the apostle Paul. These biblical leaders were prophetic intercessors either in the signs and wonders that they themselves became through their prophetic acts, or because through their intercession, they helped to shift the destiny of whole nations.[468]

Call to Africa

On December 21, 1910, Howells married Elizabeth Hannah Jones. In 1912, while at a conference in Llandrindod, Howells met some missionaries to Angola. He was stirred with compassion and offered to care for their young daughter while they were on the field. Although Howells's offer was declined, meeting these missionaries was his first connection with Africa. Immediately following this, he attended another meeting where someone stated the need for replacements for a missionary couple in Africa who had to return home. Howells received a vision of people in Africa being like sheep without a shepherd, and his heart broke for them.[469] When he returned home from the conference, he shared these things with his wife.

During their intercession over the matter that night, they felt that God was calling *them* to be the answer to their own prayers.

At the end of 1912, Rees and Elizabeth Howells had a son, named Samuel, whom they would later surrender to the Lord and leave with his uncle so that they could respond to God's call for Africa.[470] Howells received some theological training at a faith mission in Scotland for one year before going to London to study medicine for a short time. Meanwhile, his wife learned midwifery.

When the Howellses were ready to leave London for their journey to Africa, they had merely ten shillings to their name. This was only enough for a train ticket to travel twenty miles. They boarded the train and got as far as they could on that money. At their stop, they got out and had breakfast with some friends who wanted to see them and say good-bye before they went overseas.

They waited on the Lord for how to proceed. When God asked Howells what he would do if he had the money, Howells responded that he would get in line to buy a ticket. In nearly an identical situation to that of John G. Lake a couple of years previously, Howells stood in line, even though he had no money. When he had nearly reached the head of the line, someone who had to leave to open his shop stepped out of the crowd and placed thirty shillings in his hands. After Howells bought the tickets, others who arrived to see him and his wife off showered them with gifts. They departed England for Africa on July 10, 1915.[471]

Revival in Gazaland[472]

When they arrived in South Africa, they joined the mission that Andrew Murray had started. People there were hungry for an impartation from the Welsh Revival, and they asked Howells if he "had brought that blessing" with him.[473] He began to release the impartation in all the mission stations he went to, and many people were healed and converted.[474] When Howells and his wife visited a mission base that had not seen a single conversion in seven years, they were stirred to pray together that revival would sweep the land. After this prayer meeting, Howells received confirmation from God that revival was coming.

On Thursday evening, four of us were reading the Bible together and I said, "The Holy Spirit is coming down in this district and will give a Pentecost." I told them the prayer had been heard and there was no need to pray any longer. A few days before this we had begun to sing the chorus: "Lord, send a revival, and let it begin in me." Everywhere people were singing it and I knew the sound of it, a sound you cannot make, the sound of revival, something which brings you into the stillness of God. Every moment we were expecting him to come. The following Sunday was my birthday and I knew the day before that the Holy Spirit would come down on that day.[475]

On October 10, 1915, Rees Howells's thirty-sixth birthday, "like lightning and thunder the power came down."[476] Howells recounted:

It was in the afternoon that [the Holy Spirit] came upon a young girl who broke down in tears as she prayed. Within five minutes the whole congregation fell on their knees, crying to God. The Holy Spirit came with power such as I had never seen, even in the Welsh Revival, and had only heard of through reading of men like Finney and others. The meeting went on late into the night and continued day after day from 9 o'clock in the morning until 6 o'clock in the evening, for seven days. We baptised 67 on the same day and great numbers after that. Everyone who called on the name of the Lord was saved and the revival lasted for 15 months without a break, with two revival meetings every day and meetings all day on Fridays. Evangelists were going out from the station all on fire for God and hundreds were converted.[477]

Following this outbreak of revival, Howells inspired missionaries from all around South Africa to set aside time each day to pray for God to pour out His Spirit in the land. He recalled that

after a month of praying, with great liberty, the morning came when I lost myself in God and I saw the Holy Spirit descending on Africa. As surely as John the Baptist saw the Holy Spirit coming down on the Saviour, I saw him coming down on all those mission stations, and he told me that as I had prayed and believed, he would send me to every place where the Spirit was to come down. I was overcome in his presence.[478]

Not long after, Howells was invited to a conference in Durban where he ministered for three weeks and released impartation to forty-three missionaries from the various bases of the South Africa General Mission. Following this, the conference chairman sent him to every one of their mission bases in South Africa to release the blessing. He remembered that "at every mission station there was an open heaven. I laid my hand on thousands and every one came through."[479] Howells traveled over eleven thousand miles and visited five provinces. Even the Queen of Swaziland was drawn to him and allowed him to speak to her officials. It deeply impacted her that just as the Father had parted with His only Son Jesus, Howells had left his son in order to minister to the people of Africa.[480]

Protection and Healing from Influenza

Then the influenza hit Africa, and over sixty-five people in their mission were afflicted early on. Hundreds of people were dying all around them, but Howells believed he had heard from the Lord that no one in his mission base would die. When he made that declaration, a nearby chief heard about it and asked if he could bring his people there for protection from the disease. The witch doctors could do nothing to help the people. Word spread within a twenty-mile radius of the mission that "the white man was able to keep death away."[481] Beginning with five of the most hardened men, people began to flock to the mission base for safety. There was not a single death at the base during this time of tragedy.

In just under five years in Africa, Howells was used as a catalyst to spread the Welsh Revival throughout the land. Over ten thousand people were converted, and many missionaries received impartation and burned with the fire of God once again.[482]

In 1920, Howells and his wife returned to Wales, refreshed and ready to start meetings at once. They had only planned to take a furlough in their home country, but the Lord redirected their journey.

Raising Up an Army of Intercessors

For the first few years after returning from Africa, the Howellses traveled around and shared testimonies about the revival in Gazaland. Rees Howells had also been offered his dream for ministry work. His mission council had said they would pay his way to travel wherever the Spirit led him, imparting to people around the world what God was doing in Wales. However, in 1922, when he participated in the Llandrindod Convention, everything changed. Howells spoke with great power by the Holy Spirit and made a call for full surrender. Immediately following his charge, an emergency prayer meeting was called.

During this time, Howells felt led to surrender his dream of a worldwide revival ministry and instead start a Bible college in his homeland. He was to build a place where "young people might come to learn a life of faith, and above all be filled with the Holy Spirit."[483] Having already left his son to go to Africa, this new call "would now mean leaving hundreds of spiritual children in Africa."[484] Soon after this stirring, the Howells family visited D. L. Moody's Bible College in Chicago, where God further confirmed this calling.[485]

Then it was time to act. With about fifteen cents to his name, Howells stepped out in faith to secure the first building for the ministry school. Behind the scenes, Howells spent eleven hours a day for nine months on his knees praying for the finances to be released. With multiple small donations, just before payments were due, the money always arrived. The school opened in 1924 with five teachers and thirty-eight students. The next year, after some internal conflict, the school dropped to just two teachers and five students. Howells wasn't sure what to do, so they spent the whole year on their faces in prayer. That time proved foundational for the school. In the following years, more students came. Tuition was free, and room and board was made as cheap as possible. The students all had to learn how to rely on the Lord alone to meet their needs.[486]

In 1934, more than ten years after the school was launched, the Lord gave Howells a vision to release the gospel to "every creature." This vision shifted the direction of the ministry and emphasized intercession for world affairs.[487] The college eventually transitioned into something like a *"house of prayer for all nations"* (Isaiah 56:7). The whole school was mobilized. In 1936, when Germany reoccupied the Rhineland, the Holy Spirit directed them to "prevail [through prayer and fasting] against Hitler."[488] During another crisis two years later, the Spirit instructed them to pray, "Lord, bend Hitler,"[489] and Great Britain's war with Germany was averted for a time. The college specifically targeted cities and countries that they felt needed intercession for protection and for maintaining open channels for proclaiming the gospel, especially in the growing international conflict. In Howells's intercession, the Lord once revealed to him that Russia would be attacked. A few weeks later, Russia was attacked by the Nazis. The school responded by specifically interceding for Moscow, which was miraculously protected from Nazi capture.[490]

Corporate Encounter and Visitation: Fire Fell on Sacrifice (1936–1937)

On March 29, 1936, Howells was stirred to call for intercessors "who will lay their lives on the altar to fight the devil, as really as they would have to fight the enemy on the western front."[491] He saw that "prayer had failed" in the conflict with Germany and that "only intercession" would take them through. Many of the students and staff went forward and surrendered their lives for the cause that day. The very next day, March 30, the following was recorded in the diary of the college meetings:

> Fire fell on sacrifice. Holy Ghost descended on evening meeting. We went on knees and someone started the chorus, "Welcome, welcome, welcome! Holy Ghost, we welcome Thee." Liberty and power so great we continued singing this one chorus for a full hour.[492]

Into the following year, there was an "increasing consciousness of God's presence." In early 1937, these stirrings became visibly manifest when one of the staff members broke down "confessing her sense of need and crying to the Holy Spirit to meet her."[493] After she did this, *"He came"* and there was a visitation for three weeks. A heavy, weighty glory of His presence fell and lingered on the whole campus. Dr. Kingsley C. Priddy, who was the headmaster of the school at the time, recalled,

> He did not come like a rushing mighty wind. But gradually the person of the Holy Ghost filled all our thoughts, His presence filled the place, and His light seemed to penetrate all the hidden recesses of our hearts. He was speaking through the Director in every meeting, but it was in the quiet of our own rooms that He revealed Himself to many of us.
>
> We felt the Holy Spirit had been a real Person to us before; as far as we knew we had received Him; and some of us had known much of His operations in and through our lives. But now the revelation of His Person was so tremendous that all our previous experiences seemed as nothing. There was no visible apparition, but He made Himself so real to our spiritual eyes that it was a "face to face" experience. And when we saw Him we knew we had never really seen Him before....
>
> ...We were people who had left all to follow the Savior, and had forsaken all we had of this world's goods to enter a life of faith, and as far as we knew we had surrendered our lives entirely to the One who died for us. But He showed us, "There is all the difference in the world between *your* surrendered life in My hands, and Me living *My* life in your body."...
>
> One by one He met us; one by one we broke in tears and contrition before Him.... One by one our wills were broken....
>
> But far greater than anything His visitation could mean to us personally was what it was going to mean to the world....
>
> There was no excitement or enthusiasm of the flesh in those days. When His power had come upon us after March 29 we had been carried away and were singing and shouting our praises. But in these days we were so awed by the holy majesty of His Person that we hardly dared raise our voices in the meetings.
>
> Even the grounds outside seemed filled with His presence. Walking around together we would suddenly be conscious that

we were speaking in whispers. The late hours came, but no one thought of bed—for God was there.... 2 and 3 a.m. often seemed just like midday as we communed together, prayed with some who were "coming through," or waited before God in the quietness of our hearts.

His visitation lasted for some three weeks in this *special* sense although, praise God, He came to "abide," and has continued with us ever since. But no one has a monopoly of the Holy Ghost. He is God, and whatever our experience of Him, He is far greater than all we can know of Him. Whatever we know of His gifts, His manifestations and His anointings, He is greater than all those.[494]

Final Years and Legacy

Rees Howells remained the director of the college until he died on February 13, 1950, of a heart attack at age seventy. Before he passed away, he raised up his son, Samuel Rees Howells, to be his successor. Samuel (who died in 2004) later passed on the legacy to Alan Scotland, who continues to direct the ministry training center as of this writing, "equipping disciples to change nations." Scotland runs the school under the new name of Trinity School of Ministry, which was relocated to Rugby, England, in 2009.[495] The school maintains focused intercession for countries around the world.[496] In 2012, the original campus of the Bible College of Wales was purchased by Cornerstone Community Church of Singapore. They are seeking to "re-dig the wells of revival" there and to use the property to help fulfill the Great Commission.[497]

Howells's "every creature" vision that caused his heart to burn to release the gospel to the whole world has seen increasing measures of fulfillment over the years. Since 1924, thousands of students have been trained at the college, and its graduates are now serving God in about fifty-two nations.[498] In the 1950s, a young German missionary named Reinhard Bonnke attended the college.[499] Since then, Bonnke has brought into the kingdom over seventy-two million people, and he continues to evangelize and bring in millions of souls.

Prophetic Inheritance

Fighting a War That's Already Won

Few people illustrated the prayer life of spiritual warfare more clearly than did Rees Howells. There is reason to believe that he and his team had a huge impact on the course of world history in his day—specifically, on World War II. Hitler's strategies were revealed to Rees and his group of intercessors ahead of time. They would pray, and Hitler's armies would be defeated. His stories read much like those of the prophets of the Old Testament who would hear from God about the plans of an enemy king. They would inform the king of Israel, and the evil plans of their enemy would fail.

This remarkable gift to shape the course of world history is available for every believer. To put it simply, it is the ability to hear from God and to pray...without ceasing. Very rarely in modern history can we trace the effect of prayer on an international event more clearly than we can with Rees Howells, partly because of the records he and his team kept concerning their prayer assignments.

In the church today, the emphasis is on what Jesus has already accomplished for us through His death and resurrection. That really is the heart of the gospel, and I'm thankful for this emphasis. I, too, am frequently grieved over the prayers of many people who seem to be trying to fight for what they already possess in Christ. Yet this emphasis sometimes seems to be made apart from the focus of Scripture, which clearly teaches that we are still engaged in a spiritual battle with the enemy. (See, for example, 1 Peter 5:8.) Some people have gone so far as to mock those who pray with the same kind of intensity that Rees Howells did, saying that such intercession is unnecessary because "God has already given us every spiritual blessing in heavenly places in Christ." (See Ephesians 1:3.) We need wisdom to navigate these apparently conflicting ideas because, although Christ won the victory over the devil two thousand years ago at Calvary and at the empty tomb, we must still battle the enemy, applying Christ's victory to our lives and circumstances, and to the lives and circumstances of others.

Both the Holy Spirit and Jesus continuously intercede for us before the Father. (See Romans 8:26–34.) If intercession were no longer needed because of Christ's victory, then the Spirit and Jesus would no longer pray on our behalf in that way! But They model the ministry of prayer perfectly. Jesus triumphed over all the powers of darkness, once and for all. His victory is forever, and it will never be lessened or diminished, regardless of how we live. He is the absolute Triumphant One over all.

Christ's victory *for* us makes victory possible *in* and *through* us. Yet the church's conflict with the enemy will exist until the final day when all the powers of darkness are once and for all sentenced to hell. (See Revelation 20:7–10, 14.) (Hell is not the place from which the devil rules to torment humanity. It is the place of his eternal judgment.) A good way to characterize the battle we are in is to say, "We don't fight *for* victory; we fight *from* victory—the victory won by our Lord Jesus Christ."

Spiritual warfare is a challenging subject, especially in relation to revivals and outpourings of the Spirit. Ephesians 6:12 reminds us that our fight is not against other people but against the powers of darkness. Let's be clear that we are no match for the devil in our own strength. He would beat us in every area of the conflict if it were not for one important fact— Jesus is our Victor, and we are in Jesus. The devil and his hordes recognize to whom we belong. Therefore, the enemy uses lies to get us to focus our attention on the problem at hand so that it appears bigger than the answers we carry. When our focus is on the problem, we give way to fear, which invites the powers of darkness into a place of influence in our lives, even though the battle has already been won by Jesus.

Much spiritual warfare is necessary on our part in order to rescue people, cities, and nations from the influence of the rulers of darkness. Multitudes have given the enemy a legal right to invade their lives. In Christ, we have been given authority over those powers. But as we pray, we often need to follow certain processes to align people with God's will. One such process is to take thoughts captive to the obedience of Christ. (See 2 Corinthians 10:5.) Through this battling in prayer, the atmosphere from which people think, perceive, and make decisions is transformed.

The answer to the challenge of conducting spiritual warfare through prayer is not so much theological, in the sense of having the right concept or doctrine to work with. Rather, our prayers must be *Presence-centered*. To learn to pray God's way requires an increasing ability to recognize the presence of God, and the heart of God, in a matter. That is what Rees Howells did so well.

Sovereign Opportunities

The somewhat frightening part of Rees Howells's story occurred when God gave him up to a certain time to decide what kind of person he was willing to be. He wrestled with God over this issue—and, thankfully, lost. Total surrender was the result.

As God's children, greatness is always in front of us, regardless of the mistakes we've made. God is the great Restorer. He is able to make up for a lifetime of wrong decisions and lead us into significance, according to His perspective. He is that good. At the same time, there are those who assume that whatever God has promised them in one season will always be available to them. While it's important not to live in regret over foolish choices or even missed opportunities, it is equally important to realize that God is God, and He has every right to make some things available to us in one moment that will not be available in another. That fact is sobering. But sometimes we need a more sobering influence over our approach to life. We must realize that delayed obedience is disobedience.

The question comes to mind, "How do we know when we're in one of those opportunities?" First of all, it's not given to the casual of heart. It's almost as though God reserves this kind of open door for those who have already displayed a hunger that grabs His attention. That kind of hunger is costly. He therefore doesn't seem to give such options to people who don't already have the momentum to make the right choice. I believe that is a wonderful display of His mercy—to not increase judgment on people who aren't prepared to make the right choice. But those who long for more, and are willing to pay any price, are given opportunities in life that are not afforded to many others. I call this posture "leaning into God." It is that place where we best anticipate the voice and the presence of God, hearing His summons to the greater things. Rees Howells lived in that *leaning* posture. That position enabled him to see what was about to happen. He lived a beautiful picture of faith in that he sensed God's heart on a matter, prayed until the burden lifted, and was then able to declare ahead of time what would occur. This is a wonderful picture of being a co-laborer with God.

Consecration

Few have modeled the consecrated life as well as this hero of the faith who was possessed by God. His description of the moment of his absolute surrender is one of the most glorious and frightening accounts recorded in church history. I remember the sobering effect it had on me as a young man, and yet I couldn't get enough of it. It wasn't a fear of God that drove me from Him. Not hardly. It was a paradoxical fear that endeared me to Him. Joyful fear (see Psalm 2:11) is one of the greatest mysteries of life, understood only by those who live in it.

A consecration experience such as Howells had cannot be sold to someone as though they were buying a car. Nor is it something one can buy into or use one's self will to enter into and sustain. It is possible only to a person who has had a defining moment. It is the product of the Presence who has fallen upon a person. I don't think it is possible for someone to reasonably come to a place of consecrated surrender through a theological posture alone. There must be an "I was overcome in His presence" type of experience that becomes known as the "face-to-face" moment, as happened with Rees Howells.

I remember telling people about the Rees Howells moment of surrender, hoping to bring many others into the same experience. As noble as that ambition might have been, it was foolish. It's never wise to make the outcome itself our focus or priority, because it distorts the process. Some people try to do the same thing in relation to worship. It is biblical to say that the powers of darkness are driven away from a situation through worship. (See, for example, Psalm 68:1–2.) But the moment battling the devil becomes the focus, it is no longer worship. True worship is based on God's worthiness, not on our need to triumph over the devil. The devil is not worthy of such attention.

Rees Howells's consecration was the result of his encounter with Jesus, who told him things beyond his imagination. His experience seems so similar to the experience of Saul, who became the apostle Paul and heard *"inexpressible words"* (2 Corinthians 12:4) in God's presence. Paul's greatness in consecration to Christ, his accomplishments for the honor of His name, and his sufferings for the cause of the gospel were the fruit of his defining moment. They were clearly the outcome of Paul's encounter with Jesus Christ on the road to Damascus. (See Acts 9:1–31.)

After reading a book about someone's lifestyle of devotion to Christ, it is unintentional cruelty to preach it as an example to others as though they could have that lifestyle without first experiencing a defining moment. All that accomplishes is frustrating people, and piling on more guilt and shame about what they have not attained spiritually. Instead, we should be preaching about *the encounter.* Our message should be about seeking God's face, about being willing to pay any price for the "more" that God has promised to all who seek Him. Then, His presence must become more and more manifest in our corporate gatherings. The work of the gospel is so much easier when the King of Glory is gloriously manifested.

Postscript

In the life of Rees Howells, we see once again that the encounter made the person. Howells was heroic in his approach to prayer, which was the overflow of his life of total consecration to God. Again, we see that fire always falls on sacrifice. Howells became the offering that the fire of God fell upon, and the rest is history.

One of the parts of his story that is often forgotten is the fact that his personal breakthrough with God became corporate blessing. It's not that others didn't need to have their own encounter with God. They did. It's just that his community of like-minded people had available to them things that they probably wouldn't have had access to on their own. This result is consistent with the concept of biblical inheritance, in which someone receives an inheritance that someone else paid a price for. Now we just have to learn to pay a price to increase what we have freely received so that we have something to give to the next generation.[500]

Rees Howells's story, like the stories of many others who experienced God-encounters, is one of numerous defining moments. Some might call them many baptisms in the Spirit. Others might have another name for them. It really doesn't matter what they're called as long as we welcome the Holy Spirit and respond to His invitation of total abandonment to the only One who has the right to rule in our lives.

Spiritual Hunger:
Aimee Semple McPherson

"Oh, Lord, I am so hungry for your Holy Spirit.
You have told me that in the day when I seek with my whole heart
you will be found of me. Now, Lord, I am going to stay right here
until you pour out upon me the promise of the Holy Spirit for
whom you commanded me to tarry, if I die of starvation.
I am so hungry for Him I can't wait another day. I will not eat
another meal until you baptize me."[501]
—*Aimee Semple McPherson*

Aimee Semple McPherson was a household name for me when
I was growing up, because various members of my family were
connected with her ministry. My grandpa, a housepainter as well as a pastor, painted her home and did artistic work on her ceilings. My uncle, David
Morken, was a soloist in her ministry for a season. I remember my grandparents telling me stories of what it was like in her day. I now understand why

they longed for "more of God." They had tasted it for themselves through her ministry.

My wife and I attended Uncle David's ninetieth birthday party, which was attended by a number of other relatives and friends who were also a part of Aimee Semple McPherson's ministry. I'll never forget overhearing several of them talking as they sat together at a nearby table. Somehow, the subject turned to Aimee and to the days of her miracle ministry. They began to speak quite softly, as though they knew something few others could understand. Revival, miracles, and living full of the Holy Spirit were all themes that moved me in indescribable ways, so I became silent and leaned ever so slightly in their direction to hear more clearly. Finally, I heard one of them say, "It was like heaven on earth." That was it. It was like the knockout punch in a boxing match. I knew I had heard something from heaven that would forever mark my life. "Heaven on earth." It became apparent to me how the answer to the prayer *"Your will be done on earth as it is in heaven"* (Matthew 6:10; Luke 11:2) is to be manifested—through miracles, signs, and wonders that bring glory to Jesus.

Early Spiritual "Deposits" from God

Aimee Semple McPherson (1890–1944) was a woman ahead of her time who greatly impacted the church in the twentieth century. Several spiritual "deposits" in her life in her early years contributed to her impact later on. Her dedication at birth was a significant act of consecration on the part of her mother. Then, in 1907, Aimee received a special ordination from God while reading the book of Jeremiah. A year later, she was born again. It wasn't long before she was baptized in the Holy Spirit and spoke in tongues. Shortly after this, she got married and had her first child.

Following the unexpected death of her first husband, she remarried and had a second child but soon became sick. When she rededicated her life wholeheartedly to the Lord, she was healed. Her act of surrender and subsequent healing marked a defining moment in her life. Almost immediately after this, in 1915, she left her husband at home to pursue her call to ministry. She attended a camp meeting in Kitchener, Ontario, and was reignited for evangelism. From that point on, her ministry began to grow and flourish.

In the 1920s, Aimee built her 5,300-seat Angelus Temple, and during the Great Depression, she fed more people than the Red Cross and all other organizations in Los Angeles. She was one of the first women evangelists on the radio, and she also started her own radio station. While miracles, signs, and wonders followed her ministry, she was most passionate about leading people to Jesus and seeing them baptized in the Holy Spirit.[502]

Dedication at Birth

One year before Aimee was born, her mother, Minnie Kennedy, was stirred while reading about Hannah in the Bible. She then made the following vow to the Lord:

> Oh Lord, You called me to preach the Gospel, but somehow I have failed You and cannot go, but if You will only hear my prayer, as You heard Hannah's prayer of old, and give me a little baby girl, I will give her unreservedly into your service, that she may preach the word I should have preached, fill the place I should have filled, and live the life I should have lived in Thy service. O Lord, hear and answer me; give me the witness that Thou hast heard me, O Lord, for Thine own Name's sake. Amen.[503]

This seed planted in God's heart emerged a year later when Aimee was born on October 9, 1890, in Ontario, Canada. Through her mother's act of surrender, Aimee had been set aside for the Lord's work even before she was born. When Aimee was only a few weeks old, her parents dedicated her once more at their Salvation Army service.

Ordained to Preach the Gospel

Even though Aimee grew up with the influences of the Salvation Army and read the Bible, she did not have a strong faith in her early years. When she was a teenager, she struggled with the theory of evolution and called out to God to find out if He was real. Part of her struggle involved the fact that she read about miracles in the Bible but did not see any manifest in her day. Then, in 1907, she encountered God while reading Jeremiah 1:4–10. She felt that God was calling her to be a prophet to the nations, even though she was still very young. These Scriptures confirmed that God was truly calling her and that He would put His words in her mouth. Aimee later recalled that special time:

> When I was a little girl seventeen years of age, the Lord spoke these words plainly into my startled ears, as I was alone in my bedroom praying one day. It was a solemn time when He ordained me there to preach the Gospel. At first it seemed too astounding and impossible to be true that the Lord would ever call such a simple, unworthy little country girl as I to go out and preach the Gospel but the call and ordination were so real that, although later set apart and ordained by the saints of God, the memory of my little bedroom, flooded with the glory of God as He spoke those words has always been to me my real ordination.[504]

Born Again

In 1908, Aimee was introduced to Pentecostalism when she attended a meeting with her father that was led by Irish evangelist Robert Semple. He spoke on Acts 2 and called people to repent. Aimee remembered that there was "no appeal for money. Not even a collection was taken. It was just God, God, God from one end to the other, and his words seemed to rain down upon me, and every one of them hurt some particular part of my spirit and life until I could not tell where I was hurt the worst."[505] Robert Semple spoke about how salvation and the baptism of the Spirit should happen side by side because "for a Christian to live without the baptism of the Holy Spirit was to live in an abnormal condition not in accordance with God's wishes."[506] He also spoke in tongues, a practice that was unfamiliar to Aimee.

For the next three days, Aimee struggled with what she thought she would have to give up if she gave herself wholeheartedly to God: novels, dancing, the theatre, and secular music. She even asked God not to let her die until after she had participated in the Christmas play so she could make her decision for Christ after that. She could barely eat or sleep. On the third day after hearing the Pentecostal message, while coming home from school, she could not hold out any longer:

> Utterly at the end of myself—not stopping to think what preachers or entertainment committees or anyone else would think—I threw up my hands, and all alone in that country road, I screamed aloud toward the heavens: "Oh, Lord God, be merciful to me, a sinner!" Immediately the most wonderful change took place in my soul. Darkness passed away and light entered.... So conscious was I of the pardoning blood of Jesus that I seemed to feel it flowing over me. I discovered that my face was bathed in tears, which dropped on my hands as I held the reins. And without effort or apparent thought on my part I was singing that old, familiar hymn:

> "Take my life and let it be
>
> Consecrated, Lord, to Thee;
>
> Take my moments and my days,
>
> Let them flow in ceaseless praise."

> I was singing brokenly between my sobs:

> "Take my life and let it be
>
> Consecrated, Lord, to Thee."

> My whole soul was flowing out toward God, my Father....

> When I came to the part in the song that said

> "Take my hands and let them move
>
> At the impulse of Thy love"

> I knew there would be no more worldly music for me, and it has been hymns from that time forth....

> Nevertheless the succeeding days were brim full of joy and happiness. How dearly I loved God's Word! I wanted it under my pillow when I went to sleep, and in my hands when my eyes opened in the morning. At school, where I used to have a novel hidden away

inside of my Algebra and Geometry, there was now a little New Testament, and I was studying each passage that referred to the baptism of the Holy Spirit.[507]

Hungering for More

Aimee's born-again experience stirred up a new hunger within her. She was obsessed with this thing that Robert Semple had called the baptism of the Holy Spirit. She had to have it. Her mind was consumed with being fully possessed by the Holy Spirit.

> Of all the promises in which I found comfort there was none, I believe, that compared with the simple promises of Matthew 7:7 to 11. "*Ask, and it shall be given you; seek, and ye shall find; knock, and it shall be opened unto you....*"

> I would get about so far with my reading, and Oh, the Bible seemed to me all so new, so living and speaking (and it was God speaking to me), that unable to wait another moment, I would excuse myself from the room, go down to the basement, fall upon my knees and begin to pray: "Oh Lord, baptize me with the Holy Spirit. Lord, you said the promise was unto even as many as were afar off, even as many as the Lord our God should call. Now Lord, you've called me, the promise is unto me; fill me just now."

> The girls found me thus praying and did not know what to make of me, so utterly was I changed. No more putting glue in teacher's chair or helping to lock him in the gymnasium, or practicing dance steps in the corridors at noon hour. A wonderful change had taken place—all old things had passed away and all things had become new. I had been born again and was a new creature in Christ Jesus.

> Each day the hunger for the baptism of the Holy Spirit became stronger and stronger, more and more intense until, no longer contented to stay in school, my mind no longer on my studies, I would slip away to the tarrying meetings where the dear saints met to pray for those who were seeking the baptism of the Holy Spirit.[508]

Opposition

Aimee's high school principal sent a letter to her mother about how distracted she was from her studies. That same day, a Salvation Army officer warned her mother of the dangers of Aimee being associated with the Pentecostal mission because they saw that the "so-called power was all excitement or hypnotism and false."[509] When Aimee returned home from school that day, she was forbidden to go to any more Pentecostal "tarrying" meetings. She remembered,

> I went to school on the train the next morning as the roads were banked high with snow, and all the way in I was looking out of the window at the falling flakes of snow and praying for the Lord to fix it all some way so that I should be able to knock until He opened or else to baptize me at once.
>
> Walking from the train to High School it was necessary to pass both the Mission and the Sister's home where I often went to tarry for the baptism. As I went past the latter I looked longingly at the windows, hoping that she might be there and that I could speak to her from the sidewalk without going in and thus disobeying Mother's command, but not a sign of her did I see. I walked slowly past, looking sadly and hungrily back all the way; then finally came to a halt on the sidewalk and said to myself:
>
> "Well, here now, Jesus is coming soon and you know it is more important for you to receive the Holy Spirit than to pass all the examinations in the world. You need the Holy Spirit—oil in your vessel with your lamp—in order to be ready for His appearing. As you have to make a choice between going to school and seeking the baptism I guess you won't go to school at all today, but will just go back to sister's house and make a whole day of seeking the baptism."[510]

God Sent Snow

With this I turned and walked quickly back to the house, rang the doorbell and went in. I told the sister my dilemma, and she said quietly: "Let's tell Father about it." So we got down and began to pray. She asked the Lord in her prayer either to baptize me then and there or to arrange it some way that I could stay until I received my baptism. The Lord heard this prayer, and outside the window the snow which had been falling in light flakes, began to come down like a blinding blizzard. My heavenly Father sent out His angels to stir up some of those big, old, fleecy clouds of His, and down came the snow—and causing the window-panes to rattle, and one of our old-fashioned Canadian blizzards was on.

The entire day was spent in prayer and at night on going to the depot to see about my train home, the ticket agent said, through the window: "Sorry, Miss, but the train is not running tonight. The roads are blocked with snow. We are not able to get through." Oh, Hallelujah! I was not sorry a bit. Then the thought came— "This will not do you much good, for you will have to call Mother on the telephone and she will ask you to go to her friend's home to stay and warn you not to go near the Mission." But when I went to the telephone and gave the number, Central said: "Sorry, wires all down on account of the storm." This time I did shout "Glory" and ran almost all the way back to the sister's home.

The storm increased, and as fast as the men endeavored to open a pathway, the Lord filled it in with mountains of white snow, until at last all thought of getting through while the storm lasted was abandoned. Oh, how earnestly I sought the baptism of the Spirit.

...Time was precious, for while man was working so hard to shovel out the snow, and God had His big clouds all working to shovel it in, I must do my part in seeking with all my heart.[511]

Baptized in the Spirit

Friday I waited before the Lord until midnight. Saturday morning, rising at the break of day, before anyone was astir, in the house, and going into the parlor, I knelt down by the big Morris chair in the corner, with a real determination in my heart.

...Now Jesus *was* my friend; He had bidden me knock, and assured me that He *would* open unto me. He had invited me to ask, promising that I should receive, and that the empty He would not turn hungry away. I began to seek in desperate earnest, and remember saying:

"Oh, Lord, I am so hungry for your Holy Spirit. You have told me that in the day when I seek with my whole heart you will be found of me. Now, Lord, I am going to stay right here until you pour out upon me the promise of the Holy Spirit for whom you commanded me to tarry, if I die of starvation. I am so hungry for Him I can't wait another day. I will not eat another meal until you baptize me."

After praying this earnestly—storming heaven, as it were, with my pleadings for the Holy Spirit, a quietness seemed to steal over me, the holy presence of the Lord to envelop me. The Voice of the Lord spoke tenderly: "Now, child, cease your strivings and your begging; just begin to praise Me, and in simple, child-like faith, receive ye the Holy Ghost."[512]

Waves of Electricity

Oh, it was not hard to praise Him. He had become so near and so inexpressibly dear to my heart. Hallelujah! Without effort on my part I began to say: "Glory to Jesus! Glory to Jesus! GLORY TO JESUS!!!" Each time that I said "Glory to Jesus!" it seemed to come from a deeper place in my being than the last, and in a deeper voice, until great waves of "Glory to Jesus" were rolling from my toes up; such adoration and praise I had never known possible.

All at once my hands and arms began to shake, gently at first, then violently, until my whole body was shaking under the power of the Holy Spirit. I did not consider this at all strange, as I knew how the batteries we experimented with in the laboratory at college hummed and shook and trembled under the power of electricity, and there was the Third Person of the Trinity coming into my body in all His fullness, making me His dwelling, "the temple of the Holy Ghost." Was it any wonder that this poor human frame of mine should quake beneath the mighty moving of His power?

...Almost without my notice was my body slipped gently to the floor, and I was lying stretched out under the power of God, but felt as though caught up and floating upon the billowy clouds of glory.... The desire to praise and worship and adore Him flamed up within my soul. He was so wonderful, so glorious, and this poor tongue of mine so utterly incapable of finding words with which to praise Him.

My lungs began to fill and heave under the power as the Comforter came in. The cords of my throat began to twitch—my chin began to quiver, and then to shake violently, but Oh, so sweetly! My tongue began to move up and down and sideways in my mouth. Unintelligible sounds as of stammering lips and another tongue, spoken of in Isaiah 28:11, began to issue from my lips. This stammering of different syllables, then words, then connected sentences, was continued for some time as the Spirit was teaching me to yield to Him. Then suddenly, out of my innermost being flowed rivers of praise in other tongues as the Spirit gave utterance (Acts 2:4), and Oh I knew that He was praising Jesus with glorious language, clothing Him with honor and glory which I felt but never could have put into words....

Hearing me speaking in the tongues and praising the Lord, the dear Sister of the home in which I stayed, came down stairs and into the parlor, weeping and praising the Lord with me. Soon Brother Semple and other saints gathered in. What shouting and rejoicing! Oh hallelujah! And yet with all the joy and glory, there was a stillness and a solemn hush pervading my whole being....

The next day was Sunday. The storm had cleared away; the sun was shining down in its melting warmth. Attending the morning services at the Mission, we partook of the Lord's Supper, and as we meditated upon His wonderful love, His blood that was shed for us, His body that was broken on the tree, it was more than I could bear, and I went down to the floor under the power again. Oh who can describe that exceeding weight of glory as He revealed Himself, my crucified Savior, my resurrected Lord, my coming King! School-mates and friends were standing up to look over the seats to see what in the world had happened to me, but I was lost again with Jesus whom my soul loved, speaking in tongues and shaking under the power.[513]

Immediately after Aimee's powerful encounters, she experienced some resistance from those closest to her. A family friend noticed her behavior at church and called her mother, who came straight to the service, picked Aimee up, and scolded her all the way home. Her parents concluded that she must never go to the Pentecostal mission again, or they would take her out of school. Aimee acknowledged that the Word of God says to obey one's parents. She also challenged her mother to show her from the Bible where it says not to be baptized in the Holy Spirit or to speak in tongues. If her mother could prove her wrong, then she would yield.

When Aimee went off to school the next day, her mother started studying the Bible right at the breakfast table. When Aimee came home that night, she saw her mother sitting in the same spot, with her eyes swollen from crying. Her mother said, "Well, dear, I must admit that of a truth, *this is that which was spoken of by the prophet Joel, which should come to pass in the last days!*" At that, they danced and rejoiced together.[514]

Divine Healing and First Sermon Spark

In 1908, not long after her Pentecostal Spirit baptism, Aimee married Robert Semple. They planted a church in Canada and spent the next two years raising money to be missionaries in China. In 1909, they went to Chicago, Illinois, to see Pentecostal pastor and theologian William Durham, who ordained Robert. During a trip to Ohio, Durham prayed for Aimee's ankle, which had been badly injured in a fall, and she was instantly healed. Immediately after, she cut her cast off and began to dance. This introduced her to divine healing.[515]

On their way to China in 1910, the Semples stopped over in England and went to a Pentecostal meeting led by Cecil Polhill, one of the original "Cambridge Seven" who helped build the China Inland Mission. Polhill invited Aimee to speak. Without any preparation or practice, she preached for an hour to an audience of fifteen thousand people. The Lord gave her a vision of Joel 2:25 and the importance of restoring the years the locusts had eaten.[516] She believed that while she was speaking, the Holy Spirit possessed her and spoke through her in "tongues," except for this time it was in English.[517]

All this happened before Aimee turned twenty. Not long after she and her husband arrived on the mission field in China in 1910, they both contracted malaria. Sadly, Robert died on August 17, 1910, but Aimee recovered and gave birth to her first child, a daughter she named Roberta. Shortly after, Aimee returned to the United States to be with her mother.

Activation

In 1912, Aimee married Harold McPherson. In March 1913, they had a son named Rolf. Following this, Aimee went into a deep depression and became very ill. In 1914, she got sick again and, after several surgeries, was near death. Her mother remembered the promise she had made to God years before and petitioned Him for a miracle. During this time, Aimee heard God ask her again if she would go out and preach the gospel. She recalled, "I realized that I was either going into the grave or out into the field with the gospel. I made my decision and gasped out the words, 'Yes—Lord—I'll—go!' Instantly, new life and warmth surged through my being. I was healed."[518]

After her recovery, Aimee tried but failed to fit into the life of a housewife. In 1915, she left Harold to pursue her calling. She wrote him a letter inviting him to join her and the children in ministry.[519] Shortly after, she attended a Pentecostal camp meeting in Kitchener, Ontario, Canada, while her mother watched the children. While there, she wanted to do anything she could for Jesus, so she washed dishes, waited on tables, and led the choir. By the close of the weekend, the lead minister had lost his voice, and she was given the opportunity to preach in an evening meeting. Eleven people were converted that night. During the camp meeting, Aimee fell under the power of the Spirit again, and she also prayed for many to receive the baptism of the Holy Spirit.

Beginnings of Preaching Ministry

Two weeks later, she responded to an invitation to preach in the small town of Mount Forest, Ontario. She advertised an evangelistic meeting, but only three attended. She left the mission and went to the town center, stood on a chair, held her arms up high, and froze in that position for some time. This Salvation Army tactic drew a crowd of nearly fifty. After a few minutes, she jumped down and told the crowd to follow her. They ran after her right to the mission. When they had all entered, she had someone close the door behind them. Now that she had a "captive" audience, she preached the gospel. Aimee continued to conduct meetings for several days and baptized sixty in the river and saw seventy baptized in the Holy Spirit.[520] Like Maria Woodworth-Etter, Aimee used nearly all of the offering money to buy a tent so she could begin her evangelistic campaigns.[521] The momentum had begun, and Aimee's ministry began to take off.

Los Angeles

In 1916, Aimee had enough money to buy a vehicle and transform it into a "Gospel Car." She drove throughout the country, camped on the side of the road, and facilitated tent meetings as she went.[522] In 1917, she started a newspaper called *The Bridal Call*. She released her book *This Is That: Personal Experiences, Sermons and Writings of Aimee Semple McPherson* in 1919, and the same year traveled with her mother and children to set up a ministry base in Los Angeles, California.[523] In 1921, her husband divorced her on grounds of abandonment. Following this, she began to minister more internationally.

From 1917–1923, Aimee preached across the United States six times, speaking in over one hundred cities. Aimee was known for her theatrical performances in the pulpit. She creatively communicated the gospel in engaging ways that tapped into the culture and spoke the language of the people. In 1921, when Aimee arrived in San Diego to hold meetings, she first headed to the sold-out boxing ring to invite people to her services. She asked the manager if he would introduce her in between rounds. When she walked into the ring, she called for all present to find the "worst sinners" in the city and bring them to her meeting the following night. The response was great, and many were saved.[524]

Aimee stepped out in faith to pay five thousand dollars down to build a church in Los Angeles. Originally, this was just going to be a platform for her to speak, but it quickly developed into a church. After the construction had already begun, she traveled around doing revival circuits to raise the rest of the money. By the time the work was finished, she was able to pay for it in full, debt-free. On January 1, 1923, she dedicated Angelus Temple, which held up to 5,300 people, marking the foundation of the Foursquare Church denomination. In 1923, she also opened a Bible school, which later became known as L.I.F.E. (Lighthouse of International Foursquare Evangelism) Bible College.

Aimee's influence continued to spread as she utilized multimedia and the creative arts. She became the first woman preacher on the radio, and in 1924 she launched her own radio station, KFSG.

Signs and Wonders in Ministry

In her ministry, Aimee regularly invited the presence and power of God. As a result, unique signs and wonders were released. The following is a sampling of some of them.

One time, Aimee experienced a financial miracle when, having only eighteen dollars, she was able to drive from Savannah, Georgia, to Long Branch, New Jersey (over seven hundred eighty miles) without running out of gas. She even had some money left over.[525] Another time, in Wichita, when the weather would have prevented more people from making it to her meeting, she prayed that the rains would be held back. At her rebuke, the rain ceased.[526] She once spoke in tongues in Spanish and interpreted it by sharing a message in English. She later found out that she had spoken the exact translation of what she had said in Spanish.[527] People reported heavenly worship filling her meetings.[528] In a "Colored Camp Meeting" on the island of Key West, Florida, racial divides were abolished. One participant reported that "it was impossible to keep the white people away. So for the first time in the Island the white and colored attended the same place of worship and glorified the same Lord side by side."[529] While attending one of Aimee's meetings, John G. Lake's wife was baptized in the Spirit and spoke in tongues.[530] Aimee also gave space to the children who experienced God in powerful ways to preach and to minister.[531] Additionally, in her meetings, many people were healed of infirmities like cancer, blindness, lameness, and heart trouble.

The "slain in the Spirit" also became a mark of Aimee's ministry as it was of Maria Woodworth-Etter's. Elizabeth Sisson, who was at one time a coeditor with Carrie Judd Montgomery, reported on the occurrence of this sign at one of Aimee's ecumenical camp meetings.

> We had two thousand chairs in the tent. These were all filled an hour or so before preaching service began. Then all around the tent they stood, ten, fifteen deep, in profound attention for an hour and a half or two hours. Crowds composed of every nationality.... The power and demonstration of the Spirit was wonderful.... The "slain of the Lord were many." The whole altar was filled with them from end to end, daily the most wonderful baptisms in the Spirit.[532]

Aimee did not have preconceived notions about how the Holy Spirit should show up but was open to whatever His visitation might look like, manifestations or not. She said,

> So many people I find have got it all fixed up in their minds just how the Holy Spirit is going to come to them. Some feel that He is to come to them as a still, small dove, in a gentle way as they sit in their seats, or as they kneel in a dignified manner at the altar. To such He usually comes as a mighty, rushing wind, slaying them under the power and giving mighty manifestations. Others have it all figured out that the Holy Spirit is to come to them as a great dynamic, explosive power, accompanied with a mighty, rushing wind and tongues of flame and great manifestations. To these He sometimes comes as the still, small dove, and quietly fills them, speaking through them in other tongues softly and tenderly, the glorious praises of Jesus and the message of His coming. But in whatsoever form He comes, do not doubt Him. You have invited Him to come, now just receive Him. When you come to the altar, come determined to praise God. Come not to seek, but to receive.[533]

Final Days

Although many people flocked to Angelus Temple, including movie stars and the affluent, controversy surrounded Aimee later in life.[534] In May

1926, she disappeared while at the beach. Two people died while looking for her in the ocean. When she reemerged in a town far away a few weeks after this incident, she claimed kidnapping. Then, in 1931, she married a singer at her church named David Hutton but filed for divorce in 1933. Her popularity with the public suffered some as a result.

Even so, she remained very busy with her ministry endeavors. It is reported that in one 150-day period in the 1930s, she "toured the country, traveled more than fifteen thousand miles, visited forty-six cities, broadcast on forty-five radio stations and delivered three hundred and thirty-six sermons, sometimes as many as five in a single day."[535]

During the Great Depression, Aimee's ministry fed more of the poor in Los Angeles than the government did; from the late 1920s through the Depression, she provided food for over 1.5 million people.[536] Additionally, in the Second World War, "she sold more war bonds than the most famous Hollywood stars."[537] These were remarkable accomplishments in the midst of challenging times. Despite the circumstances, Aimee used the influence and platform God had given her to bless her community and nation. During hard times, she released good news and brought hope to desperate people. She did not shrink back from the crises of her day but met them head-on to pioneer a better way.

Then, tragically, on September 27, 1944, after sharing her life message to crowds of ten thousand in Oakland, Aimee died in her hotel room, reportedly of an accidental overdose of sleeping pills.[538]

Legacy

At the time of this writing, the Foursquare Church that Aimee founded had more than seventeen hundred churches in the United States, with more than sixty-six thousand churches and meeting places worldwide in one hundred forty countries and territories.[539] Aimee utilized the arts, the media, and the entertainment world to reach the lost in a way that no one had done before. Again, she spoke to her generation in a language they could understand. And she greatly impacted the city of Los Angeles during the Great Depression. Healings, signs, and wonders, including financial miracles and people being slain in the Spirit, occurred in her ministry.

Like Maria Woodworth-Etter, Carrie Judd Montgomery, Phoebe Palmer (a holiness evangelist and writer), and others who came before her, Aimee is an inspiration for women in ministry.[540] Her example helped to pave new paths for women to venture out into their God-given destinies. She is also an inspiration for all people to step outside of the boxes that confine them. She is a vanguard for releasing the gospel in creative ways that speak to the heart of the people and transform culture.

Prophetic Inheritance

Hunger for God

Aimee's hunger for God can be seen in her passion to receive the baptism in the Holy Spirit. This gift is anchored in a promise found in God's Word. Jesus said that if we were to ask our earthly father for a fish, He would not give us a serpent instead. And God, as the perfect Father, is even more committed to giving the Holy Spirit to those who ask for Him. (See Luke 11:9–13.) Aimee sought the face of God based on this promise. She believed that God was true to His Word and would give her what she asked for.

As simple as that may seem, such faith is all too uncommon. Many people are afraid to ask God for what has been made available to us through the promises in the Scriptures, as well as in the lifestyle that Jesus modeled for us. Fearmongers would warn us of possible deception when seeking the Spirit or learning to live according to His voice—creating a picture in which, in practice, the devil in bigger than their God. Leaders in the church should not fear deception more than they trust God, or they will birth the kind of unhealthy fear that defiles many.

Can spiritual deception occur? Yes, of course; history has proven that. When it happens, it's always tragic and horribly unnecessary. Being teachable and humble in studying the Scriptures, as well as living in accountability to legitimate spiritual authority, can help to keep a person from falling into deception. But we must also recognize that the person who isn't hungry for what God has promised is deceived, as well. Not to hunger spiritually is to live against our reason for being, violating our very design. We were born to step into His purposes, demonstrating His love, purity, and power. Not to hunger for "more" is to suppress our God-given appetite.

Manifestations and Power

Waves of electricity surged through Aimee's body in her Holy Spirit baptism. This kind of encounter was never meant to be only a one-time event. Some experiences that seem too good to be true are supposed to be much more frequent. And such encounters are more common in history than many might think. Extreme encounters are seldom broadcast, and they are sometimes even edited out of revival books. It is scary when history reconstructionists change the record to make a lack of spiritual experience look normal. It is not reasonable to think that the God of all power could touch a person in a transformational way without the possibility of physical manifestations. There are wonderful historical records of mighty outpourings of the Spirit, with similar results recorded from the past two thousand years of church history.

I am so thankful that some of our heroes of the faith have shared their experiences with us. While it's not wise to require that God touch us in exactly the same way as He did another, it's good to recognize how He has ministered to people throughout history. It gives us an understanding of His works so that we might be more aware of what He is doing in our own lives. Here are just a few descriptions of Aimee's experience: "My whole body was shaking under the power of the Holy Spirit"; "I was lying stretched out under the power of God"; "I went down to the floor under the power again. Oh who can describe that exceeding weight of glory...!"; and "I was lost again..., speaking in tongues and shaking under the power." The result of this encounter in her life was quite remarkable. During her ministry, the dying were often lined up all across the front of Angelus Temple for prayer. She would even host "Stretcher Days" in some of her campaigns where people brought their dying loved ones on stretchers.[541] Her faith for miracles was so great that person after person would get up off of their deathbed, healed for the glory of God. Angelus Temple still has storage rooms filled with crutches, wheelchairs, and other implements discarded by the infirm who were healed.

Creativity in Sharing the Gospel

Aimee Semple McPherson loved bringing people to Christ. It was the greatest priority of her life and ministry because the conversion of a soul is the most wonderful miracle of all. She was known for reaching the poorest of the poor, but she also reached the elite of her city through her expertise in the arts. Hollywood came to see her in order to learn from her. She presented the gospel through drama, music, and any other medium she could use to communicate it well. Her creativity is one of the rarer expressions found in the ministries of revivalists. It's one I take personal delight in because we tend to think that being filled with the Holy Spirit has to do with power alone. But in Exodus 31:1–5, we read of one who was filled with the Spirit and manifested God's nature through creativity and excellence in workmanship. To more completely display God's greatness, we must do better in our stewardship of the creative arts, and celebrate those who have such gifts instead of labeling their ministries as second-class—or even worse, as *secular*.

Aimee's creativity reached beyond the stage. True artists don't turn their gift on and off. The artistic mind-set is an approach to life that affects everything. It's not confined to a canvas, a stage, or an instrument. Artists think and see differently, and we need them.

I'm so thankful that Aimee Semple McPherson was mature enough not to assume that if she enjoyed the arts, God must be against them. I know there are times when God asks us to lay down our gifts at His feet, possibly never to pick them up again. Moses did that with his rod, which represented his personal history and livelihood. When God told Moses to pick up the rod again, it became the rod of the Lord. (See Exodus 4:1–5, 17.) God is not opposed to our gifts—He gave them to us. He is opposed to our serving our gifts instead of serving Him. Our gifts are to be called the gifts of the Lord.

Aimee became a much fuller expression of the love of a perfect Father by excelling in her gifts in a way that brought people to Him. Jesus said, *"Let your light shine before men in such a way that they may see your good works, and glorify your Father who is in heaven"* (Matthew 5:16 NASB). Aimee did this well.

Bold Faith for Finances

Many of those who have experienced defining moments have had unusual faith for finances to support their ministries. It's been that way throughout history. The Lord enabled Aimee to raise all the funds she needed to build what many would call the greatest sanctuary in North America, completing the construction debt-free. Aimee's passion for excellence was displayed in Angelus Temple, as well. There's a difference between careless extravagance and excellence. She chose the latter. And in doing so, she illustrated the perfect Father, who is the God of "more than enough."

Postscript

Defining moments change everything about us, causing us to see and to think in a new way. People who do things differently than most are often heavily criticized and opposed by the church; they are called worldly, anti-biblical, or other demeaning phrases in an attempt to manipulate them to back down. True heroes hold their course, knowing that an accurate expression of God is dependent upon their manifesting their uniqueness. For Aimee, that manifestation was the unusual combination of the arts and miracles. She valued beauty in a way that represented God well. Some people forget that God gives *"beauty for ashes"* (Isaiah 61:3). This was His idea.

A humble passion for God brought Aimee Semple McPherson into the forefront of ministry in a day when women were not usually accepted in that position. But her encounter with God made it impossible for her to keep quiet. Perhaps that is what is needed once again—people so full of God that it is impossible for them to keep quiet about Him.

Anointing:
Kathryn Kuhlman

"On the day of Pentecost, they were all filled with the Holy
Ghost. That hour is at hand, my friend, when there will be times
even in moments such as this when there will be such oneness
in the Spirit, when the Holy Ghost is come upon those in the
assembly. Those who know absolutely nothing about the Holy
Spirit, and great waves of glory will come upon them and every
person present will be filled with the Holy Spirit and receive the
baptism of the Holy Spirit. I believe that."[542]
—*Kathryn Kuhlman*

As a young man, I was privileged to see Kathryn Kuhlman minister a few times, both in Sacramento and at the Shrine Auditorium in Southern California. She was a larger-than-life figure. I only wish I had been as aware of the privilege then as I am now; the primary values of my life at that time were not *kingdom* enough to fully benefit from her ministry. Even so, I was powerfully impacted by these experiences.

The Manifest Presence of the Holy Spirit

Kathryn Kuhlman lived with such devotion to—and awareness of—the Holy Spirit that she set the standard for that spiritual value. To me, one of the huge secrets of the anointing is the manifest presence of the Holy Spirit, which enables us to do supernatural works. I have pursued this concept of "hosting the presence of God" for many years. I'm sure that somewhere in the back of my mind, I learned it from Kathryn Kuhlman. It's one thing to live in an awareness of the Holy Spirit in ministry; it's another to host Him in life itself.

Kathryn Kuhlman (1907–1976) is among the most well-known female healing evangelists. She first encountered the Holy Spirit in a profound way at her conversion when she was fourteen years old. Shortly after, she was stirred to pursue even more of the Holy Spirit. In the midst of this season, she felt God call her to a life of ministry, which she entered into with some success. Over twenty years later, in 1944, while walking on a dead-end street, she had a revelation that caused her to surrender everything, even her husband, to the Lord. Two years later, while she was teaching on the Holy Spirit in one of her meetings, a woman was healed of a tumor. After this woman gave her testimony in the meeting the next day, healings, signs, and wonders were released in great measure through Kathryn's ministry—and this lesser-known evangelist became a national sensation.

Conversion Encounter

Kathryn Kuhlman was born on May 9, 1907, in Concordia, Missouri, of German parents. One of four children, she grew up under a strict mother, from whom she was distant, and a kind, loving father, to whom she was very close. At fourteen, Kathryn attended a Methodist church meeting where she first experienced the conviction of the Holy Spirit.

I cannot tell you what the preacher said at that service, or what hymns were sung. But suddenly something happened to me.... I began to tremble. This was my first experience with the Holy Spirit. Suddenly I felt like the meanest, lowest person in the whole world. I trembled so violently I couldn't hold the hymn book. It was my first contact with the power of God. I sat down in the pew and sobbed.... On the way home from church everything looked brighter, more beautiful. My feet didn't touch the sidewalk.[543]

Call to Ministry and Increased Hunger

Within several years of her conversion, she received a clear call into ministry. She remembered, "If everybody in the world told me that as a woman I have no right to preach the Gospel, it would have no effect upon me whatsoever, because my call to the ministry was as definite as my conversion."[544] Kathryn continued to be consumed with a deep hunger for more of God.

Oh, it seemed that every atom of my being cried out for more of Him. I've known physical hunger, but I have never known a physical hunger in my whole life that was as great as the spiritual hunger that I had for Him.... And then I shall never forget those holiness camp meetings in Oskaloosa, Iowa.... I only attended years ago right after I became a Christian, and before I knew anything about the Holy Spirit, before I knew anything about the baptism with the Holy Spirit, all I knew was I had been born again, Jesus had forgiven my sins, and I could remember that old-fashioned tabernacle, saw dust on the ground.... So hungry for more, and every time an altar call was given, whether it was after the morning session, the afternoon session, or night, there was a red-headed, freckle-faced teenage girl who was first to walk down the aisle and kneel in that saw dust, crying, seeking holiness. Seeking some experience I knew not what. After every one of these morning services, that red-headed, freckle-faced girl would rush to the altar, my head buried in my arms, weeping and crying, and when the noon hour would come for dinner, everyone else would leave, but she was still there. She would still be there when the afternoon service would begin. She was the first at the altar when the call was given again for those who wanted to be completely holy and seeking holiness. I never found what I was seeking there. I was that girl. I was seeking for some experience, some ecstasy.[545]

Early Evangelistic Ministry

Following this season, Kathryn went to Oregon to visit her older sister and brother-in-law, evangelist Everett B. Parrott, for the summer. She extended her stay and lived with them for five years, helping in the ministry. Because her brother-in-law was connected to the ministry of evangelist Charles S. Price, Kathryn had the opportunity to sit under Price's ministry for some of that time. In 1928, when Everett could not be at a meeting in Boise, Idaho, Kathryn was given the opportunity to preach for him. After that meeting, a local pastor who was in attendance encouraged her to branch out on her own.[546] Helen Gulliford, a pianist who had played for Charles Price, decided to join her. Kathryn was only in her early twenties when she and Helen traveled to Idaho, Utah, and Colorado over the next few years to minister before moving to Denver, Colorado, in 1933.

In 1934, Kathryn's father died in an accident. It was at his funeral that she claimed to have overcome her fear of death. While in Denver, Kathryn also started a radio show. Then, in 1938, against the counsel of her friends, she married Burroughs Waltrip, who had just divorced his wife and left his children to be with her. This controversial marriage marred her ministry, and she had to give up her church in Denver. But during a visit to Joliet, Illinois, she was impacted when she saw someone speak in tongues for the first time.[547]

Total Surrender at a Dead-End Street

As time went on, the tension within Kathryn over her marriage continued to build. In 1944, she struggled to fully surrender her husband to the Lord, even though she knew it was the right thing to do.

I had to make a choice. Would I serve the man I loved, or the God I loved? I knew I could not serve God and live with Mister [her husband]. No one will ever know the pain of dying like I know it, for I loved him more than I loved life itself. And for a time, I loved him more than God. I finally told him I had to leave. God never released me from that original call. Not only did I live with him, I had to live with my conscience, and the conviction of the Holy Spirit was almost unbearable. I was tired of trying to justify myself. Tired.[548]

One afternoon I left the apartment—it was in the outskirts of Los Angeles—and found myself walking down a tree-shaded street. The sun was flickering through the great limbs that stretched out overhead. At the end of the block I saw a street sign. It said simply, "Dead End." There was heartache, heartache so great it cannot be put into words. If you think it's easy to go to the cross, it's simply because you've never been there. I've been there. I know. And I had to go alone. I knew nothing about the wonderful filling of the Holy Spirit. I knew nothing of the power of the mighty third person of the Trinity which was available to all. I just knew it was four o'clock on Saturday afternoon and I had come to the place in my life where I was ready to give up everything—even Mister—and die. I said it out loud, "Dear Jesus, I surrender all. I give it all to you. Take my body. Take my heart. All I am is yours. I place it in your wonderful hands."[549]

In that moment, I yielded to God in body, soul, and spirit. I gave him everything…. That afternoon, Kathryn Kuhlman died. And when I died, God came in, the Holy Spirit came in. There, for the first time, I realized what it meant to have power.[550]

Kathryn was filled with the Spirit in a powerful way that day.[551] Three days after this, she left her husband and headed to Franklin, Pennsylvania, for a series of meetings. According to biographer Jamie Buckingham, author of *Daughter of Destiny*, she then traveled to other states as an itinerant evangelist. She ministered and still drew crowds, but her past hindered her. In 1946, she returned to Franklin and preached at the Gospel Tabernacle, where the people responded positively to her ministry. Eventually, she began preaching to crowds larger than those Billy Sunday had preached to at the Tabernacle.

Healing Ministry Launched by Surprise

Kathryn soon faced the issue of divine healing head-on. She had struggled with praying for the sick because she rarely saw anyone healed.

She was frustrated and tired of seeing healing services that were devoid of miracles, because she had noted how miracles happened all the time in the Bible. While attending a camp meeting, she came across some "faith healers" but was disillusioned by the lack of power accompanying them. This stirred her to cry out in prayer for days concerning the reality of healing.[552] Her surge of prayer and desperation to see healing power manifest contributed to the spark that was to follow.

Then, in 1947, while Kathryn was preaching about the Holy Spirit, a woman was healed of a tumor.

> I was preaching in Franklin, Pennsylvania. One night my sermon was on the Holy Spirit. I hadn't mentioned healing. But the next night, before I began to preach, a woman stood up and said, "Pardon me Miss Kuhlman, but I have a testimony to give. While you were preaching last night I had a strange sensation in my body and I knew I had been healed. I knew it. Today I went to my doctor and he confirmed that I was." As I recollect, the woman had had a tumor. And that was the beginning, the first of miracles.[553]

Kathryn recognized this miracle as "the first healing after God anointed [her] with the Holy Spirit for the healing of sick bodies."[554] The very next week, a man named George Orr felt a tingling during one of her services, and his eye was restored to sight after twenty-two years of blindness.[555]

Kathryn realized that simply by honoring the Holy Spirit and by being in God's presence, healing could be released.

> *The Holy Spirit, then, was the answer,* an answer so profound that no human being can fathom the full extent of its depths and power, and yet so simple that most folk miss it! I understood that night why there was no need for a healing line; no healing virtue in a card or a personality; no necessity for wild exhortations "to have faith." That was the beginning of this healing ministry which God has given me; strange to some because of the fact that hundreds have been healed just sitting quietly in the audience, without any demonstration whatsoever, and even without admonition. This is because the Presence of the Holy Spirit has been in such abundance that by His

Presence alone, sick bodies are healed, even as people wait on the outside of the building for the doors to open.[556]

A Yielded Vessel

Even though great healing was released through her ministry, Kathryn, like Carrie Judd Montgomery and many other healing revivalists, denied having a gift of healing. In response to the question of whether she had the gift of healing, she said:

> I would never say that I have ever received any gift. I am leery of folks who boast of this or that gift. The greatest of the Christian graces is humility. All I know is that I have yielded my body to Him to be filled with the Holy Spirit, and anything that the Holy Spirit has given me, any results there might be in this life of mine, is not Kathryn Kuhlman. It's the Holy Spirit; it's what the Holy Spirit does through a yielded vessel. That is one thing I am so afraid of: I am afraid lest I grieve the Holy Spirit, for when the Holy Spirit is lifted from me I am the most ordinary person that ever lived.[557]

> As I have said before, I am not a faith healer. I have not been given anything special. What I have is something that any Christian could have if he would pay the price of full surrender and yieldedness. I am absolutely dependent on the mercy of the Lord Jesus Christ.[558]

Foundations Laid

Kathryn's husband eventually divorced her in 1947. The next year, on July 4, 1948, she held her first "miracle service" at Carnegie Hall in Pittsburgh, Pennsylvania.[559] After this, she continued to hold meetings in Pittsburgh, in Franklin, and elsewhere.[560] In 1950, she moved to Pittsburgh and lived there until 1971.

Although Kathryn's evangelistic efforts had minimal success up to 1946, after her revelation at the "dead-end" street (1944), followed by her intercession at the camp meeting, she was on the verge of her tipping point. The testimony released by the woman who was healed of the tumor broke open the floodgates of healings, signs, and wonders in her ministry. From there, the anointing fell on her in even greater measures. Biographer Allen Spraggett says that the healing of the tumor was the event that

> divided Kathryn Kuhlman's ministry into two distinct phases: before the coming of The Power, and after. In the first phase she was just another itinerant evangelist, a little more eloquent and energetic than most, perhaps, but otherwise undistinguished. In some twenty years of preaching she had whistle-stopped her way across the American Midwest several times. The second phase of her ministry was a much different story. The initial healing was the start of an unbroken succession.[561]

Following this initial outbreak of healing, Kathryn went from being relatively unknown to being one of the most famous healing evangelists in America.

Final Days

In 1955, Kathryn was diagnosed with a heart problem. Even with her health issues, she continued a rigorous schedule of traveling back and forth to Los Angeles. For ten years, she conducted meetings for up to seven thousand people at the Shrine Auditorium. She also continued to travel around the world, holding meetings and dedicating churches.

Kathryn was ordained by the Evangelical Church Alliance in 1968. In 1972, she was awarded an honorary doctoral degree from Oral Roberts University in May, and she met Pope Paul VI in October. Then, after many years of ministry, on February 20, 1976, following open-heart surgery in Tulsa, Oklahoma, she went to be with the Lord.

Legacy

Over the years of Kathryn Kuhlman's ministry, thousands of people were healed in her meetings or through her radio and television appearances. The Kathryn Kuhlman Foundation reports,

Fifty stations carried her thirty-minute broadcasts, five days a week, covering most of the nation; in Canada; and overseas broadcasts reaching much of Europe. The last ten years of her life, her weekly half-hour television programs (produced at CBS in Los Angeles) were shown throughout the United States and Canada.[562]

Kathryn also set up over twenty-four international mission bases debt-free as a gift to national leaders. Her book *I Believe in Miracles*, published in 1962, became a best seller, with over two million copies sold.[563] She walked in great anointing and saw signs, wonders, and healing released through her ministry.[564] Many people were "slain in the Spirit" and received a "fresh baptism of the Holy Spirit."[565]

Women in Ministry

Just as there are parallels between Maria Woodworth-Etter and Aimee Semple McPherson, there are also several parallels between Aimee Semple McPherson and Kathryn Kuhlman. Even though Kathryn never had the chance to meet Aimee, they both claimed to be ordained by God Himself. Following their conversions, both had an intense hunger to be baptized in the Holy Spirit; their major turning points included a hunger for more of the Spirit to the point of desperation. They both participated in camp meetings where the main speaker was unable to present the message, and they were asked to fill in. This open door to preach was significant in launching their ministries. Each also utilized the media in innovative ways to reach their generation, and each was drawn to Los Angeles. Finally, a difficult but common component of their lives was that after they yielded to God, they left their husbands before they stepped into the fullness of their callings.[566]

Total surrender preceded the defining moments not only of Kathryn Kuhlman and Aimee Semple McPherson but also of Maria Woodworth-Etter and Carrie Judd Montgomery. Additionally, all four women planted churches or movements, and healing and God's presence were prominent and consistent themes among them. The determination and courage of Maria Woodworth-Etter and Carrie Judd Montgomery paved the way for both Aimee Semple McPherson and Kathryn Kuhlman to expand the kingdom in new ways in their generations. It appears that Kathryn picked up where Aimee left off.[567] One might say that Heidi Baker has taken the torch from these female healing evangelists and is passing it on in our present day.

Environments Saturated with God's Presence

Similar to what Evan Roberts tried to foster in Wales, Kathryn sought to cultivate an environment saturated with God's manifest presence, emphasizing the importance of the Holy Spirit. Accordingly, healing became a natural outworking of her ministry. She said,

> Very often not even a sermon is preached. There have been times when not even a song has been sung. No loud demonstration, no loud calling on God as though He were deaf, no screaming, no shouting. Within the very quietness of His presence, there have been times, literally hundreds of times when in a great miracle service there has been so much of the presence of the Holy Spirit that literally one could almost hear the beating, the rhythm of the heartbeat of thousands of people as their heart did beat as one. In the stillness of that moment, I have more than once slipped my feet out of my shoes, for the ground whereon I stood was holy ground. No screaming, no manifestations of the flesh, no exhorting, no admonishing, just the very presence of the Holy Spirit.[568]

Kathryn noticed that time after time, healing was released in the presence of the Holy Spirit, and praise was a key element to inviting God to come in power.

> I realized that it [the mystery behind the miracles] was the presence of the Holy Spirit.... When the power of the Spirit is there, miracles happen. Gradually, I began to understand The Power, how it operates. I discovered that certain things bring the presence of the Holy Spirit. Praise, for instance. Just praising God— not asking for a single thing but just praising Him—always brings The Power. It's pleasing to the Lord.... You do not manipulate the Holy Spirit. The Holy Spirit is a person. He is not an *it*. He is God. He is to be reverenced, to be worshiped. He is not to be presumed upon by anyone.[569]

Anointing

Kathryn regularly waited until she felt the Holy Spirit's anointing before she stepped up to the pulpit to speak. When the anointing fell, it was as if she became a different person—as if she was, in a sense, possessed. This is similar to what happened to Aimee Semple McPherson the first time she preached. She felt the Holy Spirit speak through her in "tongues," except that the tongue was English. Kathryn claimed to experience a similar sort of Holy Spirit possession or inhabitation.

> I'm completely detached from everything that goes on in that place…. It's as if my body is possessed by the Holy Spirit. It's as though I were removed, up above somewhere, looking down on the proceedings. I see myself, and I'm shocked when I hear myself say things like, "A cancer is being healed." I'm a bystander looking on and as amazed as anyone else by the miracles. And I'm having the time of my life.[570]

> When I come out on stage, there is an anointing that comes upon me, and it is very difficult to explain. These things are supernatural. That's the reason it is so hard for the natural mind to comprehend. But there is an anointing that comes upon me. I am completely taken over by the Holy Spirit.[571]

One couple familiar with Kathryn's anointing recalled,

> When the anointing was on her a lot of times she didn't know what she was doing. She had no memory of what she did—none whatever—and she did not know what she said…. When she was in the natural, people would stop her in Pittsburg when they would see her, and they'd say, "Miss Kuhlman, pray for me." She'd say, "Don't you understand? Sometimes the anointing's on me. Other times it isn't." See, it would depend on what she was thinking, how she was feeling. Sometimes her mind would be on the Lord and going down the street she would meet somebody. She'd go to say "Hello," and they'd go down under the power.[572]

Kathryn recognized her own need for a continual baptism of the Holy Spirit, and she saw how it released the anointing, saying,

I too received the Baptism of the Holy Spirit many years ago, but there's never a time when I'm in a great miracle service but what I receive a fresh Baptism of the Holy Spirit. And when I stand to minister in Christ's name, I feel that anointing from the top of my head to the soles of my feet.[573]

Even though miracles, signs, and wonders had already been released through her, Kathryn was still desperate for, and relied upon, fresh baptisms of the Holy Spirit to flood her so that she could continue to walk in the anointing. There is much that we can learn from the way that she stewarded her anointing.

Prophetic Inheritance

Quite a number of our heroes of the faith spoke of being "possessed" by God. This term makes many people uncomfortable, yet it probably best describes the kind of lifestyle that Kathryn Kuhlman modeled for us. People who have not had a particular spiritual experience often express concerns about those who claim to have had it. But while the uniqueness of an encounter, in itself, doesn't legitimize it, neither does it necessarily disqualify it.

The idea of being possessed by God may seem out of the ordinary, but it has a strong biblical precedent. Judges 6:34 says, "*The Spirit of the LORD came upon Gideon.*" The purpose of this anointing was to enable him to lead the Israelites to victory against their enemies. In the literal Hebrew, this verse actually says, "The Spirit of the Lord clothed Himself with Gideon." This is an amazing picture of God putting on a person like clothing in order to accomplish His purposes. And it is a description of someone who is being used by God in an extraordinary way. Many times, I've heard people say that they were not even aware of all they said and accomplished in a meeting as they flawlessly followed the Holy Spirit's leading. That was Kathryn's response, too.

The Holy Spirit loved to clothe Himself with Kathryn Kuhlman. I don't think God wants us out of the picture. It's just that He can do everything much better than we can, even on our best days, and He wants the manifestation of the Holy Spirit through a person to be untarnished by human will and weakness. Kathryn clearly recognized her need and sought an ongoing manifestation of the anointing upon her life.

Sensitivity

I know someone who stood behind the curtain at one of Kathryn Kuhlman's meetings, positioned in a place where she couldn't have known he was there. He saw her alone behind that curtain, praying. The way she prayed and confessed her need of the Holy Spirit in that moment changed his life forever. It broke him, making him hungry for what she had. That moment didn't reveal great power for miracles. Neither did it display great revelation knowledge of the Word. It was a moment of such tenderness toward the Holy Spirit that this individual almost felt awkward watching it. When Kathryn finally took the stage, she was confident in the presence and power of the Holy Spirit. That confidence had no other foundation than her awareness of God and of His heart for people.

Courage often bursts forth in the heart of a person who feels God's heart for others, and so it was for Kathryn Kuhlman. She modeled a tenderness toward the Holy Spirit that few others have demonstrated, either before her or after her. She showed us that the anointing is actually a Person. Her respect for her gift in ministry and her powerful anointing illustrated how she would treat her Best Friend—the Holy Spirit.

He is the *Holy* Spirit. When we are filled with the Spirit, it must be demonstrated in power. But this emphasis is never to be at the expense of the most logical manifestation of His presence—our personal holiness. Kathryn said,

> It was years later [after her conversion] that I found out that Jesus is our holiness, and the one who has the most of His holiness is the one who has the most of Jesus. You talk about experiences of holiness, of sanctification. It is still a matter of seeking Jesus. You talk about the wonderful experience of being filled with the Holy Spirit, it's still more of Jesus. Even after one has been filled with the Holy Spirit, remember my friend, the Holy Spirit Himself always magnifies and glorifies Jesus. He is most holy who has most of Jesus within. No, it's not striving to have faith, it's not striving for some

experience, but it's looking to Jesus, receiving more of Him and that is your answer.[574]

Early in Kathryn's ministry, as she taught about the Holy Spirit, miracles began to break out in her meetings. The same result has happened numerous times throughout history. We tend to receive what we teach. The Holy Spirit is often attracted by the words of people who seek to honor Him in their teachings and proclamations. Such a focus often attracts the realm of the Spirit into one's environment. It's not as though we can control or manipulate God through our confessions. Nothing could be further from the truth. It's just that God honors His Word. And He looks for people who are willing to cooperate with the nature of His kingdom by making decrees that are aligned with His Word.

Liberty to Be Real

Of all those whom I've seen minister the gospel, Kathryn Kuhlman was unique. Her entrance onto the platform, the way she moved around the stage, and the way she talked—everything was very different. Her manner offended many people who couldn't help but judge by outward appearance. It wasn't that she did anything wrong or even questionable as she ministered. She was just different. To me, that was a personal triumph for her. She didn't allow herself to be conformed to what others thought was best. Instead, her own personality came through beautifully. And I, for one, think we are better off because of it. Most of all, her uniqueness was honest. She wasn't attempting to be different; she simply had the liberty to be real.

Love for the Whole Church

Many people have demonstrated the power of the Holy Spirit by living in the miracle realm, and that is wonderful. Again, power is an essential expression of the kingdom. The gospel is not fully good news without it. But Kathryn did more than display power. Her tenderness toward the Holy Spirit caused His nature to become hers. His tenderness became her tenderness. His compassion became her compassion. She mirrored His heart so beautifully. This was especially true of her love for the church—the whole church. She was well loved by Catholics and Protestants alike. Furthermore, she had great respect for medical science, which was a notable shift from many who had gone before her. Additionally, she somehow discovered the honorable value of each person and of their assignment in life. Significantly, she was not known for what she *didn't* believe or whom she *didn't* like. The purpose of her sermons was not to expose the errors of those who didn't agree with her. Instead, she was known for love—passionate love for God and for other people.

Kathryn Kuhlman's defining moment left such a deep impact upon her that His ways actually became her ways. When I read about someone having a profound encounter with God, I automatically look for power: power in preaching, miracles, and personal triumphs. That realm has been lacking in the church for so long that I hunger for it in ways that are hard to describe. Yet, while Kathryn illustrates each of those things so wonderfully, it's her ability to *follow God's lead in the dance*, reflecting His heart toward everyone, that impacts me the most.

Bring on the miracles! They are a necessary evidence of the resurrected Christ in us. But by all means, let's let our love for all people prove that our love for God is genuine.

Postscript

Kathryn Kuhlman demonstrated how to value the anointing. She treated her anointing as a Person and cherished her friendship with Him more than any other part of her life. But I believe she modeled something else that is rare, and that relates to the various kingdom paradoxes we read about in the Bible. We know that the kingdom of God functions in a completely different way than the world around us. For example, we are exalted by humbling ourselves (see, for example, Matthew 23:12), and we receive by giving (see, for example, Luke 6:38). I could give countless other examples. But this leads us to one more secret to Kathryn's life and ministry that is uncommon among believers: her passionate hunger and desperation for more of God actually came from her contentment in Him.

That may sound like another great contradiction, but it's not. Let me illustrate: I love my wife so much. She completely, totally satisfies me. I've never looked for another, not even for a moment. And yet I am hungry for more. My desire for her is not because of what I lack but because of what I have to gain. It is this kind of passion demonstrated in Kathryn Kuhlman's life that is so arresting. Her love for the Holy Spirit, her valuing the anointing on her life, only created in her a passionate cry for more.

Kathryn modeled this lifestyle for us wonderfully. But it all proceeded from her defining moment. She spoke of the baptism in the Holy Spirit in this way: "I believe in the baptism of the Holy Spirit with every atom of my being. He is with you, but there is an experience."[575] Her passion for the Spirit made it possible for God to entrust the atmosphere of heaven to her, so that many miracles and breakthroughs happened simply because God was there in a pronounced and manifest way.

Kathryn Kuhlman's defining moment enabled her to bring the actual atmosphere of heaven to earth in very practical and powerful ways. We, too, have the privilege and responsibility to bring heaven to earth—to help shift the spiritual atmosphere over cities and eventually even nations. We need to stand on Kathryn Kuhlman's shoulders to reach into an even higher spiritual reality than she was able to. From our place of breakthrough, we will be entrusted with the "more" that Kathryn longed for.

Impartation:
Randy Clark

"The 'impartation' experience that I am speaking about is not just receiving a 'blessing' from God. Neither is it a matter of being strengthened by the Holy Spirit or an angel of God; it is more than that. There is destiny connected with the 'impartation.'"[576]
—*Randy Clark*

R andy Clark is one of my closest friends. I don't know if I've ever met a more gracious man. He is unpretentious, extremely intelligent, and a bondservant of the Lord every day of his life to see people saved, the church strengthened, and God glorified. I've traveled with him to many nations of the world, observing and participating in this mysterious grace called *impartation*. It is one of the most unusual miracles I've ever seen. The results are obvious and measurable, as people become radically changed inside and out into a transformational force in the earth. It's simply astonishing.

Impartation is basically the *ministry grace* that is on one person's life released to another, often through the laying on of hands and prophecy. It is amazing to see the dramatic change or increase that can come on a person who has one level of anointing, or one type of gift in their life, after they receive it. In just a moment of time, that level or gift dramatically changes and/or increases. What is really hard to understand is that sometimes when a new grace is imparted, it functions at a much higher level in the person who received it than it did in the one who laid hands on that individual. For example, Randy is a wonderful church planter. But there are those he has imparted to who have now planted thousands of churches. It's the same grace that Randy carries, but it is now released through a new person, opportunity, and assignment. It fascinates me to watch this process.

While there are many who abuse this subject of impartation, thinking that it is their key to a shortcut to greater anointing, it remains a formidable force in the church for increasing our effectiveness and power in life and ministry. And I don't know of anyone who carries this grace better than Randy, whether in the past or in the present. It is a primary assignment in his life.

Transference of Anointing

One way that Randy Clark refers to impartation is "transference of anointing." He also says, in relation to impartation, "Many times it is accompanied by a prophetic word that reveals this destiny. At other times, a person's destiny has already been revealed to them. Later, they receive an 'impartation' which enables them to accomplish their God-given destiny." Randy also recognizes that "most frequently, this impartation comes to those who have been serving God faithfully for years and that it often comes at a time of brokenness and crisis."[577]

Randy Clark has emerged as a leader among leaders within our generation. He is a catalyst for apostolic and international leaders around the world, launching them into greater measures of their destiny. In January 1984, several years after he was miraculously healed of injuries from a car crash, Randy received an impartation from John Wimber. Throughout the years, he received other impartations and powerful prophetic words from people like Blaine Cook, Ron Allen, Happy Leman, Rodney Howard-Browne, and Richard Holcomb. Two significant impartations from Vineyard leaders included manifestations of electricity, while the impartation under Howard-Browne was marked by peace. After his impartation from Howard-Browne, when Randy returned to his church and prayed for people, many of them fell down. Some of them remained on the floor for many hours. A few months later, in January 1994, which was ten years to the month after his impartation from Wimber, Randy was used as a catalyst to launch the Toronto Blessing. Randy's ministry has since exploded, and he has seen increasing signs and wonders both inter-denominationally and internationally.

Early Life and Healing

Randy Clark was born on February 18, 1952, in McLeansboro, Illinois. His father worked as an oil field driller, and his family did not have a lot of money.[578] When he was five years old, his grandmother told him about a healing she experienced. This is something he never forgot. Randy grew up in a Baptist church, but when he was eighteen years old, he backslid from the Lord for eleven months. Then, on October 11, 1970, he rededicated his life to the Lord. A few days later, on October 15, he was seriously injured in a car accident that took the life of a friend. The last week of October, Randy was miraculously healed of a fractured jaw that had set itself, of paralysis of the digestive system, and of other serious head and spinal injuries. Before he was healed, he had taken 50 mg of Demerol—a morphine derivative—every three hours. He was released from the hospital about a week later, on November 4, 1970, after spending nearly twenty days there.

Following his healing, Randy asked God for three signs to verify his call into full-time ministry. The final sign was fulfilled at a Baptist revival meeting on November 20, 1970, when he watched the worship leader, who had just had a stroke, play the piano without any pain. At this confirmation, Randy publicly declared his call to become a preacher. The community surrounded him and confirmed his calling right then and there. He preached his first sermon two days later.

Shortly after this, he went off to Bible college. On his first day, he went to the bookstore and heard God impress upon him that *"the issue of your lifetime will be the Holy Spirit."*[579] Then, in 1971, after the woman he loved became engaged to someone else, Randy got married on the rebound.[580] He got divorced three years later because of her infidelity. Randy always saw this as one of the biggest failures of his life. On July 12, 1975, he married DeAnne Davenport.

Hunger to Learn More About the Holy Spirit

While Randy was talking to God one day in the summer of 1983 and thanking Him that he was not a liberal or a cessationist, he heard the Lord respond,

> So what? You might as well be a liberal or a cessationist. You say that you believe I do all these things and that you even believe in the gifts; yet you don't know how to move in them.[581]

This response caused Randy to invest over seven hundred dollars in books about Spirit baptism from different theological perspectives, as well as the manifestations of the gifts of the Spirit. A week later, he heard someone preach about the healing of the woman with the issue of blood. While the preacher did not specifically connect the woman's faith with her healing, that fact was highlighted for Randy, and it deeply impacted him. He wept and called out to God later that night. The Lord then gave him three strong impressions:

> I want you to teach this church that I still heal today. I want you to have a conference on healing at this church. I want you to preach differently.[582]

In response to this word, Randy called Dr. Larry Hart to ask him to come and speak on healing. Hart suggested he invite John Wimber from the Vineyard movement instead. Randy had never heard of Wimber before that. The very next day, however, he saw Wimber on television. Randy was very impacted by his message and his complete lack of hype. He believed it was confirmation to contact him.

Impartation from John Wimber

When Randy called Wimber to ask him to do the healing conference, Wimber said he was not available to come out himself, but he would send a team in March 1984. Randy could not wait that long to learn more. In January 1984, he and two of his deacons went to Dallas, Texas, to a James Robison Bible Conference, where Wimber was speaking, to learn more about him. On the second morning of the conference, Randy had a spiritual dream—the second such dream that he had experienced. It consisted of a series of walls and gates. On some of the walls, commandments were written. In the dream, Randy felt inspired to obey the commands to go through the gates and come up higher.[583] Later that day, John Wimber spoke to about five hundred pastors. Randy was intrigued as he watched Wimber move in the Spirit. David Yonggi Cho also spoke; his words brought conviction to Randy "for more intimacy with God and a relationship with the Holy Spirit."[584] That night, David Wilkerson addressed a crowd of eight thousand. The Holy Spirit fell, causing many to fall on their faces in repentance. Randy continued to be hit with the power of the Holy Spirit and was taken down to the ground, shaking and weeping.

The next night, Randy went up to Wimber to ask him to pray for his deacons. Wimber responded,

> I want to pray for you; but first I want to pray for your heart because you've been wounded lately in your church.... You're a prince in the kingdom of God.... There's an apostolic call on your life.[585]

The impartation Randy received from Wimber marked his life and was a powerful investment for what would come. At the time he received this word, Randy had fewer than one hundred fifty people in his congregation.

Impartation from Blaine Cook

In March 1984, Randy was to host a healing conference with Blaine Cook and a team from the Vineyard in Yorba Linda, California. Randy had been fasting for about two weeks before the conference. A few days before the team arrived, Randy called the Vineyard to learn more about words of knowledge. Lance Pittluck shared some helpful insights with him over the phone. The following Sunday night, Randy had his first word of knowledge, which resulted in a healing.[586] When the team from the Vineyard came to minister, healings, signs, and wonders began to break out in their meetings. Randy and his wife received an impartation from Cook that resulted in greater boldness. Randy recalled,

> It was so powerful that I no longer considered what happened in Dallas as an impartation. I felt like I had grabbed hold of an electric wire. I began to shake, feeling electricity flowing through my body. It was so strong that the next day all my joints ached. The anointing of God had a similar effect on my body, as the electricity was so strong I could not control the aching. It also activated the gifts of word of knowledge and healing in our lives in much greater measure.[587]

Following this, God began to move in his church in a new way. Randy also became aware of the demonic realm for the first time. During that summer, he went on his first forty-day fast, praying specifically for greater healing anointing.[588] By September 1984, he had resigned as pastor of the Baptist church and had planted a church in the town of Marion, Illinois, with the intention of one day planting a church in a city. Fifteen months later, after receiving confirmation, Randy went to St. Louis to start a Vineyard church. During the transition to St. Louis, he took a job frying doughnuts in the early hours to help pay the bills.[589]

Electricity Encounter

About five years after first connecting with the Vineyard, Randy felt dry again and was hungry for more of God. His heart burned for evangelism, but he didn't see how that would fit into his ministry. He prayed that someone would give him a prophetic word.[590] Then, on October 27, 1989, while attending a regional meeting for the association of Vineyard churches at the Champaign Vineyard in Illinois, Randy received a prophetic word from one of the regional overseers. Ron Allen told Randy that he would travel to the nations and that his son's anointing would eclipse his anointing. Later on in the meeting, Randy asked him for prayer.

> And he [Ron Allen] started praying for me and another guy [Happy Leman] blew on me, even though he didn't believe in blowing, and I hit the floor. When I hit the floor, I screamed on the way down and kept on screaming. I had electricity going through my body, and I was in pain. I was so afraid I was going to die. It was so powerful that it scared me. I heard people standing over me. I was hot, and I was sweating. I was screaming bloody murder, and I thought this was the baptism of the Spirit. I refused to consider that it might be demonic. I said to myself, "This is the baptism of the Spirit. I am feeling power. God is just empowering me." But some of the people standing over me were saying, "Do you think it is a demon?" I was unable to talk because so much was happening, but I thought, "No! Don't start yelling, 'Come out.' Don't mess this up for me! This is powerful. This is God. Don't say that." Then I heard a guy [Ron Allen] say, "I think he will become one of the greatest evangelists in the Vineyard." And I was thinking, "I like that one! I like that one!" After a while, in about 45 minutes, it ended, and then for several hours I couldn't lower my hands past my waist because they hurt so badly. The electricity would get so strong I had to pull them back up. I wish I could say that immediately there was this great change of great power. There wasn't. However, I realized a few weeks later that an issue in my life that I had never been able to get free of was gone, and I realized that both those who spoke over me were right. It was a mighty baptism of the Spirit, and I did get delivered sovereignly.[591]

When people like Ron Allen, John Wimber, and several others prophesied over Randy about going to the nations or imparting the Holy Spirit to leaders around the world, Randy didn't believe these words were from God. At the time that these things were spoken to him, he had only a small church, he had received no speaking invitations, and he had never been out of the country. He didn't even have a passport. In relation to several of the early prophetic words over his life, he admits, "I threw them away because there was too big of a gap between where I was and what I was, to what I was going to be doing. I couldn't believe it."[592]

Activation

When Randy first learned about South African evangelist Rodney Howard-Browne, he was hungry for God at any cost. He remembered praying, "God, I will go anywhere and do anything if you will just touch me again. Make me a coin in your pocket, spend me anyway you want."[593] In August 1993, Randy went to hear Howard-Browne speak for the first time. Even though the conference was in Tulsa, Oklahoma, at Kenneth Hagin Jr.'s Rhema Bible Church, a Word of Faith group Randy didn't embrace at that time, he broke out of his box and went anyway.[594] During this time, he was on another fast. This time, he purposed not to eat again until God touched him. Similar to Aimee Semple McPherson's heart-cry before she was baptized in the Holy Spirit, Randy called out,

> Lord, I want to be touched by You so desperately.… I'm not going to give up on You! I don't care what I have to do; I'm not going to eat until You touch me![595]

During the first few days of the conference, nothing really happened to Randy, and he was skeptical. But since he was not going to eat until God had touched him, he got in line along with forty-five hundred others to receive an impartation. After Howard-Browne gently slapped him on the head, Randy fell to the floor. Because he didn't shake or feel any electricity as he had in his other two major encounters, he began to question the validity of this move of God. But when he tried to get up from the floor, he couldn't move for over thirty minutes. Finally, he got back up, took off his glasses, and went to another part of the line. When Howard-Browne prayed for him, he went down again. Randy continued this several more times.[596] He believes that during this time, God changed his heart in a radical way.[597] While the main manifestations that accompanied the impartations from the Vineyard were electricity-like and caused shaking, these were ones of peace.[598]

Randy returned to his church in St. Louis, and during the first Sunday service following his impartation, everyone he prayed for fell down. Prior to this, for eight years, no one in Randy's church had ever fallen down under God's power. Not long after, Randy shared these testimonies at a Vineyard regional meeting. The Holy Spirit broke out powerfully over everyone there, including the leaders; nearly everyone was on the floor. Then, in November 1993, while at a national Vineyard Council meeting, Pastor John Arnott heard Happy Leman's testimony of revival breaking out at Randy's church. This spurred Arnott to invite Randy to his church in Toronto.

Before leaving on his first international trip, Randy went to Florida the first week of January 1994 to see Rodney Howard-Browne so he could get filled up again. He had been fasting for two weeks when he received a strong impartation in his hands at the meeting. Howard-Browne noticed this, and in front of eight thousand people, he told Randy, "This is the fire of God in your hands, go home and pray for everyone in your church."[599] When he did, the power of God fell.

The night before he left for Toronto, Randy received an important phone call from his friend Richard Holcomb, who told Randy that he believed the Lord was saying,

> Test Me now, test Me now, test Me now! Do not be afraid, I will back you up! I want your eyes to be opened to see My resources for you in the heavenlies, just as Elisha prayed that Gehazi's eyes would be opened. And do not be anxious because when you become anxious you can't hear Me.[600]

Prior to this word, Randy doubted that anything would happen in Toronto; he was fearful that God would not back him up.[601] He recalled, "That word changed my life. I got ready to leave the next day and I went from 'I hope God shows up' to saying, 'We're on an apostolic mission trip where we're going to see more than we've ever seen in our lives.'"[602] Randy also said that this word gave him "the faith to move in the anointing [he] had received when John Wimber prayed for [him] ten years earlier and when Rodney prayed for [him]."[603]

This word was significant to build Randy's confidence, and it inspired the faith necessary to step into his anointing. This word was also not a shot in the dark. Randy and Holcomb had been friends for many years. God had already used Holcomb to speak into Randy's life and to bless him in other situations over the years where the timing was crucial. Holcomb had Randy's ear; and even more important, the Lord had Holcomb's hearing ear and obedient heart.

Tipping Point: Toronto Blessing

Randy was forty-two years old when he got his passport and left the country for the first time. Not long after his impartation from Howard-Browne, and ten years to the month after his impartation from Wimber, on January 20, 1994, Randy spoke for the first time at the Toronto Airport Vineyard. After he shared his testimony to about one hundred twenty people and invited them forward, the Holy Spirit broke out.[604] John Arnott recalls, "Eighty percent of our church was all over the floor, and laughing and rolling and totally overtaken by the Spirit of God."[605]

What was intended to be a four-day conference turned into revival meetings every night. At Arnott's request, Randy delayed his flight home so he could continue to fan the flame in Toronto. He was present at forty-two of the next sixty consecutive days of meetings.[606] Randy's presence in Canada ignited what would later be called the Toronto Blessing. In the first six months of the outpouring, John and Carol Arnott's church doubled in size from three hundred fifty people to seven hundred. They had meetings every night except for Mondays (a practice that continued for more than twelve years); during those six months, over thirty thousand people went to the meetings, with a total attendance of seventy thousand. There were three hundred salvations and twenty-five hundred rededications to Christ.[607] This renewal movement spread to over fifty-five thousand churches in the first year. In the first few years of the movement, over three million people visited the outpouring in Toronto. Many people were significantly healed and touched by God during their visit. When they returned home, revival fire spread.[608]

John and Carol Arnott would become the stewards of this great move of God for over twenty years. Similar to the Welsh Revival of 1904, the meetings of the Toronto Blessing were filled with testimonies, worship, and space for the Holy Spirit to move, no matter how that might look. Both of these outpourings were centered on God's presence. Along with the Azusa Street Revival in Los Angeles in 1906, these movements acted as epicenters that drew people from around the world to "catch the fire" and then go back to their homes to spread what had been imparted to them. In the Azusa Street Revival and the Toronto Blessing, many apostolic leaders were drawn to the fire in these "hot spots." Once there, they were restored and empowered before being launched into greater levels of anointing.

Randy was perfectly positioned to step into what he was destined for. He continually kept his lamp full of oil. Despite his fears, he ventured into what would await him in Toronto. It was there that the prophetic words spoken over him and the anointings of the impartations he had received were catalyzed. The outbreak in Toronto launched him into the international and interdenominational ministry he was born for. His ministry, Global Awakening, reported the following:

> A few days after the outpouring of the Holy Spirit at the Toronto Airport Vineyard, now called Catch the Fire, John Wimber called Randy. He said, "This is the fulfillment of what God showed me about your life ten years ago." The last time Randy met with Wimber, John gave him one more word, "God told me audibly that you and (one other) [Blaine Cook] were the two Vineyard pastors who would go around the world, laying your hands upon pastors and leaders to impart gifts of the Holy Spirit to them and to impart the Holy Spirit to them."[609]

Impartations Released Through Randy

After the flame was lit in Toronto, Randy went on his second forty-day fast, this time praying specifically for breakthrough to see creative miracles. Through impartation, Randy also began to empower many apostolic leaders, specifically those from other nations or those who were working in other nations.[610] Randy realizes that "the price of revival is high, and that impartations prepare people to be willing to pay that price." When he prays for people to receive an impartation, he does not just ask God to "fill them with power," but he also asks that God would "baptize them in His love" because he realizes that it is that baptism of love that will encourage them not to give up when things get hard.[611]

In 1995, Randy prayed and prophesied over Norwegian pastor Leif Hetland. Since that impartation, Hetland has been used to bring over one million Muslims into the kingdom of God and has helped to establish over five thousand "Lighthouses of Love" in the Middle East.[612]

While ministering to one thousand pastors and leaders at the Catch the Fire Conference in Moscow in 1995, Randy prayed for Rabbi Boris Grisenko. Since then, Grisenko's Messianic congregation has grown to over one thousand people and is considered one of the largest in the world. Grisenko's best friend from the Ukraine, Oleg Scherbakov, was also deeply impacted from the impartation he received at the same conference. Scherbakov is now the "pro forma bishop of the region, serving all other Protestant congregations of Nikolaev."[613] During Randy's time in Moscow, Russian Oleg Serov was also completely healed of stuttering. Though not a pastor at the time he attended the conference, three years later, he became the pastor of the largest Protestant church in his city and has since planted other churches and ministries. Another Russian named Sasha simply read about the Toronto Blessing online, encountered the Holy Spirit, and then planted several churches.[614]

While speaking at a pastor's conference in Toronto in January 1997, Randy released a significant impartation and prophetic word over Heidi Baker that later helped reignite her ministry in explosive ways.[615] As of 2013, Randy reports that through Rolland and Heidi Baker's ministry and Leif Hetland's ministry alone, there have already been two million people saved and well over fifteen thousand churches planted. In 1999, Randy also ministered to Pastor Henry Madava, a young apostolic leader in Kiev, Ukraine. God had previously given Madava a strategy for evangelism that he had not yet put into action. After the impartation from Randy, he began healing crusades around the world. Through the ministries of Heidi Baker, Leif Hetland, and Henry Madava, three million salvations have occurred. And there have been at least another million salvations through other people who were touched in this move of God.[616]

Before Toronto, Randy had been hungry for more of God at any cost and desperate to receive impartation from other powerful leaders. After his turning point in Toronto, however, Randy became the powerful leader releasing impartation to other key leaders. What he imparted to others radically shifted their ministries and caused explosive growth in them. Randy eventually founded Global Awakening and has since traveled to over forty-five countries, releasing the kingdom in signs and wonders.[617]

Two of the primary themes that are released wherever Randy goes are healing and impartation. Brazil, specifically, has become a land of his greatest anointing and favor. From 1999–2013, Randy and his teams have seen over two hundred thousand healings there. The blind see, the deaf hear, the lame walk, and those with diseases are fully healed. Scores of thousands have been saved, and others have been empowered for ministry.[618]

Randy has also started several ministry and healing schools. He regularly leads missions trips, speaks at conferences, writes books, and releases impartation around the world. Moreover, he recently completed his doctorate at United Theological Seminary, a United Methodist school, after having previously received a bachelor's degree in religious studies, as well as a master's degree in divinity from Southern Baptist Theological Seminary.

Randy on Encounters and Spirit Baptism

Like Heidi Baker and many others, Randy is more concerned with "intimate relationship" with Jesus than anything else in his ministry.[619] For him, the secret power behind his anointing is living in the "continuing power of the Spirit," not just in one great impartation or encounter but as a lifestyle. He says,

> My emphasis has been less on the experience of receiving an impartation of the Spirit and more on the fruit of having intimate relationship with Jesus Christ. The reason I have encouraged people in my church not to ask someone if they have been baptized in the Spirit is that the answer does not really tell us much…. It is like asking people if they have had a wedding. They may answer yes, but that does not tell you anything about their relationship with their spouse. They may be living in marital hell. They may be living in

marital bliss. They may now be divorced or widowed or separated. We do not really know much about a marital relationship by asking someone if he or she has had a wedding. Rather, we learn more by asking people how intimate they are with their mate and whether they love their mate more today than when they first got married.

In like manner, people could have had an experience with God years ago—call it baptism in the Holy Spirit or some kind of impartation of the Spirit—but now they are cold or lukewarm or backslidden. Or they may be passionately in love with God. Focus on the *relationship*. In this way people cannot hide behind an experience of the past. It is not enough to have received a baptism in the Holy Spirit; we must continue being filled with the Spirit. It is not enough to have received an impartation of the Spirit; we need to live in the continuing power of the Spirit.[620]

Randy gives himself liberally to the young and old alike. His advice is simple yet profound, always drawing people into a closer relationship with Jesus. His one desire is that God be glorified. He says,

Remember that it is out of relationship that this powerful new move of God is born. As He continues to shape and perfect your relationship with Him, He will increase accordingly the anointing He has placed upon your life. When you are completely equipped to perform what He has called you to do on earth, He will release you to *go!* I would like to provide these guidelines as encouragement to those of you who wish to be used by God:

- Cultivate an attitude of humility.
- Pursue unity within the body of Christ.
- Develop a secret prayer life with God.
- Become grounded in His Word.
- Pay attention to the promptings of your heart.
- Fast and pray.
- Visit those places and people where and in whom God is pouring out His Spirit in an unusual manner.

+ Have the patience necessary to wait for the fulfillment of prophetic words with which your spirit bears witness.

+ Accept the sovereignty of God.[621]

Acts 2:42 (NASB) says of the early church, *"They were continually devoting themselves to the apostles' teaching and to fellowship, to the breaking of bread and to prayer."* This basically means that they continued to renew themselves in the basic priorities of their lives, over and over again. That's what staying filled with the Holy Spirit is—it's renewing the contract of total surrender again and again so that He might be fully manifest in and through us.

Prophetic Inheritance

Impartation

Like many before him, Randy has experienced several impartations. Living in what we've been given is what prepares us for increase. Even a life-changing impartation must be stewarded well for the purpose of staying fresh and bringing increase. If I will tend this garden, it will produce for as long as I am on this earth. But if I don't, the weeds (cares, distractions, and offenses) will choke the wonderful grace that God has planted in my life. Impartation is one of God's ways of releasing gifts. And all treasures must be treasured.

Impartation is something that God alone directs in His sovereignty. Ministers of the gospel are not vending machines that we approach with a request, pull the lever on the machine, and walk away with a life-changing experience. Seek God in secret. Cry out specifically for what your heart aches for. And when you have the chance, receive impartation, knowing that God alone releases the grace for increase.

Gifts are free; maturity is expensive.

Personal Prophecy

Very few areas frighten church leaders more than personal prophecy. And with good reason. The abuses throughout history have traumatized many. Yet prophecy is still in the Bible. The abuses of prophecy never justify its neglect. To the same degree that it has caused damage, to that degree—and more—it is to be used to build, to edify, and to set free. At several turning points in Randy's life, a prophetic word first came forth to prepare him with the courage he needed to embrace God's new endeavor. We see the same pattern in Scripture. I would like to suggest that the problem with prophecy has not been merely with wrong words given by well-meaning people. The problem has been with believers who have not learned to decipher between meat and bones. The New Testament shifts the focus from judging the prophet to judging the word, because New Testament believers have the Holy Spirit in them, enabling them to discern whether what's been given to them is from God or not.

I look to the Scriptures, and not to man, for direction from the Lord. I read the Bible with a heart open to the voice of God, who brilliantly speaks through the printed page. This is my primary source for direction. I've learned that hungering for His voice seems to attract His voice. But sometimes that voice comes through a prophetic word from another person. It is not mine to decide whether God will speak through Scripture, through His audible voice, through His still, small voice, or through a human vessel. My job is to hunger.

You can't hunger for His voice without having a passion for His will. Jesus said that the Father's will was His food. (See John 4:34.) Leaning into Him due to a love for the will of God attracts the word of the Lord.

In my forty-plus years of ministry, I know of few things that have brought freedom to people more quickly than an authentic prophetic word. There is a clear pattern set forth in Randy's life, bringing him into the greater things of God—prophecy and impartation. And these gifts remain with us to this day so that each of us might experience the greater things.

Hunger That Leads to Fasting

Fasting is not a hunger strike. It is not a time when we let God know what we want and threaten not to eat until we get it. That would be manipulation. God responds to people who cooperate with His promises and with the nature of His kingdom. He exposes us to possibilities, summons us through opportunities, and invites us to co-labor with Him to see His kingdom manifest among humanity. It's hard to imagine anyone turning down such an invitation, yet it happens all the time.

True fasting is when we hunger for God's world more than we hunger for this one. It's not escapism. It is recognizing a superior reality and not being willing to settle for less. Many people throughout history have fasted until they got a breakthrough. Randy is one of them. In his life, there is a definite trail of breakthroughs preceded by fasting. Jesus prepared us for this when He said, *"When you fast..."* (Matthew 6:16, 17). He didn't say "If you fast...."

Hunger is usually the precursor to breakthrough. In Randy's case, it was a hunger that increased through the years that brought him layer after layer of breakthrough. And I can tell you firsthand that he hungers for more.

Sometimes the hunger is not about fasting but about focus. Sometimes it's not about saying "no" to a thousand options but about saying "yes" to the one thing. I've seen this firsthand in Randy's life. He said "yes" to the one thing, and he refuses to change the subject, no matter what is popular or what latest theme is in demand. As a result, we get to see a man on a journey, driven by hunger, living with great risk, and literally changing the world.

Postscript

There are many reports of great men and women of God who thought they were going to die while experiencing a God-encounter. This is a story frequently told by those who have sought God with all their hearts, cried out for more at any cost, and ended up in their defining moment. Waves of electricity shot through Randy's body. People around him wondered at what God was doing. And yet history has proven that the unexplainable has released Randy into the unimaginable. The deeper the touch on a person, the more profound the grace released through him or her. It's time for us once again to so completely direct our hearts to the one thing that nothing else matters. From that posture, we see and think differently, live differently, and get in position to change the world.

14

Surrender:
Heidi Baker

"Anyone that discovers who He is would give everything.
He's the pearl of great price, He's the lover of our souls....
Once you see Him, you'll give anything."[622]
—*Heidi Baker*

Heidi Baker seeks to live a life of complete surrender to the Lord with full possession by the Holy Spirit. She has intentionally cultivated her heart to become a temple that God can fill with His glory and saturate with His presence. I did an interview about Heidi's life for the film *Compelled by Love*. Here is my description of this dear friend and hero of the faith:

> Heidi's life is infectious. She is totally sold out to Jesus. When you take that life and you put it in front of people, there is a certain percentage of people from that group who will do anything: they

will pay any price to have that connection with God. It has nothing to do with performance, fame, or accomplishments. It has to do with people recognizing and seeing in Heidi the supreme call on a human being. I realize it is not all about Heidi because she is made of the same stuff we're made of. But that's the thing that encourages me; she is made of the same stuff we're made of; but she said "yes."[623]

The Impact of One Surrendered Life

Heidi is an example of how one life surrendered to God can impact a nation. I've been with Heidi and her husband, Rolland, in their home, at their ministry base, and in places of ministry all over the world. I can honestly say that I've never seen anything like it. They demonstrate the most authentic model of the Jesus lifestyle I've ever seen, anywhere.

Heidi G. Baker is a missionary to the poorest of the poor, primarily in Mozambique, Africa. Heidi and Rolland Baker lead a missions movement called Iris Global that is marked by love, mercy, signs, wonders, and miracles. After spending many years of ministry to plant four churches, they touched an unfathomable acceleration point and planted over ten thousand churches in just ten years. What brought about such transformation in and through them? A defining moment through an impartation prayer from Randy Clark. Heidi's story is one of the most measurable accounts revealing the impact of a moment. While it would be foolish to ever reduce a life as rich as the Bakers' to one experience, it would also be foolish to ignore the obvious—that a moment, when it's orchestrated by God, can change *everything*. The before and after of a defining moment has never been clearer.

Heidi encourages people to live in utter dependence on God, to realize that all fruitfulness flows from intimacy, and to stop to love the one in front of them. She also encourages people to drink from both the cups of joy and of suffering. She has been used as a catalyst to wake up the church and to release revival around the world. Through the Bakers' relentless passion for Jesus and for the poor, they are not only transforming the nation of Mozambique but also continuing to bring a major paradigm shift in the West, replacing the model of how church is done with a model of family and kingdom.

Early Days

Heidi's mother, Glenetta Farrell, was barren but cried out to God for a child, promising to dedicate her firstborn to the Lord. In the meantime, she and her husband, James, decided to adopt a son named Zachary. Then, on August 29, 1959, Heidi became the fulfilled promise of her mother's prayer, the miracle child they had hoped for. Four years later, Zachary died of congenital heart disease. After this, Heidi became extremely sick with spinal meningitis. She spent six weeks in the hospital fighting for her life. Her parents pleaded with God, promising to give her completely to Him if He healed her.[624] He honored their request, and Heidi was healed. Interestingly, Heidi's early dedication to the Lord by her mother is similar to the experience of Aimee Semple McPherson.

Heidi grew up in a wealthy family in Laguna Beach, California, and attended an Episcopalian church. She always remembered having a hunger for God from a young age. Even during her first communion when she was twelve years old, she was overwhelmed in the Spirit, fell down, and had to be carried out of the church. Heidi remembered,

> I always wanted God the whole time I was growing up. "Where are you, God?" I would ask, lying on my bed at night. I prayed every prayer I was taught in my mother's Episcopal church. I prayed all the time. The Holy Spirit would touch me powerfully as I took the Eucharist. I was being prepared and called.[625]

Heidi was also exposed to missions and to the poor at a young age when her parents took her on vacations to Mexico. Further, Heidi's sixth-grade teacher, who had previously been a missionary to China, showed the class pictures of her work in the slums of Hong Kong. This sparked Heidi's interest in missions even more and stirred her to begin to pray for the time when she could go to Hong Kong to help the people there. When Heidi was thirteen, she lived as a foreign exchange student in Switzerland, where she learned German.

Saved, Baptized, Speaking in Tongues

On March 13, 1976, at the age of sixteen, while serving as an American Field Service student on a Choctaw Indian reservation in Mississippi, Heidi was led to the Lord by a Navajo evangelist. The very next day, she was introduced to the "Holy Ghost" by members of a Pentecostal Holiness church. She recalled this turn of events:

> It was storming that night, but I didn't care. I ran through the rain and puddles to the church and tried to sneak in unnoticed. But I was obvious, the only white girl, with sopping blonde hair. The preacher, wearing his bright, multi-colored native coat, was Navajo. He was preaching about his days in the Indian power movement and about how much he hated whites. I began to feel very nervous. But then I took notice. He said he met a man who taught him how to see people from the inside, and how to love. That's what I had wanted all my life. He talked about our sin, and our need for forgiveness and faith in Jesus. He gave an altar call. Nobody responded.
>
> Then I felt as if a hand physically grabbed my shirt and pulled me forward. My heart broke and I burst into tears. Sobbing I ran to the altar alone in front of five hundred [Native Americans]. The pastor's wife tried to calm me down and assure me everything was all right. "It's not all right!" I cried. "I'm a sinner!" It was March 13, 1976.
>
> Glenda, the pianist, came running over and gave me a big hug. "I'm so glad you're saved, but now you need the Holy Ghost!" I remembered something about the Holy Ghost from Episcopal prayers, and I wanted everything. Glenda invited me to her Pentecostal Holiness church the next night. I was going to go to the movies, but not any more. That next day I felt so light and free, like a butterfly. The flowers and sky were so beautiful. My mood

changed completely. I told everyone I found what had happened to me, and I wanted them to experience the same thing. I sang and sang to Jesus. I was so in love with Him. I couldn't wait for church that night.

Only about thirty people were there. It seemed like I was their first visitor in years. All eyes turned to me, the California girl in jeans and a short top. Obviously I wasn't initiated. They invited me to the altar. Again a hand was pulling me. My heart was pounding hard. All thirty laid their hands on me and prayed for my baptism in the Holy Spirit. Immediately everything went black. I've never experienced anything so dark. And then in a few minutes all became bright white, even with my eyes closed, just brilliant, blazing light. I couldn't get out a word of English. All I could do was speak in tongues. "Now you need to be baptized in water!" they said. I just nodded, unable to communicate intelligibly. Out came water and a bathtub, and I was baptized right there.[626]

Laying Down a Dream

After her life-changing experience, Heidi started to attend church regularly. She told her church leaders that she was a ballet dancer, but they told her that dancing was a sin. She also felt the Lord leading her to surrender her dancing to Him. She recalls,

God spoke to me clearly when He told me to lay down the dance. It was powerful because my whole life I wanted to be a ballerina. I studied and diligently pursued that goal. When I was born again at the age of sixteen, I felt like I heard God say, "Lay down your toe shoes. Lay down the dance. Lay it down at My altar. Give it to Me." I remember with all that is within me saying, "Yes, Lord. I don't care what it costs me." And I remember crying because it hurt so badly. To just suddenly stop dancing was even painful for my body because it was so used to ballet. But laying that down and saying, "Okay, God, I want You to possess me. I don't care what the cost is. I don't care what it's going to take, I just want to yield," I felt like I was jumping off a cliff and trusting that He was going to catch me. He did, and it was awesome.[627]

While Heidi does not now believe ballet dance is a sin in any way, she always saw what happened at that time as a good thing because it taught her how to surrender the one thing she loved to the One she loved. She learned how to die to herself. Total surrender became a consistent part of her life. Several years later, God gave her back the dance when one of her professors at Vanguard University reintroduced her to it as a medium for evangelism.

A Vision of Destiny Released

A couple of months after her surrender, while on a five-day fast, Heidi was taken up in a vision for three hours and heard the call to minister in Africa, Asia, and England. This experience marked the path of her destiny.

I continued in school, learning Choctaw and native crafts, and leading friends in my dorm to Jesus. The thought of a life of ministry never occurred to me because I had never seen a woman preacher. In May toward the end of the semester I went on a five-day fast to find out more from God about what to do with my life. On the night of the fifth day I expectantly went to the Roarks' little Pentecostal church in the country and was drawn to the altar. I knelt down and lifted my arms to the Lord. Suddenly I felt taken to a new heavenly place. Pastor Roark was preaching, but I couldn't hear his loud, powerful voice at all. God's glory came to me again, wrapping me in a pure and brilliant white light. I was overwhelmed by who He is. I had never felt so loved, and I began to weep. This time He spoke to me audibly. "I am calling you to be a minister and a missionary," He said. "You are to go to Africa, Asia and England." Again my heart was pounding and racing. I thought I might die.

Then the Lord Jesus spoke to me and told me I would be married to Him. He kissed my hand and it felt as if warm oil ran down my arm. I was overcome with love for Him. I knew at any moment that I would go anywhere anytime and say anything for Him. I was ruined for this world by His intense love and mercy in calling me to Himself. I was stunned by such a powerful answer to my cry. When His presence began to lift, I opened my eyes and noticed that only Glenda and Pastor Roark were left in the church. They told me I had been completely still on my knees with my hands lifted up for hours.... God's word to me was so strong that I began preaching the next day. I told everyone about my precious Jesus and His intense love for us.... And since no pastor asked me to preach in a church, I began preaching on the streets.[628]

Heidi recognizes this overshadowing encounter as the most powerful of her life.[629] When she returned to Laguna Beach, she lost all of her friends because of her new faith. She also became involved in ministry and missions right away. She asked her Episcopal priest if she could use the basement of their church building to open a Christian coffeehouse. Every Friday night for several years, she ministered to drug addicts, the demonpossessed, the homeless, and the sick. She used the money she earned from working to buy them popcorn and coffee.

Exactly one year after her conversion, on March 13, 1977, she had an admissions interview at Southern California College, now Vanguard University, where she met a Christian lady who encouraged her in her faith. She was accepted to the college, and during her studies there, she met someone and fell in love, but six weeks before their wedding, she felt unrest. She was torn between getting married and leading a ministry trip to Europe at that same time. She finally surrendered this man to the Lord and dove even deeper into ministry. This was another choice of surrender that Heidi had to make. She chose to trust God even when it was painful. Later, during a ministry trip to Mexico, God spoke to Heidi again while she was "lost in worship."

He told me I would go to Indonesia and preach with Mel Tari, a famous Indonesian evangelist who had been used to raise the dead. I had never met him. He also told me I would finish college that year, one year sooner than usual. And then He told me I would marry Rolland Baker. I had only met Rolland once on a church ski trip! We had talked, but I had never thought anything more about it partly because he is twelve years older than I am.[630]

Then, on May 24, 1980, Heidi indeed married Rolland Baker, a third-generation missionary raised in China, and the grandson of H. A. Baker, author of *Visions Beyond the Veil*. Rolland's grandfather was involved in a significant revival in China in which the children saw visions and had encounters with God. H. A. Baker's influence in that country continues to impact the underground church today. Heidi not only married into that missionary legacy but, interestingly enough, found out that her inspiring sixth-grade teacher was Rolland's mother! The newlyweds left for Indonesia two weeks after their wedding with one-way tickets and only thirty dollars. Heidi remembered, "We had no money. We had no support from any church. But we had a word from God."[631] They worked with Mel Tari, who was a close friend of Rolland's and was also the best man at their wedding. They eventually based in Bali in 1980 and founded Iris Ministries, now called Iris Global.

Returning to the United States, both Heidi and Rolland attended Southern California College again. In 1985, Heidi graduated with a master's degree. Following this, the Bakers moved to Indonesia, served in Asia, and eventually connected with Jackie Pullinger's work in Hong Kong.[632] Jackie Pullinger ministered to drug addicts by having people pray in tongues over them around the clock. I've been to Jackie's ministry base and have seen firsthand the mighty work that God has done through her and her team. It is astonishing. I've never seen anything like it. The Bakers were greatly impacted by Jackie Pullinger's ministry to the poor and to the outcast. They also ministered in the Philippines during this season, further fulfilling part of Heidi's prophetic word and commissioning to Asia.[633]

During their time ministering in Hong Kong for four years, they moved into the poorest part of the city, where Heidi became extremely sick. She went to the home of her mentor, Juanita Vinson, in Fairbanks, Alaska, to rehabilitate. During the next four months, when she was unable to care for herself or her family, or even to read the Bible, God gave her new direction. He called her to plant a church among the homeless in England and to get a PhD there. After returning to Hong Kong, both she and Rolland applied to King's College, University of London, to study systematic theology, and were accepted.

PhD in England on Speaking in Tongues

Fulfilling another part of the vision God had given Heidi, in the fall of 1991, the Bakers moved to London, England, to begin their PhD's. They planted a church for the homeless and drug addicts while doing their studies at the same time. Heidi recalled, "By day we wrestled with prominent theological minds. By night we reached out to the poorest lost sheep we could find."[634]

The topic Heidi chose for her PhD research was speaking in tongues. During her years at King's College, Heidi spent time studying, praying through, and processing what communion with God looks like through the medium of tongues. She reconstructed a theology of glossolalia to be a bridge to unite evangelicals and Pentecostals. In her thesis, she attempted to "interpret and reform Pentecostal glossolalic prayer."[635] She challenged the Pentecostal view of initial evidence of Spirit baptism while at the same time highlighting the value of this gift. While celebrating the gifts of the Spirit, Heidi also emphasized the fruit of the Spirit, especially love, as needing to be front and center.[636] One must wonder how Heidi's studies at this point in her life prepared, shaped, and helped to deepen some of her theological beliefs and practices. Unity in love, ecumenicalism, value for the working of the Spirit without causing division, seeking reformation, building a bridge between Christian traditions, and seeking union with God were all themes she processed through in her work.[637]

Mozambique

Immediately after Heidi finished her PhD dissertation, she was released into the land of her destiny. Heidi's first trip to Africa came nearly twenty years after she had received her initial calling to go there. In the late 1980s, God had begun to stir the Bakers' hearts for the poorest of the poor in Mozambique. For several years, they had researched and prayed into this nation. Rolland first visited Mozambique for two weeks in January 1995 to scope things out. At that time, Mozambique was considered the poorest nation in the world. After two days there, he was offered an orphanage with eighty children in Chihango in Maputo. Then, in August 1995, Heidi went to Mozambique while Rolland finished up his research in England. She immediately began to learn the language and to lead the children to Jesus. With no support, they put the gospel to the test.[638] By the end of 1996, their children's center had grown to 320. The children also began to experience healings, visions, and manifestations of the Holy Spirit, similar to what had happened at Rolland's grandfather's orphanage in China.

Toronto Blessing

The "Always Enough" Vision

The Toronto Blessing revival broke out at the Toronto Airport Vineyard church on January 20, 1994, when Randy Clark came to speak. What was supposed to be a four-day series of meetings at John and Carol Arnott's church continued well beyond that, and it continues to influence the church around the world. When Rolland first visited Toronto for the second Catch the Fire Conference in October 1995, he was totally undone by God in that place. At 2:00 a.m., he called Heidi in Mozambique to tell her all about it and to flood her with his love. That became one of the most expensive phone calls of his life. In a place so saturated with the love of the Father, Rolland was radically changed.[639]

After seeing the transformation in her husband, and through his encouragement, Heidi finally made it to Toronto for the first time in July 1996 for a healing conference.[640] At the time, she was extremely ill and desperate for healing. She was hungry for another touch from God. During the first meeting, the speaker had a prophetic word that God was going to heal a missionary of double pneumonia and encouraged that person to take a deep breath. Heidi responded, her lungs were opened, and she was healed. When Heidi was called up to the front to give a testimony, Carol

Arnott prayed for her. Heidi manifested by swimming like a fish on the stage.[641] Even at that time, Heidi was willing to let the Lord make her look foolish if need be. She was fully yielded for Him to do whatever He wanted with her laid-down life.[642]

Later on during the conference, while Heidi was on the floor "groaning in intercession" for the children of Mozambique, God gave her a powerful vision about how there would always be enough because He had died. This vision would later mark her life and ministry and be the second most powerful encounter she recognized in her life.[643] She recalled,

> Then I had a dramatic, clear vision of Jesus. I was with Him, and thousands and thousands of children surrounded us. I saw His shining face and His intense, burning eyes of love…. Then again the Lord said, "Look into my eyes. You give them something to drink." He gave me a cup of blood and water, which flowed from His side. I knew it was a cup of [suffering] and joy. I drank it and then began to give it to the children to drink. The cup did not go dry. By this point I was crying uncontrollably. I was completely undone by His fiery eyes of love. I realized what it had cost Him to provide such spiritual and physical food for us all. The Lord spoke to my heart and said, "There will always be enough, because I died."[644]

Trouble Awaits

Following this powerful vision, Heidi returned to Mozambique with great hopes of taking many more children. However, upon the Bakers' arrival, officials gave them forty-eight hours to leave the premises of their orphanage. They told them worship was no longer allowed, and they beat many of the children. A twenty-dollar contract had even been put out on Heidi's life to kill her. The children found their way to the Bakers' office fifteen miles away. During that time, more than one hundred children piled up in their small apartment, which had only one bathroom. Hearing about their distress, someone from the U.S. Embassy brought over a pot of chili and rice, just enough to feed the Bakers. As the food was served, it multiplied before their eyes to feed all of the children who had come. In the midst of this intense trouble, Heidi strengthened herself in the Lord by recalling the vision of Jesus she had received in Toronto. A few weeks after they were evicted, the local government donated land to them in Machava so they could open up another center.[645]

Million-Dollar Donation and Vision of the Lamb

During this trying season, a large church in North America that had been supporting the Bakers for years and had recently pledged a million dollars to help build a new children's center told them to steer clear of the move of God at Toronto or their donation would be revoked. Even though it would cost their losing a million-dollar pledge to associate with or return to Toronto, the Bakers decided to go back in July 1997 because they were desperate for more of God.[646] As a result, the pastor of the church pulled the pledged donation from their ministry. This became their most expensive conference ever!

The Bakers shared a brief testimony from the stage, and after this Heidi felt electricity through her body and encountered God like a lightning bolt. Carol Arnott soaked her in prayer and released the love of God over her.[647] It was during this conference that Heidi had a vision of "the wedding feast of the Lamb" that led her to later minister in the garbage dumps.[648] Following this, Heidi and Rolland returned to Mozambique where children at their center experienced a special visitation from the Lord, which included visits to heaven, dancing with angels, and sitting on the Father's lap.[649]

Randy Clark's Impartation

When the Bakers returned to Toronto for the pastor's conference in January 1998, Heidi was radically impacted. In one session, while John Arnott was speaking about anointing and the heavy weight of glory, God's presence fell on Heidi "like a heavy blanket of liquid love."[650]

During another session, when Randy Clark was sharing his message on "Pressing In," Heidi ran screaming to the front even before there was an altar call. Randy stopped his message, looked at Heidi, who had tears streaming down her face, grabbed her hand, and told her she had an apostolic anointing on her life. Then he asked her if she wanted the nation of Mozambique. She said, "*Yes!*" In Heidi's own words, here is what happened:

At one of the meetings during this conference, Randy Clark was preaching with great fire and conviction about the anointing, power and destiny of God. All of a sudden, in the middle of Randy's message, I became so desperate for God that I just could not stop myself from responding and I ran to the front before he was finished speaking, even though it was in front of thousands of people. There was no altar call or pause in his message but I ran to the front, knelt at the altar, lifted up my hands and started screaming. I wondered about what I was doing, I couldn't believe that I was acting like that, because it's not something I would naturally do. However, I became so possessed by the Holy Spirit and so full of longing and desperation for more of His Presence that I no longer cared. Randy stopped preaching, put his hands on me and said, "God wants to know, do you want the nation of Mozambique?" And he continued, "The blind will see, the deaf will hear, the crippled will walk, the dead will be raised and the poor will hear the Good News."[651]

Heidi felt the power of God hit her "like lightning." She remembers screaming and "vibrating," thinking she was going to die. She began to sweat profusely; she felt like she had been placed in an oven.[652] When she told God she was going to die, she heard Him say, "Good, I want you dead!"[653] Heidi recalled that during that conference,

For seven days I was unable to move. Rolland had to pick me up and carry me. I had to be carried to the washroom, to the hotel and back to the meeting. The weight of His glory was upon me. I felt so heavy I could not lift my head. Some passing by thought it was funny to see someone stuck to the floor for so long. If I was put in a chair, I would slide out onto the floor again. I was utterly and completely helpless. I was unable to speak for most of the seven days. This holy, fearful awesome presence of God completely changed my life. I've never been so humbled, never felt so poor, so helpless, so vulnerable. I even needed help to drink water. There was nothing funny about it. It was a most holy time. I learned more in those seven days than in ten years of academic theological study. The Lord spoke to me about relinquishing control to Him. He showed me the importance of the Body of Christ. It had taken us seventeen years to plant four churches, and two of them were pretty weak. As I lay there engulfed in His presence, He spoke to me about hundreds of churches being planted in Mozambique. I remember laughing hysterically, thinking I would have to live to be two hundred years old before that promise was fulfilled! God showed me that I needed to learn to work with the rest of the Body.[654]

During the next year and a half following this powerful prophetic word and encounter, things got worse for the Bakers. Heidi was diagnosed with multiple sclerosis (MS) and was told by the doctors that she would likely die if she went back to Africa. She returned anyway, believing in the prophetic word that had been released.[655] Then Rolland got cerebral malaria; their daughter Crystalyn got malaria several times; Heidi was in a car crash; riots broke out at the dump, where Heidi got hit in the face; and the well pump at their center broke, leaving hundreds without water.[656] It was a trying time, indeed.

Eventually, things started to turn around for the Baker family. As the children at the center prayed for Heidi, she continued to get better. Rolland and Crystalyn also recovered. After her time in Toronto, when she had been on the floor for seven days, Heidi drastically changed her leadership style. She began to empower and release leaders more. The Bakers eventually started a small Bible school and sent out pastors to evangelize. These new leaders began to see signs and wonders. During this time, Heidi wanted to get a tent that would hold the one thousand people in their church, but it would cost ten thousand dollars, which they did not have. By faith, she went to a tent store in South Africa. While she was there, the exact amount of money they needed was deposited into their account, and they were able to purchase a tent that someone had ordered but never picked up.[657]

Acceleration–Three Blind Women Named "Mama Aida"

Heidi continued to act in faith on the promises given to her, even though she had not seen the fruit she expected. She chose to put her trust in God who is unseen, rather than let her surrounding circumstances throw her off course or cause her to give up. She remembered,

> I have received prophecies for years that in our ministry the blind will see, the deaf will hear, the crippled will walk, the dumb will speak, the dead will be raised and the multitudes will come to Jesus. As time went on it seemed these prophecies became stronger. People began to minister these words over me more and more. I especially remember Randy Clark prophesying over me in 1998. After that I would literally go out and look for every blind person I could find. Living in one of the poorest nations of the earth, they're pretty easy to find.... I'd pray for them and I'd lead them to Jesus. Every one of them would get saved. I never felt like I failed because they came to Jesus, every one, but none of them saw. I must have prayed for twenty blind people, and none of them saw. But I kept praying. I kept remembering those prophetic words that the Holy Spirit poured into my heart. There was such a powerful presence of the Holy Spirit as those words were spoken over me. I just said, "I'm not giving up.... One day they're going to see."[658]

About a year after Randy's prophecy over Heidi about the blind eyes being opened and the dead being raised, Heidi and her team prayed for three blind ladies, and they all received their sight. The interesting thing was that each of their names was "Mama Aida," the same name Heidi is known by in Mozambique. She felt that the Lord spoke to her through this that she was the one who was blind. God showed her that while Africa had physical poverty, there was spiritual poverty in the Western and Eastern worlds. God was calling her to see and to love not just the poor of Mozambique but also others around the world, whether rich or poor.[659]

Floods

Following the healing of these three blind women, other signs, wonders, and miracles began to be released in greater measures, including the dead being raised. The Bakers added Surprise Sithole, a local pastor, to their team in 1998, and this also expanded their ministry.[660] He brought ninety churches with him to join their movement. Heidi and Rolland also bought land in Zimpeto, adding another children's center to their ministry.

While in Toronto again in the late 1990s, Heidi had an encounter while standing on her head. God had turned her upside down during the service. Ian Ross did a prophetic act of pouring water down her feet, and it dripped to her head. During that time, the Lord showed her that the apostolic call is upside down; it flows to the lowest place. He also showed her that He wants her to live underwater, fully immersed in the Ezekiel 47 river.[661] Then, on February 7, 2000, severe floods hit Mozambique.[662] In the midst of this tragedy, hunger for God arose in the country. Revival broke out and spread across the land at an accelerated rate.[663] By December 2000, over five hundred churches had been planted through Iris Global, fulfilling some of the prophetic words spoken over Heidi.[664]

Technicolor Vision

In December 2001, Heidi had a "Technicolor" vision in the living room of John and Carol Arnott in Toronto. In the vision, she saw chariots of fire circle the globe. The riders had huge hearts, and the reins to the chariots went straight up to heaven. The chariots released the glory and fire of God around the world.[665] After that vision, and through the other ways God had already been speaking to her, Heidi felt led to spend one third of her time preaching around the world. She remembered that "since that vision our churches jumped in number from two thousand to over five thousand between December 2001 and August 2002."[666] By 2002, the Bakers planted the first churches in the north, in Pemba. By 2004, they moved from their base in Maputo to be close to the unreached Makua tribe in Pemba. Then, in 2005, they launched their first missions school for students from around the world, at that time called "Holy Given International Missions School," and now called "Iris Harvest School."

Healed in Toronto

Your destiny is to become a resting place for the Most High God.[667]

—Heidi Baker

Then, in October 2005, Heidi was sick again, with little hope for a cure. She was diagnosed with "methicillin-resistant Staphylococcus infection," a life-threatening staph infection. Even though she had been hospitalized for over thirty days and had cancelled all of her other engagements, she believed she was still supposed to speak at the upcoming conference in Toronto. She believed that God had told her that she would be healed there. Then, in Toronto, on October 20, 2005, while speaking from the book of Zechariah about fulfilling one's destiny, Heidi was healed right there on the stage.[668] Following her message, she danced before the Lord in front of the whole crowd, celebrating the miracle of life God had just granted her. Instead of becoming a ballerina, as she had once dreamed, Heidi has been used to bring many people to the Lord in the nation of Mozambique and to ignite the world with God's love. The dream she surrendered in her teenage years has become a thanksgiving offering unto the Lord.

Impact of Randy Clark and the Toronto Blessing

Heidi's experiences within the Toronto Blessing movement shifted her paradigm and opened her heart to receive and to understand the Father's love in greater measures.[669] After the "Always Enough" vision, the impartation from Randy Clark, the seven-day encounter, and the ministry she received while in Toronto, greater signs and wonders were released in her ministry. The timing of the Bakers' intersection with Toronto, followed by the floods in Mozambique in the year 2000, birthed a catalytic synergy that accelerated and launched their ministry like never before.

In relation to the impact of the Toronto Blessing upon their lives, Rolland wrote, "We have experienced some measure of God's love, power and presence all through our lives and ministry, but we concur that through the 'Toronto Blessing' we received an additional, massive impetus from Him that enabled us not only to survive and maintain, but to bear fruit increasingly in exponential measure."[670] He added, "We point to a set of core values that spring from a broader base than the Toronto Blessing, but without the impartation we received there, we realize we could not have continued our ministry at all, much less see such growth."[671] Rolland said that when they first visited Toronto, "Heidi and I were just two more people out of hundreds of thousands at the Toronto church, and we felt we were amazingly blessed to be included at all. The fruit of Mozambique is entirely God's doing, and a complete and utter surprise to us."[672]

The Bakers' Impact on Mozambique

As of February 2014, Iris Global has over thirty bases (ten in Mozambique) in about twenty nations. It feeds over ten thousand people a day and has more than ten thousand churches, in addition to Bible schools, primary and secondary schools, vocational training schools, a professional English school, an international mission school, and other developments in the works.[673] Besides the many healings and miracles, over one hundred people have also been raised from the dead in their ministry.[674] Iris Global also includes outreach, child sponsorship, church planting, children's centers, farming, medical clinics, and more. Heidi currently continues to spend one third of her time preaching in the Western and Eastern worlds.[675] In 2013, Rolland reported the following:

> In 1995 half of Maputo's two million people were refugees from the war living in huts around the city center. There was no internet service or cell phones.... The country of Mozambique now has one of the fastest growing economies in the world, one that has grown at an average annual rate of 6%–8% in the decade up to 2012.... Iris Ministries, now renamed Iris Global, has become the largest single group of churches in the nation, with some 10,000 churches that consider themselves part of "Ministério Arco-Íris" [this is part of the Partners in Harvest network].... We have hundreds of churches in South Africa and Malawi, and our most intense front lines now are in DR Congo and South Sudan. We also have an arm called "Iris Relief," which is increasingly involved in disaster zones such as the aftermaths of earthquakes in Haiti and Japan. The percentage of Christians in Mozambique has nearly doubled since 1995 to more than 51%.[676]

Accumulatively, from their time in Mozambique from 1995 to 2013, the nation has seen profound and marked effects from the Bakers' presence and what God has done through them and their large team.

Over the years, both Heidi and Rolland have suffered greatly and have been on the verge of death more than once. Rolland recounts that "Heidi and I would both be dead now without miraculous healing…. Heidi has faced blood poisoning, double pneumonia, chronic fatigue syndrome, multiple sclerosis and terminal MRSA infection. I have faced advanced cerebral malaria, strokes and terminal dementia."[677] Despite all the setbacks, persecutions, illnesses, and resistance, they have not given up on the promises of God for their lives and for the nation of Mozambique. Their relentless pursuit of enjoying Jesus and demonstrating His love for the poor, of being fully possessed by the Holy Spirit, and of giving God glory has impacted the face of evangelical Christianity in the twenty-first century.[678]

All Fruitfulness Flows from Intimacy

In *Birthing the Miraculous*, Heidi Baker wrote, "The first part of your calling is intimacy with Him."[679] Heidi identifies her top three most powerful encounters in the following order: when she was taken up in a vision for three hours and received her calling (May 1976), her "Always Enough" vision, where she saw the face and the body of Jesus (summer 1996), and her impartation with Randy Clark, followed by her seven days on the floor (January 1998).[680] Even after all the encounters, visions, and impartations, Heidi continues to seek full possession by the Holy Spirit. She says, "These visitations have provoked me to want to live continually in the Ezekiel 47 river. I want to be fully immersed in His glory, to see His eyes, to touch His heart, and to give away His ceaseless, limitless, bottomless love to a lost and dying world. Only when we are completely yielded will nations come to Him."[681]

Heidi starts her days worshipping and praying in the secret place alone with God; she guards this time, knowing that she needs to be filled with His love if she is to have anything to pour out. She also begins most of her meetings with prayer and worship, and she communes with the Holy Spirit throughout the day. She realizes that

there is no shortcut to being full of the Holy Spirit. The only way we can be close to Him is to spend time with Him. We can't be close to Him any other way. We can't just say, "I'm going to have a radical experience, and it's going to carry me for a year." Relationships don't work like that. If you are a friend of Holy Spirit, He wants time with you.[682]

Heidi seeks to nurture this friendship by abiding in a continuing encounter with the living God. She calls this generation to be flooded by the Spirit as a way of life.[683]

I feel that the Lord is inviting us into a place we have been afraid to live in—the supernatural realm of His kingdom, where His manifest presence surrounds and holds us like water in the ocean's depths. We were created to breathe in this realm. We can be permanently immersed in the glory of His love. We simply have to drown.... God is looking for a people He can so immerse in His love that for the rest of their lives they will have to survive inside His heart. Nothing else will matter to them.... Still, He calls us deeper. No matter how deep we have gone, there is more. We need to go deeper and lower until all we have is the mind of Christ. We are called to be more than a people who can dive for brief periods but have to keep popping up our heads, trying to figure it all out. We have to be able to breathe in His atmosphere without coming up for the world's air.[684]

The Bakers continually seek to live in God's manifest presence, as I described in the documentary film *Compelled by Love*:

Anchoring to the manifest presence of the Spirit of God is the heart and soul of who the Bakers are. It's not an add-on. I think the Lord has entrusted so much to them in responsibility and favor because they've been faithful in the greatest treasure, the person of the Holy Spirit. God trusts them enough to give them Himself. Since they have stewarded that well, all the other things like the miracles, favor, and open doors that everyone works and fights for have been added to them. All of that has come because they value the presence of the living God.[685]

Surrender

Heidi believes that "yielding to Him is everything." When she hears God speak due to being in that place of total surrender, nothing can stop her from fulfilling His word. Possessing a fierce determination similar to that of Maria Woodworth-Etter, Heidi says that "no demon of hell, no difficulty, no flood, no famine, no earthquake" can keep her from going after what is revealed to her in the secret place. Heidi also says that "yieldedness is in a way self-emptying. It's like saying, 'God, I want to take everything of myself and pour it out at Your feet. I give it all to You. Then I want You to possess me with Yourself.'" Heidi's desire each day "is to give Him more" of herself because He is everything to her.[686]

In a personal interview, one word Rolland used to describe Heidi is "surrendered." He also said that "she is the one person I personally know that basically has never said 'no' to God."[687] One person totally yielded and willing to say yes to whatever God says can literally impact a nation and be used to transform it. Not only did Heidi say "yes" to God, but Rolland did, as well, multiplying the effect of the kingdom expansion in and through their unified lives.

It's always inspiring to see what simple faith does to the heart of God. The Bakers are unusual in that they are 100 percent sold out. They are not just committed when there is an altar call; they are committed in the way they do life. They are completely sold out to the purposes of Christ and to the kingdom of God in the way they approach their time, their family, and their possessions. That's how they live. Countless numbers of people make that same decision but don't know how to follow through. What the Bakers have done is to constantly put themselves back on the altar and continually renew the contact. They are constantly saying, "Everything for You." And they are stirring others to do the same, as I emphasized in *Compelled by Love*:

> I don't know anyone like Heidi and Rolland. As I look around the places where they have either established a base, or they have established relationships, more and more people are becoming contagious for Jesus like they are. Literally just putting them as an

example in front of a group causes people to find out why they are alive. They suddenly hear something they've never heard before, but it sounds familiar because it's what was written into their heart when they were created. They discover a purpose and a destiny that finally somebody addressed and called them to. It's a powerful thing to watch people all over the world step into that same "yes." They may not be in the same place on the journey, but they are on the same journey with the same devotion, commitment to Christ, and abandonment, no matter the cost. Untold thousands have said "yes" and are on that same journey with Rolland and Heidi into the heart of God. I can almost spot them when I meet them. I can almost say, "You've been with Heidi, haven't you?" because they have the same *laid-down lover* approach to life as the Bakers.[688]

Prophetic Inheritance

One of the basic aspects of being a disciple of Jesus is the responsibility to surrender everything to Him. It's actually our point of entrance into this life of faith. In that sense, every true believer reading this book lives a surrendered life. And yet looking at this present-day hero of the faith, "surrender" takes on new meaning. She models most everything she does at a new level, with new measures of breakthrough. When I'm with her, I feel like a child again—one who knows so little about this life I am living. That might sound degrading. Not so. Her life constantly summons me to the greater things.

Rolland and Heidi are two of my most treasured friends. Oftentimes, the closer we get to people, and the more we see into their private lives, our respect for them diminishes, or at least doesn't increase. Not so with the Bakers. I have been powerfully impacted by their pulpit ministry in countless meetings where we've been together over the past fifteen-plus years. The way they inspire all of us to surrender all to Jesus is unparalleled. And yet I am convicted unto righteousness even more through their personal lives. The miracles are impressive. I've been with Heidi in Pemba, Mozambique, when the blind see. I've seen, with my own eyes, someone who is completely blind have the white film over their eyes completely disappear, and beautiful eyes emerge with the overjoyed person glowing in the goodness of God. And then it has happened again only a few minutes later. And yet, that's not what impacts me the most. It's her love for Jesus, her yieldedness to the Holy Spirit, and her joy-filled life with a perfect heavenly Father that has left a permanent mark on my life. I will never be the same. I cannot ever be the same.

Power with Purpose

When the outpouring of the Holy Spirit came at Pentecost, it changed everything about life for all of Jesus' followers. His disciples were then able to see why He said it was better that He left. This indescribable gift was their key to the greater works. This wonderful baptism was, without question, for the purpose of power. Yet there's another part of the equation that isn't always emphasized but should be. It's called *endurance*. The ability to endure tough times also comes from the same power of God. In fact, it's often the profound power encounters with God that make endurance of this nature even possible.

In relation to his prophecy over Heidi about having Mozambique, Randy Clark noted that "the prophetic word is what God uses to strengthen." He went on to say, "I have noticed that there is often a relationship between the intensity of an experience with God and the degree of difficulty the person will be facing in fulfilling the call of God on their lives."[689]

In Rolland and Heidi's life, we see a beautiful combination of power for miracles and power for endurance. I don't know anyone who has endured more than these two. And yet it's the same gift, in full measure, that enables them to do what they do—the impossible.

Suffering

Many have made the mistake of thinking that God gives sickness so we can be better followers of Jesus, learning to suffer for His name's sake. That is a mockery of the cross. The same redemptive brushstroke that dealt with sin, dealt with sickness. We sometimes mistake God's ability to use something like sickness for His glory as the sign that He is the author of the sickness. We would never say that about sin. We would hopefully never say that God occasionally ordains sin for us so that we can learn more about His grace and forgiveness. That denies the power and effectiveness of the blood of Jesus to truly free us from sin. Jesus never taught or modeled sickness as a form of suffering. And He is perfect theology.

Suffering in the New Testament is about persecution and opposition to our faith. This cup of suffering must be embraced by everyone who dedicates their life to following Jesus. Rolland and Heidi illustrate this brilliantly. They've experienced more conflict for their faith than anyone I know. I've heard Heidi say that she would never be able to endure the things she's gone through without her extreme encounter with God. It gave her the confidence to endure with purpose. Her defining moment made things possible that are unthinkable without it.

Sanctified Intelligence

Rolland and Heidi are two of the most intelligent people I've ever met. One of the things that inspires me the most is to see how this gift from God is used for His glory. This husband and wife team both have earned doctorates, which they both pursued because they were called by God to do so. As a result, they are having an incredible impact on the academic world, besides the worlds of politics, church life, missions, and others.

Postscript

The dead are raised, the blind see, the deaf hear, the lame walk, and the poor receive the good news of the kingdom. (See, for example, Matthew 11:3–5.) Over one million new believers have been added to heaven's roll book, over ten thousand churches have been planted and established, and orphans are treated as sons and daughters of the King, producing the fruit of transformed lives. Iris Global feeds over ten thousand people a day. They are experiencing a genuine transformation of a nation right before their eyes. It's affecting every area of life in Mozambique. And all of this has come following the third of Heidi's three defining moments.

Heidi has also been shot at, beaten, jailed, persecuted by local militants, and slandered and lied about by the national press. She and Rolland have been opposed and rejected by some of their closest friends in ministry. Their breakthrough has provoked jealousy and envy among believers. And some from their ranks have been martyred. All of this has also come after her defining moments. It would be incorrect to say that God sent persecution their way. It would be more correct to say that once you've had a defining moment where you no longer care if you live or die yet can manifest the authentic gospel for the salvation of a soul, the healing of a disease, or deliverance from demonic torment, then and only then are you really a threat to the powers of darkness. And it is from that realm that persecution comes.

Defining moments enable us to more effectively bring light to the darkness, order into chaos, and life where there is death. These moments launch us into the impossible!

15

Just the Beginning

I have chosen these heroes of the faith rather randomly. I wanted to show the reader various kinds of encounters that people have had with God that changed them from being nice, everyday believers to radical world changers. There are countless others whose stories have every right to be listed in a book like this. They are equally important, and perhaps in some cases, more important. Their stories would no doubt add even greater insight to the purpose of this book. But I decided to reduce our efforts to this simple yet representative list. I believe it more than prophesies to the reader what is possible in our day. It prophesies what *must happen* in our day, because now we see the heart of God for our generation. The time is now to use the momentum of these stories to step into our own. Remember, fire always falls on sacrifice. Become that sacrifice.

The only real exceptions to this "random list" of heroes of the faith are Randy Clark and Heidi Baker. History is filled with these kinds of men and women of faith. But what tends to happen is that we learn to value the people of the past without recognizing who among us is living in that same grace. In the same way, Israel loved their prophets after they died but rejected the ones who were alive. I brought Randy and Heidi into the story line because, first of all, they have my deepest respect and love. But also, they are at the forefront of a wave that is impacting and changing nations of the world. By telling a small part of their story, I'm hoping to prevent readers from wishing they were alive in the "good old days." The days we are living in are the greatest days in all of history.

Rather Personal

The two most profound encounters I've had with God were very different from each other. In one case, I was "electrocuted" throughout the night, three nights in a row. It was overwhelmingly glorious, powerful, but not pleasant at all. In reality, they are death experiences, where things die in us that needed to die. In my defining moment, God was after my right to dignity in how I appeared to others. That point of surrender changed everything. Something died. And thankfully, something came to life. The second most life-changing experience was actually a revelation from a chapter in the Bible—Isaiah 60. God opened it up to me in a way that literally changed my life forever. Every day since then has come under the influence of what was given to me on that day in May of 1979. So, one encounter was power, and the other was revelatory (sometimes seen in inspired thought). For me, both were defining moments.

It's wise to hunger for more of God. But it's not wise to think we can demand how He should come and touch us. The God of amazing diversity has many ways to touch and change people's lives. Don't tell Him you want Him to touch you in one way but not another. It's not wise to tell the God of the universe, "Give me peace, but don't make me shake," or "I'd love to prophesy, but I don't want to speak in tongues." This isn't a smorgasbord where we pick and choose from the divine menu of experiences. God spoke to and activated people in different ways: through visions, impartations, reading the Word, impressions, electricity, peace, dreams, and so on. This is where the finite engages with the infinite in surrender, knowing that He knows what is best for us, and He can be trusted.

Today's Atmosphere

In the present culture, I rejoice in the countless numbers of people who stand in line to receive prayer so that they might have such an encounter with God. I have done this many times, and I know I will do it again and again. It's beautiful. The passion people have for God is quite increasing all over the world. I've lost count of the lives that have been dramatically changed through this simple but profound tool called "the laying on of hands." It is one of the foundational doctrines of Christ listed in Hebrews 6:1–2. But we should remember that while it's usually profitable to receive from the prayers of other people, there is no shortcut to maturity. Some things are given to us in seed form and must be stewarded well to bring about the increase we have cried out for.

All encounters are truly glorious. But they are also a death experience. People with these encounters are never the same again. Things that once held great importance in their lives are often forever put away in one moment. Concerns, visions, and ambitions are laid down, often never to be picked up again. On one hand, it is the ultimate promotion, yet on the other, it is the greatest invasion of the One who only comes to rule—completely. Yes, He is Father. And yes, He is Lord of all. It is costly. Oh so costly. The stories of glorious breakthroughs are real, as are the stories of opposition and downright persecution, often from other well-meaning believers. I don't know of anyone who has escaped this reality. It is intense and yet life-changing.

There is a measure of glory that is your possession. The only way you can give God glory is to have it to give. Rise in it, because in your rising, you attract greater glory to fall on you. (See Isaiah 60:1–3.) That is kingdom stewardship. It's how you move from realm to realm, from glory to glory. You have to discover the glory in the moment you are in if you are ever going to go on to greater glory. There have to be divine encounters. Every individual must pursue increasing breakthrough, increasing baptisms in the Spirit. One touch twenty years ago doesn't do it. The ongoing fire that gets ignited in us day after day, year after year, does. I don't pretend to understand it. I don't care if I understand it all. All I need is to remain as a child and to find out what He wants me to do next.

Costly

I rarely talk about the cost involved in a great move of God. The reason is that whatever we pay pales significantly in the light of what He gives us.

It would be like trading pebbles from my front yard for diamonds. Yes, they might have been my favorite pebbles. But let's be honest. It's tough to feel bad about what I gave up in light of what He has put in its place. Yet Jesus talked about counting the cost. (See Luke 14:27–30.) Not because it wouldn't be worth it, but because it's possible in the middle of the process to think what you've left behind is more valuable than what you're about to inherit.

Because of the trials that the Israelites were facing, they wanted to go back to Egypt, their land of suffering and slavery, because they didn't yet see what they were about to inherit. Hearing Kathryn Kuhlman talk about the day she *died* is one of the most convicting and sobering messages I've ever heard. She spoke at Oral Roberts University, and her talk is available online.[690] It is priceless. But watching her with her Best Friend, the Holy Spirit, you realize the exchange she made was one she never, ever regretted.

I mention this because of how lightly many people approach the subject of a life-changing encounter with God. While we can't earn it, we also are not to treat it lightly. It is a gift that comes in His timing, for His purposes, enabling us to have the God of the universe put us on like a garment. Pray. Pray much. Pray specifically until you know you have surrendered the deepest part of your heart to God in your passionate cry for more. For it's from that place of surrender that we move God. Prayers that move us, move Him. In Ephesians, it says,

> Now to Him who is able to do far more abundantly beyond all that we ask or think, according to the power that works within us, to Him be the glory in the church and in Christ Jesus to all generations, forever and ever. Amen. (Ephesians 3:20–21 NASB)

Please notice the correlation between the work of God *through* us that is beyond all we could ask or think, and the power that works *within* us. To the degree that we allow Him to work deep within us, He does the impossible around and through us. Let *deep call unto deep*—let the deep in you call to the deep in God. (See Psalm 42:7.)

Practical Steps

Spend some time with the Lord and reflect on His faithfulness in your life. Make note of the personal breakthroughs you have experienced over the years. Meditate on them, and give Him praise. It's important to keep these records available so that the next time you face an impossibility, you can feast on what God has done in the past and pull from those testimonies to launch even farther into all that He has for you. This is practical. Testimonies prophesy![691]

Personal Prayer

Stir up your faith in God who is good. I pray God would give you a major outpouring of His Spirit. It is all about the Presence. It is all about the glory, His glory. I pray for the release of a fresh baptism of fire upon us all in this hour. Invite the glory of God on your own face, on your own countenance. He wants to change the face of the church by revealing His glory to us, where we become exposed to His goodness at indescribable levels. One of the big things about receiving more is being hungry for more…knowing it exists.

Holy Spirit, come now with power. Let there not be one who is without the fire of God. We invite You to come and display Yourself strong. Do what only You can do. We give You that place. And we honor You. We celebrate You. Our love is for You. Please raise up a generation that knows and values the beauty of both purity and power, and can walk in both well. Help us to be all this and more for the honor of the name of Jesus.

The conclusion that follows could actually be the most important part of this book, because at this point, one of God's present-day generals is praying for everyone who reads it:

Prayer of Impartation from Randy Clark

Now's not the time to be backslidden or lukewarm, because something wonderfully powerful is about to hit the country. I think there's going to be a real outpouring...like the Jesus Movement. But instead of hippies, there's going to be a lot of New Agers coming. They will be touched because they are actually looking for spiritual things and for power. And what we have is so much more powerful. You definitely want to be a part of this great move of God that is about to happen.

Perhaps you were a teenager or a child when Toronto happened, and you were touched powerfully. Often, one of the things I have seen is that people who were touched in one revival when they were young become key leaders in the next revival, often twenty or so years later. Some of you who were touched then will find yourself leading in this next revival by the sovereign grace of God.

So Father, in Jesus' name, I bless everyone who is reading this. I pray that You would create a hunger, a sense in each of us that makes us say, "I want to feel the atmosphere that's pregnant with a faith that doesn't know what You're going to do next. I want to feel Your heat, Your power, Your glory on my body. I want to have my faith encouraged. I want to be used by God for His glory and for serving other people with the power of God."

I pray that the mercy and grace of God would become tangible realities to you because you've been touched by God. I pray, "Come, Holy Spirit, anoint the people. May they feel Your love, Your heat, Your tingling, Your electricity, Your power, Your compassion. Visit them in Jesus' name. More, Lord. More of Your anointing. By faith, I believe that people are going to be touched while reading this. So I bless what I believe by faith that You are doing in them, and I say, 'More, God. Increase it. More. In Jesus' name, raise up another generation to lead revival in this land and in the world.'" In Jesus' name, amen.[692]

Notes

Chapter 1: Brace Yourself!

1. C. H. Spurgeon, "The Story of God's Mighty Acts," a Sermon Delivered on Sabbath Morning, July 17th, 1859, at the Music Hall, Royal Surrey Gardens, found in *The New Park Street Pulpit Containing Sermons Preached and Revised by the Rev. C. H. Spurgeon, Minister of the Chapel during the Year 1859: Volume V* (London, England: Passmore, Allabaster, & Sons, 1894), 309–310, emphasis mine. "When people hear about what God used to do, one of the things they say is: 'Oh, that was a very long while ago.' They imagine that times have altered since then…. Has God changed? Is he not immutable God, the same yesterday, to-day, and for ever? Does not that furnish an argument to prove that what God has done at one time he can do at another? Nay, I think I may push it a little further, and say what he had done once, is a prophecy of what he intends to do again—that the mighty works which have been accomplished in the olden time shall all be repeated, and the Lord's song shall be sung again in Zion, and he shall again be greatly glorified. Others among you say, 'Oh, well I look upon these things as great prodigies—miracles. We are not to expect them every day.' That is the very reason why we do not get them. If we had learnt to expect them, we should no doubt obtain them, but we put them up on the shelf, as being out of the common order of our moderate religion, as being mere curiosities of Scripture history. We imagine such things, however true, to be prodigies of providence; we cannot imagine them to be according to the ordinary working of his mighty power. I beseech you, my friends, abjure that idea, put it out of your mind. Whatever God has done in the way of converting sinners is to be looked upon as a precedent, for 'his arm is not shortened that he cannot save, nor is his ear heavy that he cannot hear.'… Let us take the blame of it ourselves, and with earnestness seek that God would restore to us the faith of the men of old, that we may richly enjoy his grace as in the days of old. Yet there is another disadvantage under which these old stories labour. The fact is, we have not seen them. Why, I may talk to you ever so long about revivals, but you won't believe them half so much, nor half so truly, as if one were to occur in your very midst. If you saw it with your own eyes, then you would see the power of it…. Then I think the stories you have heard with your ears should have a true and proper effect upon your own lives."

2. Bill Johnson, *Release the Power of Jesus* (Shippensburg, PA: Destiny Image Publishers, 2009), 181–183. Reprinted by permission of Destiny Image.

Chapter 2: Love: John Wesley

3. John Wesley, *Directions for Renewing Our Covenant with God*, 2nd ed. (London: F. Paramore, at the Foundry, Moorfields, 1781), 13–14.

4. While John Wesley was born on June 17, 1703, according to the Julian Calendar in use, after Britain aligned with Europe's system of the Gregorian Calendar in 1752, his birthday shifted to June 28.

5. "Famous Alumni: John Wesley," Lincoln College of University of Oxford, http://www.linc.ox.ac.uk/Famous-Alumni John-Wesley-1703---1791 (accessed May 22, 2013).

6. John Telford, *The Life of John Wesley* (Wesleyan Heritage Publications, 1998), 103 [originally published by Hunt and Eaton of New York, 1924].

7. Percy Livingstone Parker, ed., *The Heart of John Wesley's Journal* (London: Fleming H. Revell Company, 1903), xxxiii. Accessible online at http://openlibrary.org/works/OL996945W/The_journal_of_the_Rev._John_Wesley. John also learned Spanish, German, Latin, and Italian.

8. Ibid., 6–8.

9. Telford, *Life of John Wesley*, 85.

10. Parker, *Heart of John Wesley's Journal*, 33. See also Telford, *Life of John Wesley*, 96.

11. Parker, *Heart of John Wesley's Journal*, 35.

12. John Wesley, Wesley Center Online, The Letters of John Wesley: 1738, letters to William Law, http://wesley.nnu.edu/john-wesley/the-letters-of-john-wesley/wesleys-letters-1738 (accessed May 22, 2013).

13. Parker, *Heart of John Wesley's Journal*, 35–36.

14. Ibid., 42–45.

15. Ibid.

16. Ibid.

17. Martin Luther, "Preface to the Letter of St. Paul to the Romans," can be accessed at http://www.ccel.org/ccel/luther/prefacetoromans.pdf.

18. Parker, *Heart of John Wesley's Journal*, 42–45.

19. Ibid., 42–45.

20. Ibid., 42–45.

21. Ernest Rhys, ed., *The Journal of the Rev. John Wesley in Everyman's Library*, vol.1 (London: J. M. Dent & Sons Limited, London, 1906), 169, http://babel.hathitrust.org/cgi/pt?id=mdp.39015041157986;view=1up;seq=10.

22. Parker, *Heart of John Wesley's Journal*, 47.

23. Ibid., 49.

24. Ibid., 58.

25. Ibid., 87–88.

26. Ibid., 258–259. This happened on Monday, August 6, 1759, in Everton.

27. Ibid., 437–438.

28. Ibid., 55–56. This was written in June 1739.

29. Ibid., 135.

30. Ibid., 155–156.

31. Ibid., 165.

32. Ibid., 156. This happened in February 1748.

33. An interesting side fact is that Charles Wesley originally wrote the song "Hark! The Herald Angels Sing" (1734) and many other songs to release the theology of the day through music.

34. Parker, *Heart of John Wesley's Journal*, 195.

35. Ibid., 392.

36. Robert Simpson, "Circuit Riders: In Early American Methodism," Archives & History, General Commission on Archives and History, United Methodist Church, http://www.gcah.org/site/c.ghKJI0PHIoE/b.3828779/k.87C4/Circuit_Riders.htm (accessed May 24, 2013). Francis Asbury became the first bishop for American Methodism. During his circuit riding, he traveled two hundred seventy thousand miles and preached sixteen thousand sermons. Many circuit riders died as a result of their arduous lifestyle, and almost half of those who died were under the age of thirty.

37. "John Wesley's Big Impact on America," http://www.christianity.com /church/church-history/timeline/1701-1800/john-wesleys-big-impact-on-america-11630220.html (accessed May 23, 2013).

38. Parker, *Heart of John Wesley's Journal*, xxxi.

39. See http://worldmethodistcouncil.org/about/member-churches/statistical-information/ (accessed October 27, 2015).

Chapter 3: Holiness: Charles G. Finney

40. Charles Grandison Finney, *Memoirs of Reverend Charles G. Finney Written By Himself* (New York: A.S. Barnes, 1876), 13–23.

41. Finney never attended college, but later on after his conversion, he was taught some Greek, Hebrew, and Latin by George Gale, a Presbyterian minister.

42. Finney, *Memoirs*, 13–23.

43. Ibid., 13–14.

44. Ibid., 13–16.

45. Ibid., 16–17.

46. Ibid., 16–17.

47. Ibid., 18, 23.

48. Ibid., 18–19.

49. Ibid., 19–20.

50. Ibid., 20–21.

51. Ibid., 21–22.

52. Ibid., 22–23.

53. Ibid., 25–26. Finney wrote, "But now after receiving these baptisms of the Spirit I was quite willing to preach the Gospel. Nay, I found that I was unwilling to do anything else."

54. Ibid., 26.

55. Ibid., 26.

56. Ibid., 27.

57. Ibid., 28–29.

58. William P. Farley, "Charles Finney: The Controversial Evangelist," *Enrichment Journal*, The General Council of the Assemblies of God, http://enrichmentjournal.ag.org/200601/200601_118_Finney.cfm (accessed October 16, 2013).

59. Finney, *Memoirs*, 179.

60. Ibid., 183–184.

61. James E. Johnson, "Charles Finney: Father of American Revivalism," *Christian History* 20 (1988), http://www.christianitytoday.com/ch/131christians /evangelistsandapologists/finney.html?start=2 (accessed January 31, 2013).

62. Finney, *Memoirs*, 321.

63. This was a bold statement as many of the things in his book went against the Presbyterian church he was operating under. By 1837, he resigned from the Presbyterian church and served at First Congregational Church in Oberlin.

64. The biography of Finney on the Oberlin College website includes this summary of his theology: "Through the Oberlin Evangelist, established in 1839, [Finney] expressed his views on doctrinal and practical matters, collectively referred to as 'Oberlin Theology' or 'Oberlin Perfectionism.' Finney taught that the individual has a limitless capacity for repentance. He also taught that an exalted state of spirituality was attainable by leading a Christian life. These New School Calvinist views, opposed by conservative Calvinists, included prohibitions against tobacco, tea, coffee, and most popular amusements." See http://www. oberlin.edu/archive/holdings/finding/RG2/SG2/biography.html. In 1839, Finney's theology produced a split within the Presbyterian Church between the Old School and the New School. Some believe that Finney's thinking was influenced by Yale professor Nathaniel William Taylor (1786–1858). See Farley, "Charles Finney: The Controversial Evangelist."

65. See "Oberlin History: Early history," http://new.oberlin.edu/about/history. dot (accessed February 5, 2013). This community was also influential in the Underground Railroad and in bringing reforms.

66. Johnson, "Charles Finney: Father of American Revivalism."

67. Finney, *Memoirs*, 288–290. He began this for the first time while in Rochester around 1830.

68. Ibid., 80–84.

69. Ibid., 77–78.

70. Ibid., 80–81.

71. Ibid., 44–45.

72. Ibid., 136–137. See also 102–104 for other accounts of what happened when Finney preached.

73. Ibid., 74–75.

74. Ibid., 36–37.

75. Ibid., 71–72.

76. Ibid., 193–194.

77. Ibid., 34–36.

78. Ibid., 44.
79. Ibid., 370–385.
80. Ibid.
81. Ibid.
82. Ibid.
83. Ibid.
84. Ibid.

Chapter 4: Laying Foundations for Legacy: Dwight L. Moody

85. Richard Ellsworth Day, *Bush Aglow: The Life Story of Dwight Lyman Moody, Commoner of Northfield* (Philadelphia: The Judson Press, 1936), 128.
86. Richard B. Cook, *Life, Work, and Sermons of Dwight L. Moody, The Great Evangelist* (Baltimore: R. H. Woodward Company, 1900), 1–15, http://www.archive.org/stream/lifeworksermonso00cook/lifeworksermonso00cook_djvu.txt (accessed October 4, 2013).
87. Ibid., 21. This was the Vernon Congregational Church.
88. Ibid., 22–23. See also "D. L. Moody Story," http://www.moodyministries.net (accessed October 4, 2012).
89. Cook, *Life, Work, and Sermons of Dwight L. Moody*, 14–15.
90. Paul Dwight Moody and Arthur Percy Fitt, *The Shorter Life of D. L. Moody: Vol. 1–His Life* (Chicago, IL: The Bible Institute Colportage Association, 1900), 30–31. Accessible online at http://babel.hathitrust.org/cgi/pt?id=mdp.39015064336806;view=1up;seq=39.
91. Don Sweeting, "The Great Turning Point in the Life of D. L. Moody," in *Mr. Moody and the Evangelical Tradition*, ed. Timothy George (New York: T & T Clark International, 2004), 42.
92. Moody and Fitt, *Shorter Life of D. L. Moody*, 32, 34. See also page 25 where he said, "If only we could make the world believe that we love them, there would be fewer empty churches and a smaller proportion of our population who never darken a church door. Let *love* replace *duty* in our church relations, and the world will soon be evangelized."
93. J. Wilbur Chapman, *The Life and Work of Dwight Lyman Moody* (London: James Nisbet & Co., Limited, 1900), 113–117.
94. Ibid., 117.
95. Ibid., 111–112.
96. See Jennifer A. Miskov, *Life on Wings: The Forgotten Life and Theology of Carrie Judd Montgomery* (Cleveland, TN: CPT Press, 2012), 29–30 for the development of healing homes. See also Donald W. Dayton, *Theological Roots of Pentecostalism* (Peabody, MA: Hendrickson Publishers, 2000 [reprint from Metuchen, NJ: Scarecrow Press, 1987]), 121–122.
97. Chapman, *Life and Work of Dwight Lyman Moody*, 117.
98. Ibid., 118.
99. "D. L. Moody Story," http://www.moodyministries.net (accessed October 4, 2012).

100. William R. Moody, *The Life of D. L. Moody by His Son* (New York: Fleming H. Revell Company, 1900), 131.

101. Ibid., 133.

102. Ibid., 134. See also Moody and Fitt, *Shorter Life of D. L. Moody*, 41–42.

103. Moody, *Life of D. L. Moody by His Son*, 139.

104. Ibid.

105. Ibid., 139–140.

106. Ellsworth Day, *Bush Aglow*, 130.

107. Sweeting, "Great Turning Point," 40.

108. Moody, *The Life of D. L. Moody by His Son*, 137. To learn more about Henry Moorehouse, see John MacPherson, *Henry Moorhouse: The English Evangelist* (London: Morgan and Scott, 1881), https://archive.org/stream /henrymoorhouseen00macp#page/n0/mode/2up and http://www.gospelhall.org /index.php?option=com_content&view=article&id=3071&Itemid=55 (accessed October 4, 2013).

109. Chapman, *Life and Work of Dwight Lyman Moody*, 122–123.

110. Moody, *Life of D. L. Moody by His Son*, 126–127.

111. Chapman, *Life and Work of Dwight Lyman Moody*, 124. See also Moody, *The Life of D. L. Moody by His Son*, 126–127.

112. Moody, *Life of D. L. Moody by His Son*, 125–127.

113. Chapman, *Life and Work of Dwight Lyman Moody*, 134.

114. R. A. Torrey, "Why God Used D. L. Moody" (Chicago, IL: The Bible Institute Colportage Ass'n/ Fleming H. Revell Company, 1923), 51–59. Torrey said that Moody "had a very definite enduement with power from on High, a very clear and definite baptism with the Holy Ghost."

115. Chapman, *Life and Work of Dwight Lyman Moody*, 412–413. See also Moody, *Life of D. L. Moody by His Son*, 146–148, especially where D. L. Moody is recorded as saying, "There came a great hunger in my soul. I did not know what it was. I began to cry out as I never did before. I really felt that I did not want to live if I could not have this power for service."

116. Over 2,100 acres were burned, over 17,450 buildings were destroyed, over 250 people died, and over 150,000 were made homeless. Ellsworth Day, *Bush Aglow*, 134.

117. Sweeting, "Great Turning Point," 44–45.

118. Moody, *Life of D. L. Moody by His Son*, 148.

119. Moody and Fitt, *Shorter Life of D. L. Moody*, 67.

120. Chapman, *Life and Work of Dwight Lyman Moody*, 106, and Sweeting, "Great Turning Point," 46.

121. Sweeting, "Great Turning Point," 46.

122. Cook, *Life, Work, and Sermons of Dwight L. Moody*, 111–112. Moody continued, "I almost prayed in my joy, 'Oh, stay Thy hand.' I thought this earthen vessel would break. He filled me so full of the Spirit....I think I have accomplished more in the last four years than in all the rest of my life."

123. Torrey, "Why God Used D. L. Moody," 51–59. F. B. Meyer's version is found in "Moody as a Prophet" in Chapman, *Life and Work of Dwight Lyman Moody*, xvi-xviii.

124. Chapman, *Life and Work of Dwight Lyman Moody*, 412–413. See also Moody, *Life of D. L. Moody by His Son*, 146–148.

125. Moody, *Life of D. L. Moody by His Son*, 152–153.

126. Ibid.

127. Ibid., 152–167. See also Moody and Fitt, *Shorter Life of D. L. Moody*, 71.

128. An interesting side story is that of Horatio Spafford, who lost everything in the Chicago fire and afterward sent his family members ahead of him so they could visit Moody in England. The family suffered another tragedy when the ship sank. Spafford's wife survived, but his four daughters died. Spafford wrote the hymn "It Is Well With My Soul" while on a later ship passing by the place where the loss occurred. See the original song at http://spaffordhymn.com/ (accessed October 4, 2013).

129. Moody, *Life of D. L. Moody by His Son*, 199, 147.

130. "D. L. Moody Story," http://www.moodyministries.net/crp_mainpage.aspx?id=64 (accessed December 22, 2013).

131. Torrey, "Why God Used D. L. Moody," 51–59. Torrey recalled that Moody "had a passion for lost souls and even made a commitment to talk to one person about Christ every 24 hours to the point where he would get out of bed and put a coat on and go outside late at night if he forgot to fulfil this."

132. Chapman, *Life and Work of Dwight Lyman Moody*, 519.

133. Moody and Fitt, *Shorter Life of D. L. Moody*, 47.

134. Ibid., 48.

135. Chapman, *Life and Work of Dwight Lyman Moody*, 511.

136. Ibid., 433.

137. Ibid., 517.

138. Ibid., 505–506.

139. Ibid., 411.

140. Dwight L. Moody, *Secret Power; or, The Secret of Success in Christian Life and Christian Work* (Chicago: F. H. Revell, 1881), 46.

Chapter 5: Courage: Maria Woodworth-Etter

141. Maria Woodworth-Etter, *Acts of the Holy Ghost; or The Life, Work, and Experience of Mrs. M. B. Woodworth-Etter, Evangelist* (Dallas, TX: John F. Worley Printing Co., 1912), 33.

142. Ibid., 23–24.

143. Ibid., 24.

144. Ibid., 24–25. See also Wayne Warner, *Maria Woodworth-Etter: For Such a Time as This* (Gainesville, FL: Bridge-Logos, 2004), 1–2, 12, which cites the following newspaper article: "Gray-Haired Man Hears His Convert. Woman Evangelist Finds in Audience the One Who Led Her to Accept Christianity," *Indianapolis Star*, September 18, 1904.

145. Woodworth-Etter, *Acts of the Holy Ghost*, 25.

146. Ibid., 32. See also Warner, *For Such a Time as This*, 8.

147. Woodworth-Etter, *Acts of the Holy Ghost*, 30.

148. Ibid., 34.

149. Ibid., 30–31.
150. Ibid., 32.
151. Ibid.
152. Ibid., 37.
153. Ibid., 42.
154. Ibid., 37–38.
155. Ibid., 31.
156. Ibid., 42–43. Just before this quote, she said, "There had been trouble in the church for a number of years. Some of the best members had left, and the church had lost its power. I felt impressed that God was going to restore love and harmony in the church. I visited those families, and the third day of the meeting the trouble was all settled. All who were present came to the altar...."
157. Ibid., 31.
158. Ibid., 418. The following thoughts on healing are included in *Acts of the Holy Ghost*. However, they may have been taken from J. W. Byer's *The Grace of Healing* (Moundsville, WV: Gospel Trumpet Publishing House, 1899 [the Church of God (Anderson) press]), as noted in Warner, *For Such a Time as This*, 204–210, 220–221. They were part of a question and answer session that went as follows: "Q. But how may I know that it is still God's will to heal? A. Just as you may know that it is his will to save—by his Word. His Word is His Will. Q. But it may be his will not to heal me. A. You must go outside of God's Word to find stating ground for such a conclusion; for there is nothing inside the Bible about healing but what corresponds with our blessed test: 'Himself took our infirmities and bare our sickness.' Most people who argue that it might not be God's will to heal them, are at the same time taking medicine and employing every possible human agency to get well. Why be so inconsistent? Why fight against God's will? If it is his will for you not to get well, then die. Stop fighting against God."
159. Wayne Warner, "Maria B. Woodworth-Etter and the Early Pentecostal Movement," *Assemblies of God Heritage* 6, no. 4 (Winter 1986–87), 11–14.
160. Woodworth-Etter, *Acts of the Holy Ghost*, 121–123, 162–165, 199, 233–239.
161. Ibid., 283. See also page 345 for an account of a raising from the dead: "Sister Woodworth-Etter says, on that occasion there was a commotion; people going out to help, and some coming back. She asked, 'What is the matter?' As they did not wish to alarm the audience they said 'She has fainted.' Sister Etter said, 'She is all right; and even if the Lord should take her, she is ready. I wish the rest of you were as well prepared.' After quite a while they carried her body in, and said, 'The pulse has ceased to beat.' There was no motion of the heart, the body was cold and limp, and the face that of a corpse. Sister Etter gathered the others around her, and spoke of Jesus being the Resurrection and the Life, and prayed and called on her in the name of the Lord, and she opened her eyes. When she opened her eyes they were yellow, and she did not seem to know anything at first; but sat in a big armchair looking like a corpse. Later on in the meeting she expressed a desire to testify, which she did. She has been attending meetings ever since, and working daily."
162. Ibid., 379–383.
163. Ibid., 185.

164. Ibid., 156.

165. Ibid., 121–123, 164.

166. Ibid., 111.

167. Ibid., 154–155.

168. Warner, "Maria B. Woodworth-Etter and the Early Pentecostal Movement," 11–14. See also Teresa A. Taylor, "Grandmother of the Pentecostal Movement," *Healing and Revival*, http://healingandrevival.com/BioMWEtter.htm (accessed December 4, 2012).

169. Woodworth-Etter, *Acts of the Holy Ghost*, 160–161.

170. Ibid., 334, 277.

171. Ibid., 45, 59, 98. Several times, Maria labored with sinners over their souls, feeling that if they didn't yield that night, it would be their last chance. In a few of these accounts, the several who did not yield either got sick, were run over by a train the very next day, or died otherwise shortly afterward. There is one account of a couple falling through the ice while ice-skating and dying after one of Woodworth-Etter's meetings.

172. Ibid., 59. This was in Monroeville, Indiana, in November 1883.

173. Ibid., 188–189. The tent held eight thousand people.

174. Ibid., 164. God regularly backed up Maria in her meetings. Many times, the antagonists would fall down like dead if they tried to oppose her. During one meeting, "an infidel in the congregation was arguing against the wonderful manifestations of power. He fell as dead, as if he had been shot, and was carried out. He found out what kind of power it was."

175. Maria Woodworth-Etter, "Mrs. Woodworth-Etter's Meetings," *Confidence* 6, no. 4 (April 1913), 72–73, 76–77.

176. Woodworth-Etter, "Mrs. Woodworth-Etter's Meetings," 72–73, 76–77.

177. Woodworth-Etter, *Acts of the Holy Ghost*, 99–104, 156. Maria wrote, "The holy fire spread from one to another, until the country for miles around was shaken by the mighty power of God. People were converted on the roads, and some in their homes. Many were struck down in trances in their homes, some miles away, and lay for hours and had wonderful visions. Infidels, skeptics, church members, drunkards, all classes were brought into the kingdom...."

178. Ibid., 121–123.

179. Taylor, "Grandmother of the Pentecostal Movement."

180. Warner, *For Such a Time as This*, 30. In addition, in "Maria B. Woodworth-Etter and the Early Pentecostal Movement," 11–14, Warner reported that Alexander Dowie, R. A. Torrey, and Charles Parham did not support Maria's ministry.

181. W. E. Warner, "Maria Beulah Woodworth-Etter," in *The New International Dictionary of Pentecostal and Charismatic Movements*, rev. and exp. ed., eds. Stanley M. Burgess and Eduard M. Van Der Maas, 1211–1213 (Grand Rapids, MI: Zondervan, 2002).

182. "Sister Etter's Homecoming," *Pentecostal Evangel* 568 (October 18, 1924), 13. See also Warner, "Maria Beulah Woodworth-Etter," 1212.

183. Warner, *For Such a Time as This*, 153–156. The span of 1904–1912 was a quieter period of her life that she did not write much about. During this time, she and her new husband bought a farm in Illinois, and she sought to set up a faith home where people could come and receive prayer and teaching.

184. Warner, "Maria B. Woodworth-Etter and the Early Pentecostal Movement," 11–14.

185. For a short account of the church's history and current ministry, see http://www.lakeviewchurch.org/about-us/brief-history/.

186. Warner, *For Such a Time as This*, 316–317. October 31 is the same date that Martin Luther, in 1517, posted the 95 Theses, initiating the Reformation, and the same date in 1904 that Evan Roberts followed the leading of the Holy Spirit and conducted the first meeting of what would later be known as the Welsh Revival. To learn more about the significance of this day in history, see Jennifer A. Miskov, "How Halloween is a Catalytic Day for Reformation, Revival, and Destiny, http://silvertogold.com/blog/2013/10/29/how-halloween-october-31st-is-a-catalytic-day-of-reformation-revival-and-destiny, and to learn more about sacred time or sacred space, see Jennifer A. Miskov, "Coloring Outside the Lines: Pentecostal Parallels with Expressionism. The Work of the Spirit in Place, Time, and Secular Society?", *Journal of Pentecostal Theology* 19 (2010), 94–117.

187. Ibid., 321–322. Maria's daughter Lizzie died on August 7, 1924, at age sixty.

188. Taylor, "Grandmother of the Pentecostal Movement."

189. Warner, "Maria B. Woodworth-Etter and the Early Pentecostal Movement," 11–14.

190. Warner, *For Such a Time as This*, 61.

191. Ibid., 23.

192. Wayne E. Warner, "Maria Woodworth-Etter: A Powerful Voice in the Pentecostal Vanguard," *Enrichment Journal* (Winter 1999), The General Council of the Assemblies of God, http://enrichmentjournal.ag.org/199901/086_woodsworth_etter.cfm (accessed December 6, 2012).

193. Woodworth-Etter, *Acts of the Holy Ghost*, 244.

194. Ibid., 32. See also Maria Woodworth-Etter, "Work of the Holy Ghost," in *A Diary of Signs and Wonders*, 7th ed. (Tulsa, OK: Harrison House, 1916), 499.

Chapter 6: The Power of the Testimony: Carrie Judd Montgomery

195. Most of this chapter is based on Jennifer A. Miskov, *Life on Wings: The Forgotten Life and Theology of Carrie Judd Montgomery* (Cleveland, TN: CPT Press, 2012). Used by permission of the publishers. See also Jennifer A. Miskov, "Carrie Judd Montgomery: A Passion for Healing and the Fullness of the Spirit," *Heritage Magazine*, August 2012, http://ifphc.org/Uploads/Heritage/2012_02.pdf, Jennifer A. Miskov, *Spirit Flood: Rebirth of Spirit Baptism for the 21st Century in Light of the Azusa Street Revival and the Life of Carrie Judd Montgomery* (Birmingham, UK: Silver to Gold, 2010), Jennifer A. Miskov, "Giving Room to the Anointing: Carrie Judd Montgomery's Impact on Women in Ministry," in *Global Pentecostal and Charismatic Studies series volume on Women in Leadership*, eds. Peg English de Alminana and Lois Olena (The Netherlands: Brill, 2016), and

Jennifer A. Miskov, "Missing Links: Phoebe Palmer, Carrie Judd Montgomery, and Holiness Roots within Pentecostalism," *PentecoStudies: An Interdisciplinary Journal for Research on the Pentecostal and Charismatic Movements* 10:1 (2011). If interested in learning more about Carrie's life and legacy, see the Carrie Judd Montgomery Project at http://silvertogold.com/carrie-judd-montgomery-project/.

196. Carrie Judd Montgomery, "The Life on Wings: The Possibilities of Pentecost," *Triumphs of Faith* 32, no. 8 (August 1912), 169–177.

197. Miskov, *Life on Wings*, 35.

198. Carrie Judd Montgomery, *Under His Wings: The Story of My Life* (Los Angeles: Stationers Corporation, 1936), 46–48.

199. Carrie F. Judd, *The Prayer of Faith* (Alemeda County, CA: Office of "Triumphs of Faith," Beulah Mills College, 1880), 10. For a full account, see Miskov, *Life on Wings*, 15–18.

200. Montgomery, *Under His Wings*, 53, and Miskov, *Life on Wings*, 17.

201. Taken from Judd, *Prayer of Faith*, 9–19. It is important to note that many in the early divine healing movement felt that it was more important to trust in the Lord for healing than to rely on medicine. The medical practices during Carrie's day were also not as advanced as they are now, and many times caused more complications than they brought health and healing. See Miskov, *Life on Wings*, and Nancy A. Hardesty, *Faith Cure: Divine Healing in the Holiness and Pentecostal Movements* (Peabody, MA: Hendrickson Publishers, 2003), for more on this.

202. Miskov, *Life on Wings*, 19–23.

203. "For and of Women," *The Buffalo Express*, October 28, 1888.

204. Judd, *Prayer of Faith*. Before her healing, Carrie had published a few poems. Carrie F. Judd, *Lilies from the Vale of Thought* (Buffalo, NY: H. H. Otis, 1878) was a compilation of some of Carrie's poems that her parents put together to raise money when she was sick.

205. Frances E. Willard and Mary A. Livermore, eds., *A Woman of the Century: Fourteen Hundred-Seventy Biographical Sketches Accompanied by Portraits of Leading American Women in All Walks of Life* (Buffalo, NY: Charles Wells Moulton, 1893), 513.

206. All the issues of *Triumphs of Faith* have been digitized and are available from the Flower Pentecostal Heritage Center, https://ifphc.org. See also Miskov, *Life on Wings*, 27.

207. Miskov, *Life on Wings*, 50.

208. Carrie F. Judd, "Faith-Rest Cottage," *Triumphs of Faith* 2, no.2 (February 1882). "Carrie can easily be called the mother of healing homes in North America," Miskov, *Life on Wings*, 294.

209. Miskov, *Life on Wings*, 37.

210. Jennifer A. Miskov, "Carrie Judd Montgomery: A Passion for Healing and the Fullness of the Spirit," *Heritage Magazine* (August 2012), 8. This article, which can be accessed at http://ifphc.org/Uploads/Heritage/2012_02.pdf, explains that "Carrie's healing homes were part of a larger trans-Atlantic movement among radical evangelicals." For a more in-depth history of healing homes, as well as the development of Carrie's healing homes, see Miskov, *Life on Wings*, 29–49. For a more general overview, see Nancy A. Hardesty, *Faith Cure: Divine Healing in the Holiness and Pentecostal Movements* (Peabody, MA: Hendrickson Publishers, 2003), and Richard M. Riss, "Faith Homes," in *New International Dictionary of Pentecostal and Charismatic Movements*, 630–631.

211. Miskov, *Life on Wings*, 48.

212. Ibid., 37. See also pages 210–227 to learn more about the different models of healing and where Carrie fit in relation to William Branham, Smith Wigglesworth, Kathryn Kuhlman, Oral Roberts, John Wimber, and others.

213. Montgomery, *Under His Wings*, 96–102, from a chapter entitled "Ocean Depths of Blessing, and Further Service."

214. Maria Woodworth-Etter and John Alexander Dowie preceded her.

215. John Alexander Dowie was an evangelist who had a powerful healing ministry that impacted many in his time. For more on Dowie, see Roberts Liardon, *God's Generals: Why They Succeeded and Why Some Failed* (New Kensington, PA: Whitaker House, 1996), 20–44.

216. For more information, go to www.homeofpeace.com. To learn more about the Carrie Judd Montgomery Project or the Healing and Revival retreats facilitated each year at Home of Peace, go to www.silvertogold.com and click on "Carrie Judd Montgomery Project."

217. Gardiner H. Shattuck, "Ambrose Jessup Tomlinson (1865–1943)," in *Encyclopaedia of American Religious History*, 3rd ed., eds. Edward L. Queen, Stephen R. Prothero, and Gardiner H. Shattuck (New York, NY: Facts on File, Inc., 2009), 991.

218. Carrie Judd Montgomery, "'The Tongue of the Wise Is Health,'" *Triumphs of Faith* 36, no. 4 (April 1916), 74.

219. Miskov, *Life on Wings*, 110–112. See also Jennifer A. Miskov, *Spirit Flood: Rebirth of Spirit Baptism for the 21st Century in Light of the Azusa Street Revival and the Life of Carrie Judd Montgomery* (Birmingham, UK: Silver to Gold, 2010) and Jennifer A. Miskov, "Coloring Outside the Lines: Pentecostal Parallels with Expressionism. The Work of the Spirit in Place, Time, and Secular Society?", *Journal of Pentecostal Theology* 19 (2010), 94–117. For a more in-depth study of the revival, see Cecil M. Robeck, Jr., *The Azusa Street Mission and Revival: The Birthplace of the Pentecostal Movement* (Nashville, TN: Thomas Nelson, Inc., 2006).). To see Welsh Revival influences for Azusa Street, see Jennifer A. Miskov, "The Liturgy of the Welsh Revival and the Azusa Street Revival: Connections, Similarities and Development," in *Scripting Pentecost*, eds. A. J. Swaboda and Mark Cartledge (United Kingdom: Ashgate, 2016).

220. During this time, early Pentecostals commonly considered speaking in tongues to be a sign that would soon follow one's Spirit baptism. See Carrie Judd Montgomery, "Recent Trip to Mexico," *Triumphs of Faith* 33, no. 12 (December 1913), 271.

221. Montgomery, *Under His Wings*, 164.

222. Carrie Judd Montgomery, "Beulah Notes," *Triumphs of Faith* 27, no. 7 (July 1907), 168.

223. Jennifer A. Miskov, *Spirit Flood: Rebirth of Spirit Baptism for the 21st Century in Light of the Azusa Street Revival and the Life of Carrie Judd Montgomery* (Birmingham, UK: Silver to Gold, 2010), 31–32.

224. Carrie Judd Montgomery, "'The Promise of the Father.' A Personal Testimony," *Triumphs of Faith* 28, no. 7 (July 1908), 145–149.

225. Carrie Judd Montgomery, "Miraculously Healed by the Lord Thirty Years Ago," *Latter Rain Evangel* 2, no. 1 (Oct. 1909), 8.

226. Montgomery, "'The Promise of the Father,'" 145–149. The original text uses the word "endurement."

227. Montgomery, *Under His Wings*, 165. It is spelled "fulness" in original text.

228. Montgomery, "'The Promise of the Father,'" 145–149.

229. Montgomery, "Life on Wings," 169–177. See also Carrie Judd Montgomery "Christ's Quickening Life for the Mortal Body," *Triumphs of Faith* 28, no. 8 (August 1908), 169–170, "A Year with the Comforter," *Triumphs of Faith* 29, no. 7 (July 1909), 145–149, "'The Glory of His Grace,'" *Triumphs of Faith* 29, no. 1 (Jan 1909), 2–3, and Montgomery, *Under His Wings*, 170.

230. Carrie Judd Montgomery, "Some Important Changes," *Triumphs of Faith* 28, no. 12 (December 1908), 267.

231. Carrie had ministered with her husband in Mexico before this, but that had been the extent of her international travel.

232. Carrie Judd Montgomery, "Together in Love," *Triumphs of Faith* 28, no. 9 (September 1908) and "'By this all Men Shall know,'" *Triumphs of Faith* 28, no. 11 (November 1908).

233. Gastón Espinosa, "El Azteca: Francisco Olazábal and Latino Pentecostal Charisma, Power, and Faith Healing in the Borderlands," *Journal of the American Academy of Religion* 67:3 (1999), 606, 612–613.

234. Ibid., 598. Olazábal was said to have attracted "over 250,000 Mexicans, Puerto Ricans, Anglo-Americans, Italians, and blacks to his evangelistic services throughout North America and the Latin Caribbean." By the time he died, he had one hundred fifty churches with fifty thousand members in his denomination. See also Homer A. Tomlinson, *Miracles of Healing in the Ministry of Rev. Francisco Olazábal* (Queens Village, NY: Homer A. Tomlinson, 1939), 7.

235. Carrie Judd Montgomery, "Cazadero World-Wide Camp Meeting," *Triumphs of Faith* 34, no. 1, (January 1914), 23.

236. Jennifer A. Miskov, "Missing Links: Phoebe Palmer, Carrie Judd Montgomery, and Holiness Roots within Pentecostalism," *PentecoStudies: An Interdisciplinary Journal for Research on the Pentecostal and Charismatic Movements* 10:1 (2011), 8–28.

237. Jennifer A. Miskov, "Kindred Spirits," *Alliance Life*, March 1, 2011, accessible online at http://www.alliancelife.org/article.php?id=580.

238. Miskov, *Life on Wings*, 288–290.

239. Montgomery, "Possibilities of Pentecost," 169–177.

240. Carrie Judd Montgomery, "'The Tongue of the Wise Is Health,'" 74. In relation to Ezekiel 47, Carrie saw that healing and all her previous encounters with God symbolized stepping deeper into the waters of the Spirit. After 1908, she concluded that in her experience of speaking in tongues, she went all the way under the waters of the Holy Spirit the first time.

Chapter 7: Prevailing Faith: Smith Wigglesworth

241. Stanley Howard Frodsham, *Smith Wigglesworth: Apostle of Faith* (London: Elim Publishing Co., Ltd, 1949), 82.

242. Ibid., 104.

243. Ibid., 3.

244. Ibid., 3.

245. Ibid., 4.

246. Ibid., 5–6.

247. Ibid., 8, 23–24.

248. Smith Wigglesworth, *Faith That Prevails* (Springfield, MO: Gospel Publishing House, 1938, 1966), 61.

249. David W. Dorries, "The Making of Smith Wigglesworth, Part 1: The Making of the Man," *Assemblies of God Heritage* 12, no. 3 (Fall 1992), 4–8, 32, http://ifphc.org/pdf/Heritage/1992_03.pdf. See also Gary B. McGee, "The Revival Legacy of Smith Wigglesworth," *Enrichment Journal*, The General Council of the Assemblies of God, http://enrichmentjournal.ag.org/199801/070_wigglesworth.cfm (accessed October 30, 2013).

250. Frodsham, *Apostle of Faith*, 19.

251. Ibid., 21–22.

252. Smith Wigglesworth, *Ever Increasing Faith* (New Kensington, PA: Whitaker House, 2001), 143–144. See also Wigglesworth, *Faith That Prevails*, 33, and Wigglesworth's letter to the Boddys dated November 5, 1907 in "Forty Years Ago," *Redemption Tidings* (February 17, 1947), 4–5.

253. Frodsham, *Apostle of Faith*, 25–26.

254. Ibid., 26.

255. Ibid.

256. Wigglesworth, *Ever Increasing Faith*, 144–145. For an earlier version, see Smith Wigglesworth, "'BRADFORD. Testimony of Smith Wigglesworth' (first given Nov. 1907, now reprinted)," *Confidence* No. 7 (October 15, 1908), 11, 15–16.

257. Frodsham, *Apostle of Faith*, 27.

258. Ibid.

259. Wigglesworth, *Ever Increasing Faith*, 147.

260. Wigglesworth, *Faith That Prevails*, 36. See also Wigglesworth's account in Frodsham, *Apostle of Faith*, 28.

261. Roberts Liardon, *God's Generals: Why They Succeeded and Why Some Failed* (New Kensington, PA: Whitaker House, 1996), 210.

262. Albert Hibbert, *Smith Wigglesworth: The Secret of His Power* (Tulsa, OK: Harrison House, 1982), 75.

263. Frodsham, *Apostle of Faith*, 29.

264. Gary B. McGee, "The Revival Legacy of Smith Wigglesworth," *Enrichment Journal*, The General Council of the Assemblies of God, http://enrichmentjournal.ag.org/199801/070_wigglesworth.cfm (accessed October 30, 2013).

265. Frodsham, *Apostle of Faith*, 29.

266. Ibid., 30–31.

267. Smith Wigglesworth, "The Ministry of the Flaming Sword," *Redemption Tidings*, March 1931, in *Smith Wigglesworth: The Complete Collection of His Life Teachings*, comp. Roberts Liardon (New Kensington, PA: Whitaker House, 1996), 733.

268. Frodsham, *Apostle of Faith*, 76.

269. Smith Wigglesworth, "Our Great Need: Paul's Vision and the Baptism of the Holy Ghost," published in *Confidence* from an address Wigglesworth gave in London on May 28, 1917, in Liardon, *Smith Wigglesworth*, 76–77. See also Smith Wigglesworth, "The Baptism of the Holy Spirit," *Triumphs of Faith* 45, no. 6 (June 1924), 124–128, and Wigglesworth, *Ever Increasing Faith* (Springfield, MO: Gospel Publishing House, 1924), 48, 86. In *Ever Increasing Faith*, Wigglesworth said, "I can never estimate what the Baptism of the Holy Ghost has been to me these past fifteen years. It seems that every year has had three years packed into it, so that I have had forty-five years of happy service since 1907. And it is getting better all the time."

270. Smith Wigglesworth, "Present-Time Blessing for Present-Time Saints," *Pentecostal Evangel*, April 14, 1923, in Liardon, *Smith Wigglesworth*, 328.

271. Wayne E. Warner, ed., *Only Believe* (Orlando, FL: Bridge-Logos, 2005), xxi.

272. Carrie Judd Montgomery, "Cazadero Camp Meeting," *Triumphs of Faith* 34, no. 8 (August 1914), 171. See also Smith Wigglesworth, "The Spirit of the Lord Is Upon Me," *Triumphs of Faith* 34, no. 9 (September 1914), 204–206, "Possession of the Rest," *Triumphs of Faith* 45, no. 3 (March 1925), 53–57, Stanley Frodsham, "Smith Wigglesworth, A Tribute from an Old Friend, Stanley Howard Frodsham," *Redemption Tidings* 23, no. 8 (April 11, 1947), 1–3, Montgomery, *Under His Wings*, 215, and Frodsham, *Apostle of Faith*, 80.

273. Harry V. Roberts, *New Zealand's Greatest Revival (by an eye witness)* (Aukland, New Zealand: The Pelorus Press Ltd, 1951), 8. Roberts wrote, "Evangelist Smith-Wigglesworth was unknown to New Zealand. He came on his own charges, not knowing if anyone would meet him—a stranger in a strange land. There were no Churches to stand behind him. No organization to finance his campaign: BUT he was leaning on an Almighty Arm, FOR GOD WAS WITH HIM. He arrived at the end of May 1922." This was very similar to John G. Lake's adventure to South Africa.

274. Frodsham, *Apostle of Faith*, 52.
275. Roberts, *New Zealand's Greatest Revival*, 27–28.
276. Frodsham, *Apostle of Faith*, 50–51.
277. Ibid., 69.
278. Smith Wigglesworth, "Immersed in the Holy Ghost," *Triumphs of Faith* 41, no. 5 (May 1921) 113–114.
279. A. H. Badger, "God Blessing in Switzerland," *Pentecostal Evangel*, April 17, 1920, 15, http://www.smithwigglesworth.com/life/switz1920.htm.
280. *Confidence* (April–June 1920), 19–21, letter from Mr. Anton Reuss to Mr. and Mrs. Boddy describing Wigglesworth's visit, http://www.smithwigglesworth.com/life/switz1920.htm.
281. Frodsham, *Apostle of Faith*, 40–41. People later referred to this as his "wholesale healing" method. See also Smith Wigglesworth, "Filled with God," *Triumphs of Faith* 42, no. 8 (August 1922).
282. Smith Wigglesworth, "Filled with God," *Triumphs of Faith* 42, no. 8 (August 1922). This comes from an extract from an address delivered at Carrie Judd Montgomery's Monday Meeting at Danish Hall in Oakland, CA.
283. "Brother Wigglesworth in Ceylon," *Pentecostal Evangel*, May 29, 1926, 10, http://www.smithwigglesworth.com/life/india1926.htm.
284. Keith Malcomson, "Smith Wigglesworth," from Keith Malcomson, *Pentecostal Pioneers Remembered* (2008), http://pentecostalpioneers.org/SmithWigglesworth.html.
285. Liardon, *God's Generals: Why They Succeeded*, 197–226.
286. Smith Wigglesworth, "Higher Life," *Pentecostal Evangel*, September 25, 1925, a message given at Bethany Pentecostal Mission Room Pudsey, in *Smith Wigglesworth: The Complete Collection of His Life Teachings*, comp. Roberts Liardon (New Kensington, PA: Whitaker House, 1996), 525–526.
287. Hibbert, *Secret of His Power*, 69.
288. Smith Wigglesworth, "The Gifts of Healing and the Working of Miracles," *Pentecostal Evangel*, August 4, 1923, in *Smith Wigglesworth: The Complete Collection of His Life Teachings*, comp. Roberts Liardon (New Kensington, PA: Whitaker House, 1996), 346.
289. Hibbert, *Secret of His Power*, 72–73.
290. Liardon, *God's Generals: Why They Succeeded*, 215–216.
291. Hibbert, *Secret of His Power*, 36–37.
292. Ibid., 67–68.
293. George Stormont, *Wigglesworth: A Man Who Walked with God* (Tulsa, OK: Harrison House, 1989), 93–94.
294. W. [William] Hacking, *Smith Wigglesworth Remembered* (Tulsa, OK: Harrison House, 1981), 51.
295. Frodsham, *Apostle of Faith*, 103–105.
296. Hibbert, *Secret of His Power*, 109–110.
297. Ibid., 44–45.
298. Frodsham, *Apostle of Faith*, 50–51. A handkerchief that Wigglesworth prayed over was given to King George V when he was sick.

299. Roberts, *New Zealand's Greatest Revival*, 29–30.

300. Smith Wigglesworth, "Flames of Fire," May 24, 1926, an address given at Kingsway Convention, in *Smith Wigglesworth: The Complete Collection of His Life Teachings*, comp. Roberts Liardon (New Kensington, PA: Whitaker House, 1996), 565.

301. Hacking, *Smith Wigglesworth Remembered*, 82. See also Hibbert, *Secret of His Power*, 68. Wigglesworth said, "You don't tarry for the Holy Ghost. He has already been given; He is here. You don't tarry; you receive."

302. Hibbert, *Secret of His Power*, 72.

303. Ibid., 106.

304. Frodsham, *Apostle of Faith*, 84–85.

305. Wigglesworth, *Ever Increasing Faith*, 184.

306. Hacking, *Smith Wigglesworth Remembered*, 29–30.

307. Wigglesworth, *Faith That Prevails*, 36.

308. Smith Wigglesworth, "The Substance of Things Hoped For," *Pentecostal Evangel*, October 25, 1924, in *Smith Wigglesworth: The Complete Collection of His Life Teachings*, comp. Roberts Liardon (New Kensington, PA: Whitaker House, 1996), 464–465.

309. Smith Wigglesworth, "God's Treasure House," August 1927, *Bridal Call Foursquare*, in *Smith Wigglesworth: The Complete Collection of His Life Teachings*, comp. Roberts Liardon (New Kensington, PA: Whitaker House, 1996), 640.

Chapter 8: Dominion: John G. Lake

310. John G. Lake, "The Baptism of the Holy Ghost" (February 23, 1921), in *John G. Lake: The Complete Collection of His Life Teachings*, comp. Roberts Liardon (Tulsa, OK: Albury Publishing, 1999), 371.

311. Roberts Liardon, *God's Generals: Why They Succeeded and Why Some Failed* (New Kensington, PA: Whitaker House, 1996), 169–193, and "Jesus the Healer," Healing and Revival Press (2004), http://healingandrevival.com/BioJGLake.htm.

312. Lake, "The Baptism of the Holy Ghost" (February 23, 1921), 370–71.

313. Liardon, *God's Generals: Why They Succeeded*, 170, and Gordon Lindsay, comp., *John G. Lake: Apostle to Africa* (Dallas, TX: Christ for the Nations, 1981), 3.

314. Liardon, *God's Generals: Why They Succeeded*, 170–171.

315. Ibid., 171.

316. Lindsay, *Apostle to Africa*, 11–12.

317. Ibid., 12–13.

318. Ibid., 14.

319. Ibid.

320. Ibid., 14–15.

321. Ibid., 3, and Liardon, *God's Generals: Why They Succeeded*, 175.

322. Lindsay, *Apostle to Africa*, 16.

323. Ibid., 16–17.

324. John G. Lake, first diary entry, n.d., in *John G. Lake: The Complete Collection of His Life Teachings*, comp. Roberts Liardon (Tulsa, OK: Albury Publishing, 1999), 81.

325. Lake, "The Baptism of the Holy Ghost" (February 23, 1921), 371.
326. John G. Lake, *The Astounding Diary of Dr. John G. Lake* (Dallas, TX: Christ for the Nations, 1987), 20–21.
327. Lindsay, *Apostle to Africa*, 17–18.
328. Lake, first diary entry, in *John G. Lake: The Complete Collection*, 78–80.
329. Lindsay, *Apostle to Africa*, 18–19.
330. Lake, first diary entry, in *John G. Lake: The Complete Collection*, 78–80. For another version of this account, see Lindsay, *Apostle to Africa*, 18–19.
331. Ibid., 80. See also John G. Lake, "The Baptism of the Holy Ghost: And Some of the Things It Has Produced in My Life" (Sermon 3), in *John G. Lake: The Complete Collection of His Life Teachings*, comp. Roberts Liardon (Tulsa, OK: Albury Publishing, 1999), 392.
332. Lindsay, *Apostle to Africa*, 20.
333. John G. Lake and Kenneth Copeland, *John G. Lake: His Life, His Sermons, His Boldness of Faith* (Fort Worth, TX: Kenneth Copeland Publications, 1994), 495–497.
334. Ibid., 484.
335. Ibid., xxi–xxii, 484. See also Lake, "The Baptism of the Holy Ghost" (February 23, 1921), 372.
336. Lake, "The Baptism of the Holy Ghost" (February 23, 1921), 373.
337. Lake, first diary entry, in *John G. Lake: The Complete Collection*, 84. For a fuller account, see Lindsay, *Apostle to Africa*, 21–22, and Gordon Linsday, ed., *The John G. Lake Sermons on Dominion over Demons, Disease and Death* (Dallas, TX: Christ for the Nations, 1949 [1998 reprint]), 10–11.
338. Lake, first diary entry, in *John G. Lake: The Complete Collection*, 83, and John G. Lake, *Adventures in God* (Tulsa, OK: Harrison House, Inc., 1991).
339. Lake and Copeland, *His Life, His Sermons, His Boldness of Faith*, 256.
340. To learn more about George Müller's development of faith homes, see Jennifer A. Miskov, *Life on Wings: The Forgotten Life and Theology of Carrie Judd Montgomery* (Cleveland, TN; CPT Press, 2012). To see how Lake was influenced, see John G. Lake, *Astounding Diary of Dr. John G. Lake*, 12.
341. Ward M. Tannenberg, PhD, "The Healer: Dr. John Graham Lake," in *John G. Lake: The Complete Collection of His Life Teachings*, comp. Roberts Liardon (Tulsa, OK: Albury Publishing, 1999), 12–13. Two thousand dollars was miraculously given to Lake by someone from a place where he had never spoken before.
342. Ibid., 13.
343. Liardon, *God's Generals: Why They Succeeded*, 179, and Lindsay, *Apostle to Africa*, 22–24.
344. Lake and Copeland, *His Life, His Sermons, His Boldness of Faith*, 256.
345. Ibid., 488–489. Taken from Lake's sermon of February 23, 1921.
346. Liardon, *God's Generals: Why They Succeeded*, 188.
347. Lake and Copeland, *His Life, His Sermons, His Boldness of Faith*, 488–489.
348. Ibid.
349. Tannenberg, "The Healer," 13.

350. Liardon, *God's Generals: Why They Succeeded*, 182. See also Lake, *Astounding Diary of Dr. John G. Lake*, 59–60, and Lindsay, *Apostle to Africa*, 28–29. Regarding Jennie's ministry, according to W. F. Burton's report, when someone did not receive healing, they would be brought to Lake's wife in another room. She apparently was able go directly to the root of a problem and let the person know if they had some blockage to healing, such as unforgiveness. When they dealt with the blockage, they would be healed.

351. Gordon Linsday, ed., *The John G. Lake Sermons on Dominion over Demons, Disease and Death* (Dallas, TX: Christ for the Nations, 1949 [1998 reprint]), 107–108.

352. Ibid. For a similar account, see Lake and Copeland, *His Life, His Sermons, His Boldness of Faith*, xxi-xxii.

353. Lindsay, *John G. Lake Sermons*, 107–108.

354. John G. Lake, sermon, "[Untitled, on the Triune God]," Spokane, Washington, September 27, 1914, in *John G. Lake: The Complete Collection of His Life Teachings*, comp. Roberts Liardon (Tulsa, OK: Albury Publishing, 1999), 146–149. See also Liardon, *God's Generals: Why They Succeeded*, 185.

355. Lindsay, *Apostle to Africa*, 53. See also Tannenberg, "The Healer," 15.

356. Lindsay, *Apostle to Africa*, 41–52.

357. Ibid., 53.

358. Lake and Copeland, *His Life, His Sermons, His Boldness of Faith*, 488–489.

359. Lindsay, *Apostle to Africa*, 4.

360. Tannenberg, "The Healer," 17.

361. Lindsay, *Apostle to Africa*, 36.

362. Lake and Copeland, *His Life, His Sermons, His Boldness of Faith*, 139–141.

363. "Where We Came From," Christ for the Nations Institute, http://www.cfni.org/explore-about-where-we-came-from (accessed December 20, 2013).

364. "Cal Pierce, Director of Healing Rooms," Healing Rooms Ministries, http://healingrooms.com/index.php?page_id=421 (accessed December 20, 2013). The website states, "On July 22, 1999 the Spokane Healing Rooms of John G. Lake were re-opened in the same location they were 80 years ago."

365. Administrator of Healing Rooms Ministries, Spokane, Washington, e-mail message to Jennifer A. Miskov, December 31, 2013. This number is always changing.

366. Lake and Copeland, *His Life, His Sermons, His Boldness of Faith*, 236.

367. Lake, "The Baptism of the Holy Ghost" (February 23, 1921), 378–379.

Chapter 9: Led by the Spirit: Evan Roberts and the Welsh Revival

368. Awstin [T. Davies], *The Religious Revival in Wales: Contemporaneous Newspaper Accounts of the Welsh Revival of 1904–05 Published by the "Western Mail"* (Shropshire, England: Quinta Press, 2004), 122. Roberts made these comments on December 23, 1904.

369. S. [Solomon] B. [Benjamin] Shaw, *The Great Revival in Wales* (Chicago, IL: S. B. Shaw Publisher, 1905), 15.

370. Preceding this, there had been a prayer meeting in the village of Abermeurig, Cardiganshire, from the time of the 1859 revival all the way to 1904. See Noel Gibbard, *Fire on the Altar: A History and Evaluation of the 1904–05 Welsh Revival* (Bryntirion, Bridgend, Wales: Bryntirion Press, 2005), 17.

371. Brynmor Pierce Jones, *An Instrument of Revival: The Complete Life of Evan Roberts 1878–1951* (South Plainfield, NJ: Bridge Publishing, 1995), 5.

372. Awstin, *Religious Revival in Wales*, 216–220. This account is from a letter by Roberts to Rev. Thomas Francis, a Calvinistic Methodist minister, dated December 28, 1904. See also Shaw, *Great Revival in Wales*, 60–63.

373. Awstin, *Religious Revival in Wales*, 216–220.

374. Jones, *An Instrument of Revival*, 12.

375. Ibid., 10–11. Years later, the Vineyard Movement was birthed in "afterglow" meetings that had expectations very similar to those that Roberts laid for his early meetings. John Wimber's future brother-in-law, Bob Fulton, set similar expectations for meetings that would later be catalytic in birthing the Vineyard Movement, saying, "One: No prayer requests for anyone else but yourself; you are here from you, not for anyone else. Two: We are going to sing to God, not about him, and we are going to learn to worship, whatever that means. Three: Different ones will share and no one will monopolise. Four: No bringing up church problems and no church criticism. Five: Let's leave our places and positions and trophies and badges and honours at the door, and all come together on equal ground while God teaches us about himself." Carol Wimber, *John Wimber: The Way it Was* (London, England: Hodder & Stoughton, 1999), 116.

376. Daniel M. Phillips, *Evan Roberts: The Great Welsh Revivalist and His Work*, 2nd ed. (London, England: Marshall Brothers, 1906), 113, www.welshrevival.org.

377. Awstin, *Religious Revival in Wales*, 216–220. Roberts's personal companion and biographer Daniel M. Phillips recalled the same series of encounters in Phillips, *Evan Roberts*, 119.

378. Shaw, *Great Revival in Wales*, 11.

379. Jones, *An Instrument of Revival*, 18–19.

380. Phillips, *Evan Roberts*, 464. Roberts made this statement at Porth, June 29, 1906, during a missionary service.

381. Jessie Penn-Lewis, *The Awakening in Wales* (Northhamptonshire, England: Stanley L. Hunt and The Overcomer Literature Trust, 1905), 38. See also Awstin, *Religious Revival in Wales*, 216–220.

382. Awstin, *Religious Revival in Wales*, 216–220. See also Shaw, *Great Revival in Wales*, 60–63.

383. Rev. Thomas Francis adds to the account of Roberts's defining moment in Awstin, *Religious Revival in Wales*, 216–220. See also Jessie Penn-Lewis, *Awakening in Wales*, 40.

384. Phillips, *Evan Roberts*, 130, 133–134.

385. Eifion Evans, *The Welsh Revival of 1904* (Bridgend, Wales: Evangelical Press of Wales, 1969), 73 [referenced from Phillips, *Evan Roberts*, 8th ed. (1923), 142.]

386. Phillips, *Evan Roberts*, 147–148.

387. Ibid., 124–125.

388. Awstin, *Religious Revival in Wales*, 216–220. See also Shaw, *Great Revival in Wales*, 60–63.

389. Awstin, *Religious Revival in Wales*, 216–220. See also Shaw, *Great Revival in Wales*, 60–63, and Phillips, *Evan Roberts*, 131–132.

390. Phillips, *Evan Roberts*, 135–136, 151–154.

391. Evans, *Welsh Revival of 1904*, 71.

392. Roberts Liardon, *God's Generals: Why They Succeeded and Why Some Failed* (New Kensington, PA: Whitaker House, 1996), 84.

393. Jones, *An Instrument of Revival*, 29. See also Shaw, *Great Revival in Wales*, 12.

394. George T. B. Davis, *When the Fire Fell*, rev. ed. (Philadelphia, PA: The Million Testaments Campaigns, 1945), 75. See also Robert Pope, "Demythologising the Evan Roberts Revival, 1904–1905," *Journal of Ecclesiastical History* 57:3 (July 2006), Cambridge University Press, 523. See also Awstin, *Religious Revival in Wales*, 216–220, and Shaw, *Great Revival in Wales*, 60–63.

395. Phillips, *Evan Roberts*, 164.

396. Ibid., 164–165.

397. "Evan Roberts and the Welsh Revival," http://www.pentecostalpioneers.org /EvanRobertsWelshRevival.html (accessed July 18, 2013). Article edited from Keith Malcomson, *Pentecostal Pioneers Remembered* (2008). See also Evans, *Welsh Revival of 1904*, 83, in which the author talks about how Roberts also inspired his family to do family worship for the first time.

398. Phillips, *Evan Roberts*, 226. Letter from Evan Roberts to Elsie Phillips, November 5, 1904.

399. Ibid., 190.

400. Ibid., 233–234. Letter from Evan Roberts to Elsie Phillips, likely November 8, 1904.

401. Awstin, *Religious Revival in Wales*, 8, and Phillips, *Evan Roberts*, 235.

402. Awstin, *Religious Revival in Wales*, 540–548. See also Phillips, *Evan Roberts*, 426–443.

403. Evans, *Welsh Revival of 1904*, 158–159, 161. Amy Carmichael with the Tamil people of Dohnaver, India, and Pandita Ramabai with the children in her orphanage in Mutki, India, both experienced a significant outpouring of the Holy Spirit in 1905. See also Joseph R. Joute, "The Welsh Revival of 1904: A Revival of Significance for the Hmars," February 1, 2013, Hmar Online Theological Journal, http://www.hotjournal.org/the-welsh-revival-of-1904-a-revival-of-significance-for-the-hmars/ (accessed August 26, 2013).

404. Shaw, *Great Revival in Wales*, 37.

405. Ibid., 98. From a sermon by G. Campbell Morgan, "Lessons of the Welsh Revival," delivered in Westminster Chapel on December 25, 1904.

406. Evans, *Welsh Revival of 1904*, 46, 161.

407. Shaw, *Great Revival in Wales*, 98.

408. Ibid., 66.

409. Ibid, 45.

410. Ibid., 47.

411. Ibid.

412. Ibid., 118–119.

413. Jennifer A. Miskov, "The Liturgy of the Welsh Revival and the Azusa Street Revival: Connections, Similarities and Development," in *Scripting Pentecost*, eds. A. J. Swaboda and Mark Cartledge (United Kingdom: Ashgate, 2016), and Gary B. McGee, "William J. Seymour and the Azusa Street Revival," *Enrichment Journal*, The General Council of the Assemblies of God, http://enrichmentjournal.ag.org/199904/026_azusa.cfm (accessed August 27, 2013).

414. Robert Pope, "Demythologising the Evan Roberts Revival, 1904–1905," *Journal of Ecclesiastical History* 57:3 (July 2006), Cambridge University Press, 530.

415. Noel Gibbard, *Fire on the Altar: A History and Evaluation of the 1904–05 Welsh Revival* (Bryntirion, Bridgend, Wales: Bryntirion Press, 2005), 200.

416. Awstin, *Religious Revival in Wales*, 270, 282–284, 298–299. This was recorded February 23, 1905.

417. See "The Welsh Revival of 1904–1905," http://truthinhistory.org/the-welsh-revival-of-1904-1905.html (accessed August 26, 2013).

418. Roberts's friend and fellow minister Daniel M. Phillips interpreted Roberts's defining moment to have come as a result of a tipping point of preceding years of prayer and preparation: "He [Roberts] emphatically states that the chief cause of the course he took in proceeding with the Revival as he did, is found in the thirteen years of constant prayer, the burden of which, for the greater part, was an earnest pleading with God for a Revival. Therefore, it is a great mistake to think that he is the result of one meeting, or a series of religious services." Phillips, *Evan Roberts*, 111.

419. Shaw, *Great Revival in Wales*, 84–85.

420. Ibid., 15.

421. Ibid., 92–93.

422. Phillips, *Evan Roberts*, 215. From a letter dated November 5, 1904. See also Shaw, *Great Revival in Wales*, 67–68.

423. Phillips, *Evan Roberts*, 222–223. Letter from Evan Roberts to his friend Sydney Evans, November 11, 1904.

424. Ibid., 65–66. See also "Statement of Lady Henry Somerset," in Shaw, *Great Revival in Wales*, 160–161.

425. Phillips, *Evan Roberts*, 93.

426. Awstin, *Religious Revival in Wales*, 10. This was recorded November 11, 1904.

427. See Shaw, *Great Revival in Wales*, 9, 41, 65–66.

428. A present-day version of this song called "Diolch i'r lòr / Thank you, my Lord," by Bryn Terfel, Gareth Jones, and the Welsh National Opera Orchestra, is accessible on iTunes under their names or at https://itunes.apple.com/album/diolch-ir-lor-thank-you-my-lord/id4419784?i=4419747&ing-mpt=uo%3D5.

429. Shaw, *Great Revival in Wales*, 33–34. See also 49–50.

430. Ibid., 13–14.

431. Phillips, *Evan Roberts*, 147–148.

Chapter 10: Prophetic Intercession: Rees Howells

432. Doris M. Ruscoe, *The Intercession of Rees Howells* (Blowing Rock, NC: Zerubbabel Press, 1983), 42–43.

433. Howells and his wife continued to live by faith, trusting completely in God to supply the needs of the Bible College of Wales. In 1939, the school received, through donations, the exact amount that was needed to run the school for the entire year, *down to the penny*. See a copy of the 1939 cash statement for the Bible college, under the heading "The Founder's Desire," at http://www.byfaith.co.uk /paulreeshowells.htm.

434. This town is less than fifteen miles from Moriah Chapel in Loughor, a hot spot of the Welsh Revival.

435. Norman Grubb, *Rees Howells, Intercessor*, © 1952 by Lutterworth Press, 13. Used by permission of CLC Publications. May not be further reproduced. All rights reserved.

436. Ibid., 14–15.

437. Ibid., 17–18.

438. Ibid., 21–22.

439. Ibid., 26–27.

440. Ibid., 29–30.

441. Ibid.

442. Ibid. "Under the influence of the Spirit there was an irresistible power."

443. Ruscoe, *Intercession of Rees Howells*, 89.

444. Grubb, *Rees Howells, Intercessor*, 33–34. Besides Howells's new birth, this was to be "the most revolutionary event in his life."

445. Ibid., 34.

446. Ibid., 35.

447. Ibid., 36–37.

448. Ibid., 38. See also Ruscoe, *Intercession of Rees Howells*, 43–44.

449. Ruscoe, *Intercession of Rees Howells*, 42–43.

450. Grubb, *Rees Howells, Intercessor*, 39.

451. Ruscoe, *Intercession of Rees Howells*, 42–43.

452. Grubb, *Rees Howells, Intercessor*, 39.

453. Ibid., 40. Hundreds were impacted by Howells's message and sought him out the following week to learn "how the Holy Ghost had entered him."

454. Ibid., chapter 6, "Loving an Outcast," 41–47. To help establish a man in the faith, Howells, out of his own funds, gave the man enough money to pay two years' back rent so he could get out of debt.

455. Ibid, 40.

456. Ibid., 52.

457. Ruscoe, *Intercession of Rees Howells*, 79.

458. Ibid., 45. "Once the Holy Spirit had taken you into the presence of God you have more fellowship 'on the other side' than down here. Put the man of God where you like but if God is there it is heaven upon earth."

459. Grubb, *Rees Howells, Intercessor*, 114. See also Ruscoe, *Intercession of Rees Howells*, 44.

460. Grubb, *Rees Howells, Intercessor*, 128–129.

461. Ibid., 119.

462. Ibid., 43.

463. Ruscoe, *Intercession of Rees Howells*, 61–62.

464. Grubb, *Rees Howells, Intercessor*, 97.

465. Ruscoe, *Intercession of Rees Howells*, 88–89.

466. Ibid., 50–54.

467. Ibid., 58.

468. Ibid., 101–125. See also pages 19–20.

469. David Edward Pike, "Marriage & Call to Mission: Rees Howells (Part 3)," http://daibach-welldigger.blogspot.com/2013/01/marriage-and-call-to-mission-rees.html (accessed December 12, 2013).

470. Ruscoe, *Intercession of Rees Howells*, 92–93.

471. Grubb, *Rees Howells, Intercessor*, 149–154.

472. Gazaland is present-day Mozambique. See also Rees Howells, *Christian Workers Magazine* 16:1 (September 1915), 706, for a testimony of the revival in that nation.

473. Ruscoe, *Intercession of Rees Howells*, 94.

474. See Grubb, *Rees Howells, Intercessor*, 155–156, for the concept that people wanted Howells to release the blessing of what God was doing in the Welsh Revival.

475. Ruscoe, *Intercession of Rees Howells*, 95–96. See also Grubb, *Rees Howells, Intercessor*, 156.

476. Grubb, *Rees Howells, Intercessor*, 156–157. This outpouring took place in Rusitu, Gazaland. See also Ruscoe, *Intercession of Rees Howells*, 94–95.

477. Ruscoe, *Intercession of Rees Howells*, 95–96.

478. Ibid., 96–97.

479. Ibid., 97.

480. Grubb, *Rees Howells, Intercessor*, 162–163. David Edward Pike has also done some research on Rees Howells and his impact. See http://daibach-welldigger.blogspot.com/.

481. Ruscoe, *Intercession of Rees Howells*, 98–99, and Grubb, *Rees Howells, Intercessor*, 168–169.

482. Ruscoe, *Intercession of Rees Howells*, 90.

483. Ibid., 100.

484. Grubb, *Rees Howells, Intercessor*, 174.

485. Grubb, *Rees Howells, Intercessor*, 174–176. See also David Edward Pike, "The Bible College of Wales: Rees Howells (Part 5)," http://daibach-welldigger.blogspot.com/2013/02/the-bible-college-of-wales-rees-howells.html (accessed December 13, 2013).

486. Grubb, *Rees Howells, Intercessor*, 185–187.

487. This included praying for Ethiopia during a major crisis in that nation. Surprisingly, the emperor of Ethiopia later ended up visiting the college.

488. Grubb, *Rees Howells, Intercessor*, 207.

489. Ibid., 209. Remember that it was when Evan Roberts prayed for the Lord to "bend" him that he had a significant encounter. They were praying for the same to happen to Hitler.

490. Ruscoe, *Intercession of Rees Howells*, 28.

491. Grubb, *Rees Howells, Intercessor,* 208. See also http://www.byfaith.co.uk /paulreeshowells.htm.

492. Grubb, *Rees Howells, Intercessor,* 208.

493. Ibid., 217.

494. Ibid., 218–221.

495. See the following: http://trinityschoolofministry.org/tsm/about-tsm/; http://www.global-horizons.org/about/history/; http://www.byfaith.co.uk /paulreeshowells.htm.

496. Ruscoe, *Intercession of Rees Howells,* 13.

497. See http://bcwales.org/.

498. "Bible College of Wales: Reclaiming Our Inheritance: 'Most Successful Student,'" http://bcwales.org/bcw-most-successful-student/.

499. Ibid. See also http://www.theremnant.com/07-06-00.html.

500. This concept of giving to the next generation is covered well in the book coauthored by my son, Eric Johnson, and me, entitled *Momentum: What God Starts, Never Ends* (Shippensburg, PA: Destiny Image Publishers, 2011).

Chapter 11: Spiritual Hunger: Aimee Semple McPherson

501. Aimee Semple McPherson, *This Is That: Personal Experiences, Sermons and Writings of Aimee Semple McPherson* (Los Angeles, CA: The Bridal Call Publishing House, 1919), 48.

502. Ibid., 431. Aimee said, "If there is any humble little ministry that the Lord has given me, it has been mainly that of praying for those seeking the baptism of the Holy Spirit."

503. Ibid., 14–15.

504. Ibid., 11.

505. Ibid., 38.

506. Ibid., 39.

507. Ibid., 42–43.

508. Ibid., 43–52.

509. Ibid.

510. Ibid.

511. Ibid.

512. Ibid.

513. Ibid.

514. Ibid., 43–57.

515. Stanley H. Frodsham, "Aimee Semple McPherson," *Pentecostal Evangel,* June 5, 1926, 2–3.

516. Ibid., 2–3.

517. Aimee Semple McPherson, *Aimee: Life Story of Aimee Semple McPherson* (Los Angeles, CA: Foursquare Publications, 1979), 46–47.

518. Ibid., 75.

519. Ibid., 76. Aimee sent her husband a telegram, saying, "I have tried to walk your way and failed. Won't you come now and walk my way? I am sure we will be happy."

520. E. Sharp, "The Mighty Power of God Manifested at Mount Forest, Ontario," in *This Is That: Personal Experiences, Sermons and Writings of Aimee Semple McPherson*, Aimee Semple McPherson, 253–261 (Los Angeles, CA: The Bridal Call Publishing House, 1919).

521. Daniel Mark Epstein, *Sister Aimee: The Life of Aimee Semple McPherson* (Orlando, FL: Houghton Mifflin Harcourt, 1994), 79–80.

522. McPherson, *This Is That*, 178–179.

523. Edith L. Blumhofer, *Aimee Semple McPherson: Everybody's Sister* (Grand Rapids, MI: William B. Eerdmans Publishing Company, 1993 [reprint, 1998]), 140. In 1918, Aimee was ordained with the Assemblies of God; she also was licensed by both the Methodists and the Baptists. She later returned her credentials to the Assemblies of God so she could reach more people outside of that denomination.

524. Ibid., 157–158.

525. McPherson, *This Is That*, 138–139.

526. Blumhofer, *Everybody's Sister*, 184.

527. McPherson, *This Is That*, 170.

528. George Lloyd, "Memories of the Camp," in *This Is That: Personal Experiences, Sermons and Writings of Aimee Semple McPherson*, Aimee Semple McPherson, 267–269 (Los Angeles, CA: The Bridal Call Publishing House, 1919).

529. McPherson, *This Is That*, 161–164.

530. Ibid., 121–122.

531. Ibid., 164, 191–192.

532. Elizabeth Sission, "Some Things Which I Saw," in *This Is That: Personal Experiences, Sermons and Writings of Aimee Semple McPherson*, Aimee Semple McPherson, 273–274 (Los Angeles, CA: The Bridal Call Publishing House, 1919). See also McPherson, *This Is That*, 149.

533. McPherson, *This Is That*, 439, 441.

534. In 1922, Aimee was kidnapped by the Ku Klux Klan so they could hear her preach. See Roberts Liardon, *God's Generals: Why They Succeeded and Why Some Failed* (New Kensington, PA: Whitaker House, 1996), 234–235.

535. "Aimee Semple McPherson," http://www.foursquare.org/about/aimee_semple_mcpherson/p3 (accessed January 29, 2013). See also McPherson, *Aimee: Life Story*, 239.

536. "Foursquare History," http://www.foursquare.org/about/history (accessed January 29, 2013).

537. Ibid.

538. See Matthew Avery Sutton, *Aimee Semple McPherson and the Resurrection of Christian America* (Cambridge, MA: Harvard University Press, 2009), 267–68, and Blumhofer, *Everybody's Sister*, 8, 379. The causes of her death are controversial to this day.

539. "Foursquare History."

540. Wayne Warner, *Maria Woodworth-Etter: For Such a Time as This* (Gainesville, FL: Bridge-Logos, 2004), 316–317.

541. Blumhofer, *Everybody's Sister*, 171.

Chapter 12: Anointing: Kathryn Kuhlman

542. Kathryn Kuhlman, chapel service at Oral Roberts University, October 1, 1973, accessible online in video form at https://www.youtube.com /watch?v=mJ8EB136rP8 and also from the General's Library, which is Bill Johnson's revival history library in Redding, California.

543. Allen Spraggett, *Kathryn Kuhlman: The Woman Who Believes in Miracles* (New York, NY: The New American Library, 1970), 112. This material comes from personal interviews the author conducted with Kathryn Kuhlman in either 1964 or 1968.

544. Kathryn Kuhlman, "Healing in the Spirit," *Christianity Today*, July 20, 1973, 5.

545. Kathryn Kuhlman, "Surrender Brings Abiding Victory." Transcription of recording accessed from General's Library.

546. Kuhlman, "Healing in the Spirit," 5.

547. Kuhlman, chapel service at Oral Roberts University.

548. Jamie Buckingham, *Daughter of Destiny: Kathryn Kuhlman* (Plainfield, NJ: Logos International, 1976), 88–89.

549. Ibid., 89. See also interview with Helen and Joe Labash, July 7, 1985, accessed from General's Library.

550. Spraggett, *The Woman Who Believes in Miracles*, 114. See also Roberts Liardon, *Kathryn Kuhlman: A Spiritual Biography of God's Miracle Working Power* (Laguna Hills, CA: Embassy Publishing, 1990), 59–60.

551. Kuhlman, "Healing in the Spirit," 6.

552. Kathryn Kuhlman, "The Ministry of Healing," from a sermon given at Melodyland Christian Center, California. Transcription of recording accessed from General's Library.

553. Spraggett, *Woman Who Believes in Miracles*, 110.

554. Kathryn Kuhlman, "The Ministry of Healing."

555. Buckingham, *Daughter of Destiny*, 105–106.

556. Kathryn Kuhlman, *I Believe in Miracles* (Eaglewood Cliffs, NJ: Prentice-Hall, Inc., 1962), 197–198.

557. Kuhlman, "Healing in the Spirit," 9.

558. Ibid., 5.

559. "Purpose," the Kathryn Kuhlman Foundation, http://kathrynkuhlman.com /about.html (accessed November 9, 2015).

560. Buckingham, *Daughter of Destiny*.

561. Spraggett, *Woman Who Believes in Miracles*, 110.

562. "Purpose," http://kathrynkuhlman.com/about.html (accessed September 12, 2013).

563. Helen Kooiman Hosier, *Kathryn Kuhlman: The Life She Led, the Legacy She Left* (Old Tappan, NJ: Fleming H. Revell Company, 1976), 106–107.

564. Ibid., 112, and Kuhlman, "Healing in the Spirit," 10.

565. Hosier, *Life She Led, Legacy She Left*, 79.

566. For parallels preceding this, see Jennifer A. Miskov, "Missing Links: Phoebe Palmer, Carrie Judd Montgomery, and Holiness Roots within Pentecostalism," *PentecoStudies: An Interdisciplinary Journal for Research on the Pentecostal and Charismatic Movements* 10:1 (2011), 8–28.

567. Kuhlman, "Healing in the Spirit," 5.

568. Kathryn Kuhlman, "Jesus' Life—Secret of Miracles." Transcribed recording accessed from General's Library.

569. Spraggett, *Woman Who Believes in Miracles*, 115.

570. Ibid.

571. Stephen Strang, "A Gift of Healing," *Charisma*, October/November 1975, 8.

572. Interview with Helen and Joe Labash, July 7, 1985. Accessed from General's Library.

573. Hosier, *Life She Led, Legacy She Left*, 79.

574. Kathryn Kuhlman, "Surrender Brings Abiding Victory." Transcription of recording accessed from General's Library.

575. Kathryn Kuhlman, chapel service at Oral Roberts University.

Chapter 13: Impartation: Randy Clark

576. Randy Clark, *There Is More: Reclaiming the Power of Impartation* (Mechanicsburg, PA: Global Awakening, 2006), 4–6.

577. Ibid., 4–6, 10.

578. "Randy Clark," http://globalawakening.com/home/speakers/randy-clark (accessed June 10, 2013).

579. Bill Johnson and Randy Clark, *Healing Unplugged* (Minneapolis, MN: Chosen Books, 2013), 94.

580. In 1971, Randy also received his "prayer language," which did not coincide with a baptism of the Holy Spirit. See Clark, *There Is More: Reclaiming the Power*, 223.

581. Randy Clark, *Lighting Fires* (Mechanicsburg, PA: Global Awakening, 1998 [reprint, 2011]), 42. A "cessationist" is someone who does not believe in the gifts of the Spirit for today.

582. Ibid., 42–43.

583. Ibid., 49–50.

584. Randy Clark, *There Is More!: The Secret to Experiencing God's Power to Change Your Life* (Minneapolis, MN: Chosen Books, 2013), 30–31.

585. Clark, *Lighting Fires*, 52. See also Clark, *There Is More!: The Secret to Experiencing God's Power*, 31–32, and "Global Awakening History," http://globalawakening.com/home/about-global-awakening/history-of-global-awakening (accessed June 10, 2013).

586. Clark, *Lighting Fires*, 45–47.

587. Clark, *There Is More!: The Secret to Experiencing God's Power*, 32–33. See also Bill Johnson and Randy Clark, *The Essential Guide to Healing* (Minneapolis, MN: Chosen Books, 2011), 27.

588. Johnson and Clark, *Healing Unplugged*, 107–108.

589. Clark, *Lighting Fires*, 73–74.

590. Randy Clark, *Pressing In* (Mechanicsburg, PA: Global Awakening, 2009), 26.

591. Ibid., 26–28. See also Clark, *Lighting Fires*, 77–78, and Clark, *There Is More!: The Secret to Experiencing God's Power*, 34.

592. Randy Clark, interview with Jennifer A. Miskov, January 28, 2014, Redding, California.

593. Randy Clark, e-mail message to Jennifer A. Miskov, January 2014.

594. Richard M. Riss, *A History of the Awakening of 1992–1995*, Revival Library, http://www.revival-library.org/index.php/catalogues-menu/pentecostal/a-history-of-the-awakening-of-1992-1995 (accessed Nov. 12, 2015).

595. Clark, *Lighting Fires*, 80.

596. Richard M. Riss, "Chapter 14: Randy Clark," in *A History of the Awakening of 1992–1995*, Revival Library, http://www.revival-library.org/index.php /catalogues-menu/pentecostal/a-history-of-the-awakening-of-1992-1995 (accessed Nov. 12, 2015). See also Jerry Steingard with John Arnott, *From Here to the Nations: The Story of the Toronto Blessing* (Toronto, Canada: Catch the Fire, 2014), 50.

597. Clark, *There Is More!: The Secret to Experiencing God's Power*, 35–36.

598. Clark, interview with Jennifer A. Miskov.

599. Clark, e-mail message to Jennifer A. Miskov.

600. Clark, *There Is More: Reclaiming the Power*, 139–140, 36. See also Jerry Steingard with John Arnott, *From Here to the Nations: The Story of the Toronto Blessing* (Toronto, Canada: Catch the Fire, 2014), 52, in reference to Clark's *Lighting Fires*, 85. This is in reference to 2 Kings 6:27.

601. Jerry Steingard with John Arnott, *From Here to the Nations: The Story of the Toronto Blessing* (Toronto, Canada: Catch the Fire, 2014), 52.

602. Clark, interview with Jennifer A. Miskov.

603. Clark, *There Is More: Reclaiming the Power*, 36.

604. Steingard with Arnott, *From Here to the Nations*, 64.

605. Ibid.

606. Randy Clark took a few trips back home to see his family during this time.

607. Steingard with Arnott, *From Here to the Nations*, 87.

608. "Global Awakening History," http://globalawakening.com/home/about-global-awakening/history-of-global-awakening (accessed June 10, 2013). See also Stephen Strang, "More, Lord!" *Charisma*, May 1995, in Steingard with Arnott, *From Here to the Nations*, 94.

609. "Global Awakening History."

610. In his interview with Jennifer A. Miskov, January 28, 2014, Randy Clark mentioned that it was usually two years or longer after he released an impartation that things changed for the people he prayed for or that he heard about the fruit in their lives. With Heidi Baker, it was about two years before he found out the change that occurred. With Leif Hetland, it was six years.

611. Clark, *There Is More: Reclaiming the Power*, 183, 193–194. Randy Clark also realizes that love will take people where power cannot go and that impartation is not a onetime experience.

612. "Global Awakening History." Randy Clark updated these numbers in an e-mail message to Jennifer A. Miskov, January 2014. These numbers were not updated on the website at the time.

613. "Global Awakening History."

614. Ibid.

615. Randy Clark's ministry, Global Awakening, reported this in "Global Awakening History." Learn more about this impartation in Heidi's own words in Rolland Baker and Heidi Baker, *There Is Always Enough* (Lancaster, England: Sovereign World Ltd, 2003), 67–70.

616. "Global Awakening History," and Randy Clark, e-mail message to editor, May 29, 2015.

617. Randy Clark claimed to hear the Lord clearly say, "You are to be a fire lighter, vision caster and a bridge builder." Clark, *There Is More!: The Secret of Experiencing God's Power*, 212.

618. "Global Awakening History." "In four years (1999–2004) approximately 100,000 healings occurred when Randy and Global Awakening teams prayed for the sick."

619. Clark, *Lighting Fires*, 126.

620. Clark, *There Is More!: The Secret of Experiencing God's Power*, 220–222. See also Randy Clark, *Pressing In*, 17–18.

621. Clark, *Lighting Fires*, 126.

Chapter 14: Surrender: Heidi Baker

622. Heidi Baker, quoted in *Compelled by Love: The Film*, directed by Shara Pradhan (Iris Global Films, 2013). See also Heidi Baker, testimony given at Toronto Airport Christian Fellowship, July 29, 1997, Toronto Airport Christian Fellowship media archives.

623. Bill Johnson, quoted in *Compelled by Love: The Film*, directed by Shara Pradhan (Iris Global Films, 2013).

624. Heidi Baker, text message to Jennifer A. Miskov, February 4, 2014. She wrote, "My Mother was barren and I was her miracle child but when I got very sick after my adopted brother died she and my father gave me totally to God and said if He would heal me He could have me completely for Himself." See also Randy Clark, *There Is More: Reclaiming the Power of Impartation* (Mechanicsburg, PA: Global Awakening, 2006), 109–122.

625. Rolland Baker and Heidi Baker, *There Is Always Enough* (Lancaster, England: Sovereign World Ltd, 2003), 23–24. Reprinted by permission. All rights reserved.

626. Ibid., 23–27. Heidi Baker requested the additions in brackets in an e-mail message to Jennifer A. Miskov, February 23, 2014, replacing the term "Indians" with "Native Americans." See also Randy Clark, *There Is More: Reclaiming the Power of Impartation* (Mechanicsburg, PA: Global Awakening, 2006), 107–122. To view a video of Heidi sharing this story, go to http://www.youtube.com /watch?v=VlRQ334sXZQ.

627. Heidi Baker, interview with Jennifer A. Miskov, January 3, 2012, Redding, California.

628. Baker and Baker, *There Is Always Enough*, 23–27. See also Heidi Baker with Shara Pradhan, *Compelled by Love* (Lake Mary, FL: Charisma House, 2008), 139–140, Heidi Baker, *Birthing the Miraculous* (Lake Mary, FL: Charisma House, 2014), 14, and Heidi Baker, "The Revelation of Jesus and His Call on My Life," *Revival Magazine* [Toronto, Canada], August 1, 2003, http://revivalmag.com /article/revelation-jesus-and-his-call-my-life (accessed February 8, 2014).

629. Heidi Baker, interview with Robin Steinberg, National Critics Choice, about her book *Birthing the Miraculous*, October 13, 2013, https://www.youtube.com /watch?feature=player_embedded&v=rbE4Wdn4NTE (accessed January 30, 2014).

630. Baker and Baker, *There Is Always Enough*, 29.

631. Ibid., 12, 23, 30. They had a lunch of Chinese food together, and a few weeks later got married.

632. To learn more about Jackie Pullinger's ministry to the drug addicts and outcasts in one of the most dangerous parts of Hong Kong, see Jackie Pullinger with Andrew Quicke, *Chasing the Dragon: One Woman's Struggle Against the Darkness of Hong Kong's Drug Dens* (London: Hodder and Stoughten, 1980).

633. Donald R. Kantel, "The 'Toronto Blessing': Revival and Its Continuing Impact on Mission in Mozambique" (doctoral thesis, Regent University, Virginia Beach, VA, 2007), 120.

634. Baker and Baker, *There Is Always Enough*, 34. See also Rolland and Heidi Baker, "There Is Always Enough," in *Experience the Blessing: Testimonies from Toronto*, ed. John Arnott, 47–61 (Ventura, CA: Renew [an imprint of Regal Books], 2000).

635. Heidi G. Baker, "Pentecostal Experience: Towards a Reconstructive Theology of Glossolalia" (doctoral thesis, King's College, University of London, 1995), 3, 23. On page 153, Heidi also said that "a reformation of a theology of glossolalia is needed which takes into account both the insights of Pentecostal pioneers and the riches of Christian tradition. The primary motive for such an undertaking is to promote an understanding of their charismatic experience of glossolalia and thereby 'open the door' for Pentecostalism to make its greatest contribution to contemporary Christian spirituality." See also pages 203–208.

636. Ibid., 111, 133–134, 172.

637. Ibid., 280. Heidi said, "Glossolalic prayer signifies an abiding communion with God." See also pages 236, 254.

638. Rolland Baker and Heidi Baker, "There Is Always Enough," in *Experience the Blessing: Testimonies from Toronto*, ed. John Arnott (Ventura, CA: Renew [an imprint of Regal Books], 2000), 51.

639. Rolland Baker, conversation with Jennifer A. Miskov, 2014, Redding, California. See also Heidi Baker, testimony given at Toronto Airport Christian Fellowship, January 18, 1998, Toronto Airport Christian Fellowship media archives, Randy Clark, *There Is More: Reclaiming the Power of Impartation* (Mechanicsburg, PA: Global Awakening, 2006), 107–122, and Baker and Baker, "There Is Always Enough," 52–53.

640. Randy Clark, *There Is More: Reclaiming the Power of Impartation* (Mechanicsburg, PA: Global Awakening, 2006), 115. See also Baker and Baker, "There Is Always Enough," 50.

641. "History," http://www.irisglobal.org/about/historyIris (accessed January 15, 2014). Iris missionary Donald R. Kantel wrote about the impact that the Toronto Blessing had on Iris Ministries in "The 'Toronto Blessing' Revival and Its Continuing Impact," 167–169. See also Jerry Steingard with John Arnott, *From Here to the Nations: The Story of the Toronto Blessing* (Toronto, Canada: Catch the Fire, 2014), 183–184.

642. In the fall of 1996, both Heidi and Rolland attended a conference in Toronto where the Holy Spirit fell on Heidi, and she had to be carried out of the meeting. See Clark, *There Is More: Reclaiming the Power*, 115.

643. See also "Iris History," http://www.irisglobal.org/about/history (accessed January 29, 2014).

644. Baker and Baker, *There Is Always Enough*, 49–50. Also found in Rolland Baker, "Toward a Biblical 'Strategy' of Mission: The Effects of the Five Christian 'Core Values' of Iris Global" (doctoral project, United Theological Seminary, Dayton, Ohio, 2013), 65. The original version said "bitterness and joy"; however, in an e-mail message to Jennifer A. Miskov, February 23, 2014, Heidi suggested replacing the word "bitterness" with "suffering." See also Heidi Baker, "Lay Down & Let Him Love You," a message given at the Show Me Your Glory Conference, Toronto Airport Christian Fellowship, March 5, 2004, recording transcribed by Jennifer A. Miskov; Heidi Baker, testimony at Toronto Airport Christian Fellowship, January 18, 1998, Toronto Airport Christian Fellowship media archives; and Baker and Baker, "There Is Always Enough," 55. For additional accounts at Toronto, see Heidi Baker, "Soaking in His Presence, Ministering to the Poor," *Revival Magazine* [Toronto, Canada], May 1, 2001, http://revivalmag.com/article/soaking-his-presence-ministering-poor (accessed February 8, 2014).

645. Clark, *There Is More: Reclaiming the Power*, 121. See also Baker and Baker, "There Is Always Enough," 54–56.

646. Clark, *There Is More: Reclaiming the Power*, 115.

647. Baker and Baker, "There Is Always Enough," 56–57.

648. Ibid., 57–58.

649. Ibid., 58.

650. Ibid.

651. Jennifer A. Miskov received this excerpt in an e-mail message from one of Heidi Baker's personal assistants. This is restated in Heidi Baker, *Birthing the Miraculous* (Lake Mary, FL: Charisma House, 2014), 8–9. See also Baker with Pradhan, *Compelled by Love*, 1–7, and Heidi Baker, "Lay Down & Let Him Love You," a message given at the Show Me Your Glory Conference, Toronto Airport Christian Fellowship, March 5, 2004, recording transcribed by Jennifer A. Miskov. To read this account from Randy Clark's perspective, see Clark, *There Is More: Reclaiming the Power*, 116–117.

652. Heidi Baker, *Birthing the Miraculous* (Lake Mary, FL: Charisma House, 2014), 8–9. See also Clark, *There Is More: Reclaiming the Power*, 116.

653. Baker and Baker, *There Is Always Enough*, 68. See also Clark, *There Is More: Reclaiming the Power*, 115–116.

654. Baker and Baker, *There Is Always Enough*, 67–70.

655. Clark, *There Is More: Reclaiming the Power*, 118.

656. Heidi Baker, "Lay Down & Let Him Love You," a message given at the Show Me Your Glory Conference, Toronto Airport Christian Fellowship, March 5, 2004, recording transcribed by Jennifer A. Miskov. See also Clark, *There Is More: Reclaiming the Power*, 118–120, and Baker and Baker, *There Is Always Enough*, 60–70.

657. Baker and Baker, *There Is Always Enough*, 50–54.

658. Ibid., 171–175.

659. Baker with Pradhan, *Compelled by Love*, 1–7. See also C. Hope Flinchbaugh, 'Floods of Love in Mozambique,' *Charisma*, May 31, 2000, http://www.charismamag.com/spirit/evangelism-missions/21-floods-of-love-in-moambique (accessed Sept. 18, 2012).

660. Rolland Baker, "Toward a Biblical 'Strategy' of Mission: The Effects of the Five Christian 'Core Values' of Iris Global" (doctoral project, United Theological Seminary, Dayton, OH, 2013), 76–77.

661. Jerry Steingard with John Arnott, *From Here to the Nations: The Story of the Toronto Blessing* (Toronto, Canada: Catch the Fire, 2014), 185.

662. Many things literally began to multiply, including Christmas presents for the children and bread for the people in the refugee camps.

663. Rolland Baker, "About Us," http://www.irisglobal.org/about (accessed January 15, 2014). Rolland wrote, "Then revival was fueled exponentially by the desperation caused by catastrophic flooding in 2000."

664. Margaret M. Poloma, *Main Street Mystics: The Toronto Blessing and Reviving Pentecostalism* (Oxford, UK: AltaMira Press, 2003), 229. See also Baker and Baker, *There Is Always Enough*, 182.

665. Heidi Baker, e-mail message to Jennifer A. Miskov, February 23, 2014. See also Baker and Baker, *There Is Always Enough*, 181–182.

666. Baker and Baker, *There Is Always Enough*, 182.

667. This comes from a message that Heidi gave on October 20, 2005, when she was in Toronto. A video of her talk can be viewed at http://www.youtube.com/watch?v=2zXpPt-NEsQ.

668. Kantel, "The 'Toronto Blessing' Revival and Its Continuing Impact," 150–151. A video of this event can be viewed at http://www.youtube.com/watch?v=2zXpPt-NEsQ.

669. This paradigm shift of understanding the Father's love also happened when she was encouraged to eat a cookie and not feel guilty about it. See interview with Heidi at http://stopfortheone.org/videos/13-11-2013/prophetic-conference-2013 (accessed January 15, 2014).

670. Baker, "Toward a Biblical 'Strategy' of Mission," 70, in reference to Kantel, "The 'Toronto Blessing' Revival and Its Continuing Impact." Rolland Baker concurs with Kantel's conclusions in his thesis in regard to the impact Toronto has had on Iris Global.

671. Baker, "Toward a Biblical 'Strategy' of Mission," 70.

672. Ibid., 69.

673. Heidi Baker, *Birthing the Miraculous* (Lake Mary, FL: Charisma House, 2014), 8–9.

674. Baker with Pradhan, *Compelled by Love*, 48. The number of those raised from the dead reflects total as of 2008.

675. Baker, "About Us," http://www.irisglobal.org/about.

676. Baker, "Toward a Biblical 'Strategy' of Mission," 13–16. Partners in Harvest network was birthed out of the Toronto Blessing movement. See https://www.partnersinharvest.org/about/.

677. Baker, "Toward a Biblical 'Strategy' of Mission," 26. See also Baker and Baker, *There's Always Enough*, 65.

678. Rolland says that for Iris Global, "we have only one destination, one home, one reality, one resting place, one source, one motivation, one reward, one possession, one point of contact with God, one source of real satisfaction—and that is Jesus. We cannot overemphasize Him in any way. He is all we have and everything we need. All we do is come to Him like children for everything. His is the only name under heaven in which we trust. He is our wisdom, sanctification and joy. In Him we have no anxiety about anything. He provides our guidance. He is able to speak to us, to guide us, to thrill us by His Spirit. Our souls find our greatest delight in Him and He gives us the desires of our hearts. Our five core values can be condensed into one: in Jesus we must enjoy life!" To see this quote and learn more about the core values, see Baker, "Toward a Biblical 'Strategy' of Mission," 234–243. This quote is now accessible online in Rolland's thesis at http://www.irisglobal.org/pdf/Rolland-Toward-a-Biblical-Strategy-of-Mission.pdf, pages 237–238.

679. Baker, *Birthing the Miraculous*, 8–9.

680. Baker, interview with Robin Steinberg, National Critics Choice.

681. Baker with Pradhan, *Compelled by Love*, 90.

682. Heidi Baker, interview with Jennifer A. Miskov, 2010, Oxford, England.

683. Baker, interview with Jennifer A. Miskov, January 3, 2012. Heidi said, "All fruitfulness flows from intimacy. You can't fulfill your destiny or do anything for God unless you're intimate with Him and let Daddy God love you."

684. Baker, *Birthing the Miraculous*, 38–40.

685. Bill Johnson, quoted in *Compelled by Love: The Film*.

686. Baker, interview with Jennifer A. Miskov, January 3, 2012. Heidi said, "I feel like a lot of Christians want someone to lay hands on them and immediately be in the fullness of their destiny right now. They want the stadium; they want the millions and billions. God is saying, 'I want you to yield, to lay down, and to pay the price, I want you to give everything within you.'"

687. Rolland Baker, quoted in *Compelled by Love: The Film*, directed by Shara Pradhan (Iris Global Films, 2013).

688. Bill Johnson, quoted in *Compelled by Love: The Film*.

689. Clark, *There Is More: Reclaiming the Power*, 118.

Chapter 15: Just the Beginning

690. Kathryn Kuhlman spoke at Oral Roberts University in 1972 when the university awarded her an honorary Doctor of Humane Letters degree. A recording of her message can be viewed at http://www.youtube.com/watch?v=mJ8EB136rP8&sns=em.

691. See also Jennifer A. Miskov, "Tapping into the Power of the Testimony: Launching into Greater Destiny," October 8, 2014, accessible at http://silvertogold.com/blog/2014/10/8/tapping-into-the-power-of-the-testimony.

692. Randy Clark, interview with Jennifer A. Miskov, January 28, 2014, Redding, California.

About the Authors

Bill Johnson is a fifth-generation pastor who lives a life rich in the things of the Spirit, using heaven as a model for his life and ministry. In 1968, at the end of his high school years, he moved from the Los Angeles area to Redding, California, where his parents became the pastors of Bethel Church, and two years later, the Holy Spirit began to move powerfully in that community of believers. It was about this time that Mario Murillo visited the church, speaking about being absolutely abandoned to Christ. One Saturday night, Bill said yes to God—the absolute yes—and everything changed for him.

In 1978, Bill was invited to pastor Mountain Chapel in Weaverville, California, and he served there for seventeen years. The presence of God was very strong, and the church extended its times of worshipping and glorifying God, even though, in the first years, they saw few miracles, despite praying for many. Bill's greatest breakthrough in ministry came after attending two conferences in 1987 organized by John Wimber. Bill realized he needed to "put a demand" on what he believed—his risk factor had to line up with the boldness of his beliefs. As he did this, there was an immediate change in his ministry, and the church began to see an increase in healing and miracles.

Bill moved back to Bethel Church in Redding in 1996, where he and his wife, Beni, are the senior pastors. An outpouring of the Spirit began almost immediately. It grew rapidly, and there were many healings, including, in multiple cases, of cancer. Today, healings and miracles are the norm at Bethel. Bill and Beni have a heart to see the values of the kingdom of heaven fill the earth. Together, they serve a growing number of churches that have partnered together to work toward global revival.

⌒

Jennifer A. Miskov, PhD, is an author and a speaker, as well as the founding director of Destiny House, a ministry that cultivates a community of worshippers who fulfill their own destinies and also help to release healing, blessing, and breakthrough into destiny for leaders, missionaries, and all others whom God sends. Jennifer believes that the keys to our destiny are found in intimacy with God and connection with family.

Jennifer is originally from Anaheim, California, where she grew up attending the Anaheim Vineyard under John Wimber's leadership. She also served with Iris Global in Mozambique in 2000 where she helped to plant a church. From 2007–2011, she studied revival history while living in England and specifically looked at the life and legacy of Carrie Judd Montgomery, who was a catalyst for the divine healing movement. While there she helped set up Healing in the Streets in her city. Jennifer was ordained by Heidi Baker of Iris Global on New Year's Eve 2011, and she established Destiny House in February 2012. Jennifer teaches classes at Bethel School of Supernatural Ministry, speaks at various churches and events, and hosts workshops entitled "Writing in the Glory: How to Write and Publish Your 1st Book." She is also the author of *Writing in the Glory, Life on Wings, Water to Wine, Spirit Flood,* and *Silver to Gold.* You can learn more about her and Destiny House at www.silvertogold.com.

Welcome to Our House!

We Have a Special Gift for You

It is our privilege and pleasure to share in your love of Christian books. We are committed to bringing you authors and books that feed, challenge, and enrich your faith.

To show our appreciation, we invite you to sign up to receive a specially selected **Reader Appreciation Gift**, with our compliments. Just go to the Web address at the bottom of this page.

God bless you as you seek a deeper walk with Him!

WE HAVE A GIFT FOR YOU. VISIT:

whpub.me/nonfictionthx

WHITAKER
HOUSE